POLAND, 1918–1945

In the turbulent history of twentieth-century Europe, the reborn Polish State faced the most formidable and diverse array of problems imaginable. From 1918 until the end of the Second World War, Poland struggled to retain and consolidate independence, finally falling prey to the alien ideology and political system of Communism. The period of the Second Polish Republic, from its establishment in 1918 until its end in 1945, has often been viewed in the context of its negative aspects and failures. This lucid new study demonstrates that a far more positive assessment is needed, through an informed, balanced and objective approach.

Based on an extensive range of Polish, British, German, Jewish and Ukrainian primary and secondary sources, this work provides an objective appraisal of the interwar period. Peter Stachura demonstrates how the Polish Republic overcame giant obstacles at home and abroad to achieve consolidation as an independent state in the early 1920s, made relative economic progress, created a coherent social order, produced an outstanding cultural scene, advanced educational opportunity, and adopted constructive and even-handed policies towards its ethnic minorities. Without denying the defeats suffered by the republic, Peter Stachura demonstrates that the fate of Poland after 1945, with the imposition of an unwanted, Soviet-dominated Communist system, was thoroughly undeserved.

Poland, 1918–1945 is a controversial and challenging revisionist analysis and interpretation, making essential reading for all those who study Modern European History.

Peter D. Stachura is Professor of Modern European History and Director of the Centre for Research in Polish History at the University of Stirling. He has published extensively, including *Themes of Modern Polish History* (1992), *Poland Between the Wars* (1998), *Poland in the Twentieth Century* (1999), *Perspectives on Polish History* (2001), and *The Poles in Britain, 1940–2000* (2004).

POLAND, 1918–1945

An Interpretive and Documentary History of the Second Republic

Peter D. Stachura

Routledge
Taylor & Francis Group

LONDON AND NEW YORK

First published 2004
by Routledge
2 Park Square, Milton Park, Abingdon,
Oxfordshire OX14 4RN

Simultaneously published in the USA and Canada
by Routledge
29 West 35th Street, New York, NY 10001

Routledge is an imprint of the Taylor & Francis Group

Typeset in Times New Roman by
Keystroke, Jacaranda Lodge, Wolverhampton
Printed and bound in Great Britain by
Biddles Ltd, King's Lynn

British Library Cataloguing in Publication Data
A catalogue record for this book is available from the British Library

Library of Congress Cataloging in Publication Data
Stachura, Peter D.
Poland, 1918–1945: an interpretive and documentary
history of the Second Republic / Peter D. Stachura.
p. cm.
Includes bibliographical references and index.
1. Poland–History–1918–1945. I. Title.
DK4400.S73 2001
943.8′04–dc22
2003026325

ISBN 0–415–34357–7 (hbk)
ISBN 0–415–34358–5 (pbk)

In memory of
Henryk Stachura (1920–1939)
who fell in defence of the Second Republic
on the last day of the Polish–German War

ABBREVIATIONS AND GLOSSARY

AK Home Army (*Armia Krajowa*: the principal wartime Polish resistance).

AL People's Army (*Armia Ludowa*: Polish Communist, 1944–5).

Apparatchik Member of the Communist Party Establishment.

Ausgleich 'Compromise' between the Habsburgs and the Magyars in 1867 which established the Dual Monarchy.

BBC British Broadcasting Corporation.

BBWR Non-Party Bloc for Co-operation with the Government (*Bezpartyjny Blok dla Współpracy z Rządem*: in Poland 1928–35).

BCh Peasant Battalions (*Bataliony Chłopskie*: Polish, 1940–4).

Bund Abbreviated name of the General Jewish Workers' Union, a radical left-wing Jewish political party.

'Curzon Line' Named after the British Foreign Secretary, George, Lord Curzon, who proposed in 1920 a Polish–Russian border unacceptable to Poland.

Cysho Central Yiddish School Organisation (in the Second Polish Republic).

DDP German Democratic Party (*Deutsche Demokratische Partei*: liberal party in Weimar Germany).

DNVP German National People's Party (*Deutschnationale Volkspartei*: radical right-wing party, 1918–33).

Duma Russian parliament, introduced by the tsar in 1906.

DVP German People's Party (*Deutsche Volkspartei*: centre-right party in Weimar Germany).

Endecja Polish name for the right-wing, nationalist National Democratic Party and its successors in the Second Republic.

Endek Polish name for a follower of the *Endecja*.

Führer The Leader (Adolf Hitler's title).

Gestapo German Secret Police in the Third Reich (*Geheimes Staatspolizei*).

CONTENTS

Gulag The Soviet penal labour camp system.

Konarmiya Elite Bolshevik Cossack cavalry.

KOP Border Defence Corps (*Korpus Obrony Pogranicza*: Polish, 1924–39).

KPD German Communist Party (*Kommunistische Partei Deutschlands*: 1918–33).

KPP Communist Party of Poland (*Komunistyczna Partia Polski*: 1926–38).

KRN National Council for the Homeland (*Krajowa Rada Narodowa*: Communist).

Kulturkampf Descriptive term for the clash between the Bismarckian Reich and the Catholic Church in Germany.

Liberum Veto Polish parliamentary device until abolished by the constitution of 3 May 1791.

Mazurka Polish lilting melody (such as the Polish national anthem).

MP Member of Parliament.

NATO North Atlantic Treaty Organisation (Western military alliance).

NKVD Soviet Secret Police of the Stalinist era (*Narodnaya Kommissiya Vevnutrikh Dyel*).

NSDAP National Socialist German Workers' Party, or Nazi Party (*Nationalsozialistische Deutsche Arbeiterpartei*).

NSZ National Armed Forces (*Narodowe Siły Zbrojne*: ultra-nationalist Polish underground resistance in the Second World War).

numerus clausus A device to reduce the number of Jewish university students in the Second Polish Republic, especially in the 1930s.

ONR National Radical Camp (*Obóz Narodowo-Radykalny*: extremist offshoot of the *Endecja* in the mid-1930s).

Operation Barbarossa Code-name for the German invasion of the Soviet Union in summer 1941.

OUN Organisation of Ukrainian Nationalists.

OZON Camp of National Unity (*Obóz Zjednoczenia Narodowego*, 1937–9).

PKWN Polish Committee of National Liberation (*Polski Komitet Wyzwolenia Narodowego:* Soviet-sponsored Communist organisation, 1944).

PPR Polish Workers' Party (*Polska Partia Robotnicza*: Communist, 1942–4).

PPS Polish Socialist Party (*Polska Partia Socjalistyczna*).

PSL Polish Peasant Party (*Polskie Stronnictwo Ludowe*: 1895–1947).

PZPR Polish United Workers' Party (*Polska Zjednoczona Partia Robotnicza*: post-1948 Communist).

Reichsführer National leader (as in head of a Nazi organisation).

Reichsrat Federal parliament (Habsburg).

Reichstag Federal German parliament.

Reichswehr The name of the German Army, 1918–34 (when changed to *Wehrmacht*).

Sanacja Name of the Polish regime 1926–39 (denoting a 'cleansing' or 'purification' of political and moral life).

SDKPiL Social Democracy of the Kingdom of Poland and Lithuania (*Socjal-demokracja Królestwa Polskiego i Litwy*: radical left-wing political party).

Sejm Polish parliament (lower house).

SPD Social Democratic Party of Germany (*Sozialdemokratische Partei Deutschlands*: moderate left-wing party before 1933).

SS Nazi élite formation (*Schutzstaffel*).

Szlachta Polish gentry.

SZP Service for the Victory of Poland (*Służba Zwycięstwa Polskiego*).

TRJN Provisional Government of National Unity (*Tymczasowy Rząd Jedności Narodowej*: formed in Poland, 1945; Communist-dominated).

UB Polish Secret Police (*Urząd Bezpieczeństwa*: Communist, post-1945).

Ugoda Polish Government–Jewish Agreement (1925).

USA United States of America.

USPD Independent Social Democratic Party of Germany (*Unabhängige Sozialdemokratische Partei Deutschlands:* radical socialist party, 1917–22).

USSR United Soviet Socialist Republics (Soviet Union).

UVO Ukrainian Military Organisation.

Völkisch Racist-nationalist (extreme element of German nationalism).

Wehrmacht German armed forces in the Third Reich (invariably used specifically to mean the army).

Weltanschauung Philosophical/ideological outlook.

WiN Freedom and Independence (*Wolność i Niezawisłość*: patriotic, anti-Soviet and anti-Communist organisation, 1945–7).

Żegota Council for Aid to the Jews (Polish clandestine group, 1942–5).

ZLN Popular National Union (*Związek Ludowo-Narodowy*: new right-wing Polish political party 1919–28 representing the *Endecja*).

Złoty Polish currency introduced in 1924 (literally means 'gold crown').

ŻOB Jewish Combat Organisation (*Żydowska Organizacja Bojowa*: small anti-German underground formation).

ZPP Union of Polish Patriots (*Związek Patriotów Polskich*: Soviet-sponsored Polish Communist group, founded in the USSR in March 1943).

Żydokomuna Polish term for 'Jewish Bolshevism'.

ŻWW Jewish Military Union (*Żydowski Związek Wojskowy*: small wartime anti-German resistance group).

ZWZ Union for Armed Struggle (*Związek Walki Zbrojnej*: 1939–42, precursor of the AK).

ACKNOWLEDGEMENTS

The publishers and the author would like to thank the following for their permission to reproduce material used in the book: Michael Gibson, the Hoover Institution Archives, the Sikorski Historical Institute, Allen & Unwin, Minerva, Victor Gollancz, the Royal Institute of International Affairs. Every care has been taken to trace copyright holders and obtain permission to reproduce the material. If any proper acknowledgement has not been made, we would be grateful if copyright holders would inform us of the oversight.

INTRODUCTION

The re-establishment of Poland as a sovereign, independent state in 1918, in the form of the Second Republic, was made possible by a fortuitous convergence of external and internal factors. The collapse in 1917–18 of the three empires – the tsarist, Hohenzollern and Habsburg – which had partitioned Poland on three occasions in the eighteenth century, created a political vacuum that was filled, above all, by the commitment of the Western Allies to the Wilsonian principle of national self-determination as the basis for a postwar peace settlement in Europe and by an equally significant Polish contribution nurtured for 123 years, following the Third, and final, Partition. That contribution comprised entrenched cultural and religious values, resilience, physical and moral courage and, of course, a deep sense of patriotism, reinforced by military and diplomatic initiatives once war had broken out. But Poland quickly discovered that the regaining of independence was the comparatively easy part. An even greater challenge in the years ahead was to retain and consolidate that independence, for she was confronted by the most formidable and diverse array of problems imaginable. In every major sphere of national activity, Poland had to struggle against overwhelming odds. How effectively she coped has been analysed, particularly since 1945, by many historians, who have none the less reached an historiographical consensus that the Second Republic was largely a failure.[1]

A note of caution is needed, however, because this verdict has often been shaped, or at least influenced to one degree or another, by political and ideological perspectives, most obviously during the Communist era in Poland, from 1945 until 1989. During that time, when an alien ideology and corresponding political system had been imposed on Poland at the end of the Second World War by the Soviet Union, with the connivance of the United States and Britain, many Polish historians – willingly or not – felt it expedient to follow the party line that the Second Republic had been a bourgeois, reactionary, even fascist state which had mercifully been

1

superseded by the putative egalitarian-proletarian 'People's Poland'. The intensity and nature of official pressure on historians to conform varied from time to time. It was probably at its height during the Stalinist era, which in Poland extended for some years after Stalin's death, in 1953. But even during the slight thaws in official attitudes, especially in the 1970s, restrictions were never far away. Admittedly, despite all the constraints, a number of valuable scholarly studies were published – for example, on several political parties, organisations and leading personalities. However, it was also the case that a considerable number of historians employed in the universities or in other academic institutions were themselves either card-carrying Communists or sympathisers, and therefore had not that much difficulty in observing the restrictions and avoiding embarrassing taboo themes, such as the Polish–Soviet War of 1919–20, the Soviet invasion and occupation of 1939–41, and the Katyń Massacre. Consequently, too much of the 'scholarly' literature on the Second Republic that was published before 1989, when the Communist regime finally collapsed, was rather limited and censorious in an unmistakably unbalanced way.

The same strictures cannot be applied entirely, of course, to the small band of Western historians who have written about the Second Republic, though some of them were undoubtedly supportive or sympathetic, at least in an abstract, intellectual manner, to the Polish Communist regime as well as to the Soviet Union: Slavic scholars at the University of California provide a well-known example. No such dubious ideological baggage can be attributed, however, to arguably the most eminent scholar of modern Poland in the English-speaking world, Norman Davies, whose magisterial two-volume study, *God's Playground*, raised the standard to a completely new level which has yet to be surpassed, let alone emulated. However, even he, as arguably the most knowledgeable and fair-minded scholar in the field, states that, despite the cultural, intellectual and educational achievements of the period, the Second Republic was characterised by failure. He concludes: 'No one can claim that the policies of the Second Republic were an unbounded success', and more emphatically: 'If the Second Republic had not been foully murdered in 1939 by external agents, there is little doubt that it would soon have sickened from internal causes', and further, 'The Second Republic was indeed destined for destruction'.[2]

Another British historian, Antony Polonsky, speaks in similar vein: 'It is in many ways a disheartening experience to recount the history of the reborn Polish state. Independence . . . presented the Poles with daunting and, in the end, insuperable problems.' He admits a few successes, but these were overshadowed, in his view, by a wide range of weaknesses and inadequacies in too many areas of development, including the economy, the army, the national minorities and foreign policy.[3] Almost all other accounts echoed a similar appraisal for a long time.

The beginnings of a noteworthy departure from this pessimistic school of thought could be detected in Poland during the 1990s. Although many of the Communist-era historians were (and are) still holding down public posts – Poland having unfortunately escaped the clear-out of Communist Party hacks and fellow-travellers that occurred in the former German Democratic Republic after German reunification in 1990 – a younger, more questioning generation of historians began to make an impact through a stream of well-researched monographs on the inter-war period, with local and regional studies figuring prominently. The overall aim of these scholars, of whom Marek Jan Chodakiewicz, Tomasz Strzembosz and Wojciech Roszkowski are outstanding examples,[4] is to critically examine, on the basis of new and reliable documentary evidence, established opinion on important aspects of the Second Republic's history. The outcome has been an increasingly better-informed and far more appreciative assessment which has already succeeded in debunking some of the myths, distortions and misrepresentations that previously furnished a disproportionate amount of the historiography. This most encouraging trend in Polish scholarship, which is being emulated by a small number of Western scholars writing in English, such as the Canadian Mark Paul,[5] is certainly bound to accelerate in the years ahead.

The leading questions consequently arising are clear enough: to what extent should the older views, some now dating from thirty, forty, even fifty years ago, be revised? How far can they withstand critical scrutiny from the fresh perspective of the early twenty-first century? This is the essential task and *raison d'être* of the present study.

In considering the principal areas of the Second Republic's development, this book seeks to provide a vigorous interpretative analysis and commentary, with factual information confined to what is deemed absolutely necessary, complemented by a selection of documents and documentary extracts whose purpose is to illuminate further the themes that are reviewed, and sometimes to corroborate the arguments that are adduced. Moreover, this study aims to provide a platform for further discussion and debate among as wide a readership as possible. The documents have been taken from a broad and multifarious range of Polish, German, Jewish, Ukrainian and British primary and secondary sources. Included is archival material from the Archiwum Akt Nowych in Warsaw, the Polish Institute and Sikorski Museum and the Public Record Office (now renamed the National Archives) in London, the Berlin Document Center, Institut für Zeitgeschichte and Bundesarchiv Koblenz in Germany, and the Hoover Institution and YIVO Institute for Jewish Research in the

United States. This corpus is supplemented by material from published documentary collections, contemporary books, biographies, periodicals, newspapers and journals, parliamentary records, official surveys and reports; private papers, memoirs, diaries and autobiographies, which were found at the following locations: the Bibliotek Narodowa in Warsaw, the Main Library of the Jagiellonian University in Kraków, the libraries of the universities of Glasgow, Edinburgh and Stirling, and the Mitchell Library, Glasgow. A few extracts were obtained from Polish-language monographs published after 1945, and a small amount of additional material was kindly supplied by private sources in Warsaw, Kraków and Stirling. Translations from foreign language documents into English are my own, imperfections and errors included.

For the purposes of undergraduate courses, some of the documents included have more or less picked themselves, in so far as they are of a type that could not possibly be omitted from a book that is aimed at a broad readership. Into this category fall, for instance, the Minorities' Treaty of 1919, the Polish–German Non-Aggression Pact of 1934 and August Cardinal Hlond's well-known and important pastoral letter of 1936 on the Jews. Similarly, statements made on important issues by the two dominant personalities of the interwar era in Poland, Józef Piłsudski and Roman Dmowski, necessarily find a place here. Many other documents, however, are new and unfamiliar, except perhaps to a few specialists in the field, but they are all, in their own way, of significance.

To facilitate the interaction between the analytical and interpretative text and the documents, conventional foot- or endnotes have been dispensed with, particularly as many would have been to Polish-language works, and thus of little or no use to the vast majority of readers. Instead, it was considered more apposite to provide a selection of exclusively English-language books at the start of the General Bibliography.

The overall aim is to present as full and informative an account of the Second Republic as possible in an even-handed and balanced manner. Inevitably, of course, the opinions and interpretations offered in this book will not be to everyone's taste. How could they be, when, after all, the subject has aroused considerable passion over the years. Many of the themes covered, notably the Polish–Soviet War of 1919–20, the Piłsudski *coup* of 1926, relations between the ethnic minorities and the Polish State, the Polish–Jewish symbiosis, the nature of the Soviet occupation of eastern Poland in 1939–41, the role of the exiled Polish Government during the Second World War and its dealings with the Allies, and, last but not least, the international conferences at Tehran and Yalta, fall into the 'highly controversial' and/or 'very sensitive' category. In 'People's Poland', few if any of these were allowed to be discussed in the public domain.

Finally, I am very pleased to acknowledge the valuable assistance in the general preparation of this work provided through seminar discussion by the large number of undergraduates who have taken the third-year course on the Second Polish Republic at the University of Stirling from the mid-1990s until the present, by my small but eager group of postgraduates, and also by those who have participated in the seminars and conferences organised at the university's Centre for Research in Polish History since its creation on 3 May 2000. It is, as always, a further pleasure to record my thanks to the Centre's sponsors, the M. B. Grabowski Fund (London) and the Polonia Aid Foundation Trust (London). The Centre, which provides an indispenable focus for my own work, aims to promote knowledge and informed understanding of Polish history through regular conferences, seminars, public lectures, postgraduate studies and publications, while maintaining the highest standards of international research and scholarship. My research in archives and libraries in the UK and Poland was facilitated by grants from the British Academy, the Carnegie Trust and the University of Stirling, for which I am most grateful.

NOTES

1 For a fuller historiographical review, see my essay in Peter D. Stachura (ed.), *Poland Between the Wars, 1918–1939* (London: Macmillan), 1998, pp. 1–12.
2 N. Davies, *God's Playground: A History of Poland*. Volume II: *1795 to the Present* (Oxford: Clarendon Press, 1981), pp. 426, 431, 434.
3 A. Polonsky, *Politics in Independent Poland, 1921–1939: The Crisis of Constitutional Government* (Oxford: Oxford University Press, 1972), pp. 506 ff.
4 See, for instance, M. J. Chodakiewicz, *Żydzi I Polacy, 1918–1955. Współistnienie – Zagłada – Komunizm* (Warsaw: Biblioteka Frondy, 2000); T. Strzembosz (ed.), *Studia z dziejów okupacji sowieckiej (1939–1941)* (Warsaw: ISP PAN, 1997); W. Roszkowski, *Historia Polski, 1914–2000* (Warsaw: PWN, 2001).
5 M. Paul, *Neighbors on the Eve of the Holocaust: Jewish–Polish Relations in Soviet-Occupied Eastern Poland, 1939–1941* (Toronto: PEFINA Press, 2002).

1

INDEPENDENCE REGAINED

The history of Poland in the modern era has been characterised by salient vicissitudes: outstanding victories and tragic defeats, soaring optimism and the deepest despair, heroic sacrifice and craven subservience. Underpinning all of these experiences and emotions, however, are the interrelated themes of national freedom, independence and sovereignty, which were sometimes lost, then regained, but never forgotten or abandoned. They, more than anything else, shaped Poland's destiny in the modern era. And if there is one single, fundamental point of reference, then it is unquestionably the Partitions of the eighteenth century which resulted in Poland's disappearance from the map of Europe for well over a century.

The Polish-Lithuanian Commonwealth, as the Polish State was constituted since the mid-sixteenth century, was for the next two hundred years one of the largest and most powerful in Europe, occupying a huge swathe of territory stretching from the area around Poznań in the west to far-off Muscovy in the east, and from Livonia in the north to the edge of the Ottoman Empire in the south. Famous kings, such as Stefan Batory (1575–86) and Jan Sobieski III (1674–96), and great landowning families, the Lubomirskis, Radziwiłłs, Zamoyskis, Czartoryskis and the like, played a leading role in moulding the economic, political and social life of the country and bringing it unprecedented international prestige. By the beginning of the eighteenth century, however, the first unmistakable signs of decline appeared, and were accentuated by the emergence of ambitious and expansionist neighbours in Russia, Prussia and Austria. The balance of power in Central Europe swung towards these increasingly powerful empires, while the Polish Republic grew progressively and conspicuously weaker, culminating in her partition in 1772, 1793 and 1795. Thereafter, the so-called 'Polish Question' became an important item of European diplomacy, at least in the first half of the nineteenth century, only to be resurrected during the course of the First World War.

The reasons for Poland's collapse at the end of the eighteenth century may be explained with reference not merely to the rapacity of her neighbours, but also to her long-standing, but growing and unresolved, internal weaknesses. For a start, the Commonwealth was rather more of an unwieldy federation than a unified, cohesive state. It is very doubtful whether King Jan Sobieski's successors, the Saxons Augustus II (1697–1733) and Augustus III (1733–63), had Polish interests at heart. They were increasingly subservient to Russia, who had been behind their election in the first place, and who came to regard Poland as her rightful sphere of influence, if not domination. A Russian protectorate was *de facto* established over Poland as early as 1717. Under the Saxon kings, Poland became a byword throughout Europe for economic decline and political disorder – in fact, the 'Republic of Anarchy'. Poland was a major battleground for wars, including the War of Polish Succession (1733–5) and later the Seven Years' War (1756–63), and suffered widespread devastation. The towns fell into serious decline, while the peasantry, constituting the bulk of the population, led a miserable existence.

The Polish monarchy had always been elected by the nobility, so that instead of a smooth transition from one king to another, royal elections were occasions for endless and corrupting intrigue. Above all, this system permitted foreign powers, notably Russia, to intervene on behalf of a favoured candidate, as occurred in 1697, 1733 and 1764. The outcome was a series of weak kings ultimately beholden to Russia and her interests. Moreover, the Polish parliament (*Sejm*) was prevented from playing a constructive role in the affairs of state, not only because of Russian interference, but also, to a large extent, because of the exercise of the *Liberum Veto*. In practice, this meant that every member of parliament had the right of veto. Thus, it required only one, lone voice of dissent to kill off any piece of legislation. As there was no middle ground between total harmony and total disagreement, parliament was frequently paralysed and ineffective. Between 1697 and 1762, for example, only 12 out of 37 parliamentary sessions enacted legislation. Naturally, Russia was one of the staunchest defenders of the *Liberum Veto*, as was also the nobility (*szlachta*), who selfishly wanted to keep royal power at the centre to a minimum. As a result, control of government in the provinces lay in the hands of the most powerful magnates. Unfortunately, they, with a well-deserved reputation for being incorrigibly disputatious, were hardly a stabilising influence, so that the country as a whole was often plunged into turmoil. Compounding this dismal situation was the practice of confederacy, by which a noble who had a grievance of any kind could assert his case by force. This right allowed, in effect, a legalised form of civil war. It was invoked on a number of occasions, most notably in the Confederacy of the Bar (1768–72), causing lengthy periods of wasteful conflict. All the time, of course, Poland's enemies were eager for their own ends to encourage the continuation of these deleterious practices.

It is not surprising that, thanks to calculated foreign interference and internal weakness, by the time the Saxon era of kingship was brought to an ignominious close by the election in 1764 of Stanisław-August Poniatowski (1732–98) as king, Poland had already lost much of her independence and integrity as a state. Most contemporary observers were convinced at first that Poland's fall from grace would proceed further, particularly as Poniatowski owed his elevation to Catherine the Great of Russia (1729–96), whose lover he had once been. However, although his reign did indeed result in the disaster of partition, the king aided an attempt by some Poles such as Stanisław Konarski (1700–73) who were influenced by the ideas of the Enlightenment to implement a programme of reform in the Polish State with the eventual aim of restoring its full sovereignty. A Commission for National Education, the first embryonic ministry of education in Europe, was created in 1773 to oversee the establishment of a new school and university system. Public services and agencies, including the army, police, judiciary, press, local government and the post, were modernised to an extent, while encouragement was given to the arts, principally music, painting and architecture.

Above all, plans were laid for constitutional reform and these were designed to restore political stability. However, this is where the ubiquitous Russians drew the line. They were simply not prepared to tolerate any reform that might threaten their hold over Poland, a view vigorously shared by Prussia and Austria. All three self-styled but spurious 'Enlightened Despots' used the prospect of this constitutional reform as a pretext for carrying out the First Partition, by which Poland was deprived of about 30 per cent of her territory and 35 per cent of her population of about 14 million. The episode underlined the severe constraints on Poland's capacity for independent action, and simultaneously the vulnerability of her position *vis-à-vis* rapacious neighbours, especially when they acted in consort.

Very limited reforms of a non-political nature continued in Poland after 1772, and there were still a small number of Poles who, acutely resentful of external meddling in their affairs, were on the alert for circumstances more propitious to bolder measures. That type of situation did not arise, in fact, until the later 1780s, when Russia was distracted by her conflict with Turkey in 1787–92 and Sweden in 1788–90, and when Poland began to savour something of the revolutionary atmosphere emanating from France. For there is no doubt that reform-minded circles in Poland were

8

greatly encouraged by the developments that resulted in the Fall of the Bastille and the eruption of the French Revolution. Many Poles, led by their flawed but patriotic king, immediately looked upon republican, particularly Jacobin, ideas as a means of reversing the decline and humiliations of the previous decades and of re-establishing Poland as a truly independent and liberal country once more.

The major achievement of the Polish reformers, building on the limited advances of the 1770s and 1780s and emboldened by the French Revolution, was the constitution of 3 May 1791, the first written constitution in Europe. It was a noticeably liberal document by contemporary standards, promising a raft of political, legal, educational and administrative measures that would benefit all sections of society. The constitution also upheld the long-standing Polish tradition of religious toleration, above all towards the Jews, who had originally found a welcome home in Poland in the Middle Ages. The overall aim of the constitution was to lay the basis for bringing Poland into a new era of hope and recovery as a hereditary but progressive constitutional monarchy. Both the destructive *Liberum Veto* and the right of confederacy were abolished. A reconstituted parliament with voting by majority and ministerial responsibility was to be the prime source of authority. Civil rights were extended to the peasantry and townspeople, a Polish army was to be set up for defence, and local government was to be streamlined.

These lofty if understandable ideas duly attracted the disapproval and alarm of the conservative partitionist powers, who regarded this sequence of developments in Poland as an intolerable revolutionary challenge to the entire old order in Europe. They acted accordingly. Russia took the lead in declaring war, with the avowed aim of destroying the 1791 constitution and everything that had helped pave the way for its introduction. Confronted once again by overwhelming odds, the Poles could not prevent the inevitable outcome: a Second Partition in 1793 which took yet another substantial amount of territory and population from Poland. Outraged and still inspired by the ongoing radicalisation of the revolution in France, marked by the execution of the king, Louis XVI, the Poles made in the following year a final, desperate effort in a national rising under the leadership of Tadeusz Kościuszko (1746–1817). Proclaiming the slogan 'Liberty, Equality, Independence', this patriotic *levée en masse* in the classic French revolutionary fashion came close to realising its objectives of national independence and social revolution, by which the peasantry was to be freed from serfdom. The political price of glorious military failure was catastrophic: a Third Partition in 1795 which erased Poland from the map of Europe altogether, while the Russian, Prussian and Austrian empires expanded still further at her expense.

Even if much of the aristocracy became resigned and fatalistic, many other Poles never lost the vision and aspiration of national independence. In the short term, this found expression in the many Polish soldiers who enlisted in Napoleon's armies across the continent, fighting for the freedom of others as well as their own. They established a reputation for being the bravest of the brave, personified by Prince Józef Poniatowski (1763– 1813), and another of them, General Jan Henryk Dąbrowski (1755–1818), even composed a lilting *mazurka*, with defiant lyrics written by Józef Wybicki (1747–1822), which was later to become the national anthem. Poles made up the largest foreign contingent of the *Grande Armée* which marched into Russia in 1812, despite the fact that Napoleon had not fulfilled Polish hopes with the creation under his control of the small Duchy of Warsaw in 1807. His disastrous Russian campaign and subsequent defeat at Waterloo also signalled the end, for the time being at least, of Polish hopes for independence, a fate emphasised by the decisions of the Congress of Vienna in 1815 to re-establish much of the *ancien régime* across Europe. As a mere token gesture, the congress allowed the so-called Kingdom of Poland, which was a fraction of the size of pre-partition Poland, to be set up under Russian tutelage, as well as the even more insignificant Republic of Kraków. The tsar was king of Poland, and a large Russian army was stationed in Poland. The other partitionist powers retained, of course, a strong presence in the Polish lands.

Poland provides a clear example of a European country which responded enthusiastically to the clarion call of the French Revolution for liberation from oppressive, reactionary subjugation to foreign states but which also ultimately had to acknowledge superior military power and admit defeat. The romantic-insurrectionary tradition of the 1790s in Poland, which had been sustained by a growing national consciousness, may have been defeated but it was by no means extinguished. On the contrary, it continued after 1815 to inspire successive generations of Poles to explore all possible means of reclaiming their freedom and sovereignty. At the same time, the 'Polish Question' assumed its place on the agenda of international diplomacy throughout the long nineteenth century, though with varying degrees of importance, until a solution was finally located in 1918.

The road towards that dénouement was complex and often discouraging for Poles, not least because the movement for independence spawned various groups and personalities both within and outside Poland with their own particular approaches. Consequently, internecine squabbling emerged as a distinctive feature which was eagerly exploited by Poland's enemies. However, in the first half of the nineteenth century, a certain strand of Polish opinion, encouraged by the growth of Romantic nationalism in Europe, still supported the idea and practice of an armed uprising, especially against Russia, as the way forward. This view was strengthened when the relatively liberal reforms introduced by Tsar Alexander I (1777–1825) after 1815 in the congress kingdom were increasingly replaced in the late 1820s by reactionary measures by his successor, Tsar Nicholas I (1796–1855).

The principal and most famous episodes within the insurrectionist tradition, the November Rising in 1830, the Galician *jacquerie* in 1846, and the January Rising in 1863, all ended in failure, triggering the emigration abroad, invariably to France, as with the 'Great Emigration' of 1831, of many of the most active and talented Poles. Oppression in Poland intensified. The insurrectionist strategy, it then seemed to most Poles, was no longer a viable option, and in any event, the Polish cause ceased attracting official sympathy from European governments and peoples. *Realpolitik* dictated that as a united Germany emerged under Chancellor Otto von Bismarck (1815–98) after 1871, as the Habsburgs settled on a new, apparently more stable constitutional basis following the 1867 *Ausgleich*, and as Russia remained powerful, the Poles would have to find other, as yet untried, means of regaining their independence in a new era.

In the face of the inexorable processes of Russification and Germanisation from the 1860s and 1870s, Poles generally sought to sustain their hopes through a more pronounced emphasis on what had already emerged in the 1840s as a programme of 'Organic Work'. Overtly non-political, influenced philosophically by the rationalist empiricism of Warsaw Positivism, and inspired by a messianic vision of Poland as the 'Christ of Nations', the programme stressed the need to cherish and develop the Polish language, literature, education, social norms and economy as far as was possible within the restrictive framework of partition. The ultimate goal was an inclusive, modernised, anti-obscurantist Poland. It involved necessarily the concept and reality of 'tri-loyalism', a temporary and expedient acceptance of, even collaboration with, the partitionist powers.

During the twenty years or so after the 1863 Rising, therefore, impressive advances were recorded in the main spheres of 'Organic Work', so that a genuine sense of Polishness was kept alive and even extended to more and more of the peasantry. The Catholic Church, to which the mass of Poles owed allegiance, played a pivotal role, especially as almost all other Polish institutions and organisations had been forbidden in Russian Poland. The Church, particularly in the face of the *Kulturkampf* and colonisation initiatives in the Polish-populated eastern provinces of the German Reich, provided the essential ingredient of spiritual and moral leadership to the Polish nation, though was criticised by some as being too willing to accept the political status quo in the Russian partition.

As a whole, however, there can be little doubt that 'Organic Work' was a multifaceted phenomenon which contributed significantly to the longer-term aim of achieving independence for Poland. It sustained a sense of optimism during a period when national morale was very low, and it also allowed the creative energies of Poles to be channelled in a constructive manner. It also gave rise to a new leadership class, an urban, bourgeois intelligentsia dedicated to perpetuating the values of the *szlachta*. None the less, 'Organic Work' could not last forever in a Polish and European environment that was rapidly changing in response to industrialisation, urbanisation, and the emergence of fresh ideas and militant ideologies in the last quarter of the century. Of the latter, nationalism and socialism, in particular, exerted, in their different ways, a profound influence on the development of the Polish movement for independence.

The foremost exponent of modern Polish nationalism was the political movement that started life in 1893 as the National League and which four years later was remodelled as the National Democratic Movement, soon to be popularly referred to as the *Endecja*, with Roman Dmowski (1864–1939) as its leader and main ideologue. Dmowski, helped by a number of other right-wing, nationalist thinkers such as Zygmunt Balicki (1858–1916) and Jan Ludwig Popławski (1854–1908), sought to define the philosophical and political ideology of the nationalists in numerous writings and publications, of which Dmowski's 'Thoughts of a Modern Pole' (1903) is perhaps the best known. They felt it was important to clarify who should be considered Polish and what was the physical extent of 'Poland', and to establish precisely what their movement stood for.

The National Democrats asserted the right to have a 'Poland for the Poles' in which non-Polish peoples would play a subordinate role, though some of them, such as Ukrainians and Byelorussians, but not Germans or Jews, could be assimilated over time into Polish society. Poland was to have a conservative, Catholic ethos in deference to predominant Polish attitudes, and Poland was to aspire to the status of a Great Power, as she had been in earlier centuries. In political terms, the stridently anti-German *Endecja* believed that as the insurrectionist tradition was now obsolete, the most feasible option was to secure as much autonomy as possible from Russia as an essential preliminary stepping-stone to full independence in the longer term. Its representatives in the Duma after 1905 promoted, therefore, a policy of loyal co-operation with the tsar. In addition, in view of the prominence allotted by the nationalists to the role of the Jews in Polish society, anti-Semitism was widely and rightly perceived to be a major characteristic of the *Endecja*, as its boycott in 1912 of Jewish businesses in Warsaw as part of an electoral wrangle underlined. On this basis, the nationalists attracted a broad spectrum of support from across the three partitions, from middle-class professionals, artisans, better-off peasants, patriotic youths, to many Catholic clergy.

Alternatives to the nationalists existed, of course, on the left, with particular reference to the Polish Socialist Party (PPS), which was established in 1892 and whose most notable leader was to be Józef Piłsudski (1867–1935), and more radical groups, such as, from 1898, the Social Democracy of the Kingdom of Poland and Lithuania (SDKPiL). These disparate groups at least subscribed to one fundamental point: they were vehemently anti-tsarist. For Piłsudski, his sense of Polish patriotism transcended his socialism, and he firmly believed in the need to engage in armed conflict to overthrow tsardom and realise the goal of an independent, socialist Poland. He was the heir of the insurrectionist tradition and invited all Poles, including Polish Jews, to answer his rallying call. Consequently, quite a few of his comrades and even his closest associates in the PPS were of Jewish background, which only served to deepen the *Endecja*'s hostility towards him personally and the socialist movement as a whole. Piłsudski's banishment to Siberia from 1887 to 1892 for his political activity only hardened his resolve to effect radical change in Poland's position.

If Dmowski and Piłsudski and their respective parties largely constituted the new and most visible face of Polish politics by the turn of the century, neither seemed likely to succeed, such was the tight grip still of the partitionist powers over Poland, while only the most modest of gains and concessions for Poles had been recorded by Polish deputies in the Duma, the German Reichstag and the Austrian Reichsrat. Moreover, both the nationalist and socialist movements, bitter enemies that they were, were confronted, despite a growing sense of Polish national identity and heightened cultural and paramilitary activity in Galicia, by the apathy towards politics of a majority of Poles, who were far more concerned with everyday matters in an atmosphere of continuing, if somewhat modified, repression. The reality that partitioned Poland was a mosaic of variegated and often divisive economic, social, political, ideological, ethnic and religious elements, according to local and regional circumstances, created what seemed like an intractable impasse over the question of independence. That stalemate was broken, not from within Poland, but only from the events that culminated in the outbreak of the First World War.

Piłsudski, who had been predicting for several years that a major conflict would engulf the leading states of Europe and that this would at last create an opportunity for Poles to seize their independence, responded in the best way he knew how – by forming the Polish legions to fight the Russians on the side of the Central Powers, and thereby demonstrate a military capability on the part of Poles which would mark an indispensable step towards their independence. For the nationalists, the military option was simply not a serious consideration. Instead, Dmowski pinned his hopes on diplomatic manoeuvring to secure his more limited goal of autonomy from Russia, which meant, at least initially, supporting Russia and the Western Powers against Germany and the Habsburgs.

The political and military complexities of the war inevitably brought about changes to the paths chosen initially by Piłsudski and Dmowski. For the former, the military option proved to be of very limited value and, of course, he was imprisoned by the Germans during the last year of the war. For Dmowski, his Polish National Committee, which was set up in 1917, was able to gather a certain but hardly conclusive degree of support in the corridors of Allied power in Paris, London and Washington. Meanwhile, the partitionist powers had from the beginning of the conflict sought the support of their respective Polish subjects by making vague, hastily conceived promises of autonomy or quasi-independence. A striking example was the German and Austrian emperors' proclamation of 1916 restoring a semi-independent Kingdom of Poland in union with them. Later, in Warsaw, the German occupation authorities made strenuous efforts to enlist Polish support by setting up a number of governmental bodies, including a Council of State and a Regency Council. Both of these proved to be singularly ineffectual.

The decisive breakthrough as far as the cause of Polish independence was concerned came with the collapse of the tsarist autocracy in early 1917 and the outbreak of the Bolshevik Revolution six months later, and as a result of the actions of the United States and its President, Woodrow Wilson (1856–1924). His conversion to the Polish cause was motivated primarily by American interests, of course, but also owed much to his high-principled personal sense of justice and humanity, from which evolved the notion of national self-determination, as well as to the more pragmatic influence of the renowned international pianist and staunch Polish patriot, Ignacy Jan Paderewski (1860–1941). Paderewski's celebrity status had allowed him to move in the most exclusive social and political circles in the United States, and through friends such as the presidential confidant Colonel Edward House, he managed to establish a close and friendly relationship with the President. Wilson first gave public intimation of his support for an independent Poland in January 1917, which was then firmed up a year later when he issued his Fourteen Points as the foundation for a lasting peace in Europe: Point Thirteen referred explicitly to Poland.

Less than six months later, the Western Allies recognised Poland as 'an Allied belligerent nation' and endorsed Wilson's commitment to an independent Poland. The collapse in November 1918 of the remaining former partitionist powers, Germany and the Habsburg Empire, removed the last major obstacle to long-nurtured Polish dreams being fulfilled. The Poles themselves were now ready and eager to seize the opportunity for a momentous change in their fortunes. The Paris Peace Conference in 1919 provided the political and diplomatic framework within which the 'Polish Question' could be finally and satisfactorily resolved.

Document 1

From a manifesto of the National League to the people of Russia, Warsaw, 1894:

One hundred years of oppression have not weakened our strength, have not made us doubt our faith in the manifestation of the ideals of truth, justice, liberty, equality, and brotherhood of nations. With or without you, in accordance with or against your intentions, we will continue to conduct our struggle for our freedom and yours. The moment will come when the enslaved nations will arise in unison, an uprising of all the oppressed and exploited. And there will be no more strong or weak, slaves or masters, nationalities without rights or states artificially held together . . . The struggle for an independent Poland is a struggle for a free Russia.

Source: W. Pobóg-Malinowski, *Narodowa Demokracja, 1887–1918: fakty i dokumenty* (Warsaw: Zjednoczona Polska, 1933), pp. 101–2

Document 2

Józef Piłsudski on the Catholic Church's attitude to Polish independence, May 1895:

The higher Catholic clergy take part in a dinner given by Hurko [Russian Governor of Warsaw] . . . the Archbishop [Wincenty] Popiel [of Warsaw] confirms in Russian the oath of fidelity to the new tsar, and Father Dudkiewicz in Dąbrowa [a major industrial district] implores his parishioners from the pulpit not to learn to read, because they would then be able to get to know the contents of socialist pamphlets . . . This is the Polish clergy, the ally of tsarist rule in our country, and the loyal defender of our exploiters. It might have been thought that a despotic government, especially a foreign one, would have been met with decisive opposition . . . But where?

Source: From the socialist paper *Robotnik*, May 1895

Document 3

Józef Piłsudski on his political ideals:

The People's Republic, which we will build after casting off the Muscovite yoke, will be a republic of brotherhood and community, where the door to happiness and freedom will be fully open for all and where the welfare of its citizens will take precedence. Instead of the right of property, we will introduce another right – 'all is for all'. Instead of a government, we will declare unrestricted freedom for everyone . . . Instead of a multitude of duties which are presently imposed by the state, we will acknowledge only one duty, that of brotherhood and mutual help. The achievement of this kind of republic is the ultimate aim and major task of the working class. It is our leading principle, our ideal.

Source: From the socialist paper *Robotnik*, April 1897

Document 4

Roman Dmowski defines a Pole and Poland:

We are a nation, a single, indivisible nation, because we have a feeling of our unity, we have a common, collective consciousness, a common national spirit. That national spirit has been nurtured through centuries of common state existence, and is a feeling of unity in the fight for a common existence, in success and collective failure, in the aspiration to collective aims, a feeling of distinctiveness from the alien traditions of neighbours. That national spirit, created through a long process of history, finds in history the justification for its existence and its hopes. Clearly, 'historical rights' is not an empty phrase, not an empty formula without meaning. Yes, we are one nation, because we are united by a common feeling, a common national thought, and finally a common will directed towards one national aim that every Pole, even if only poorly educated, is aware of.

And further:

For us, Poland is above all the Polish nation, with its culture and tradition, with a separate soul and separate civilising needs; it is a living, organic union of people having common needs and interests in a certain area, a union demanding specific duties, including personal sacrifice, and work for collective needs and struggle in defence of common interests. The nation is a loose collection of individuals, groups, or strata, having nothing more in common than the fact that they live on one land, that they speak one language. They are not bound by deeper moral ties, they do not have common needs, nor common duties above the needs of justice . . . We demand of everyone that in relations between their nation and foreign nations, they feel above all that they are Poles.

Source: R. Dmowski in the journal *Przegląd Wszechpolski*, March 1892 and November 1902

Document 5

Roman Dmowski in 1902 on the Jews:

. . . In the character of this race so many different values, strange to our moral constitution and harmful to our life, have accumulated that assimilation with a larger number of [them] would destroy us, replacing with decadent elements those young creative foundations upon which we are building the future.

And further, in 1913:

There has not been anything so contrary to conservative principles, so hostile to them, as the programme of the assimilation of Jews, of bringing them into the midst of Polish society . . . A Jew cannot be a conservative in European society, even if for some reason he should decide to be one. The whole tradition of European society is alien to him, contrary to all that the Jewish soul has absorbed during countless generations. He treats the entire past of European peoples with disgust, harbours hatred towards their religion, looks upon every hierarchy . . . as usurping the place of the 'chosen people'.

Instinctively, the Jew seeks to destroy in his European environment respect for tradition, attachment to religion, recognition of hierarchy; he besmirches and ridicules all that which for every honest conservative is sacred . . . The incursion of a large wave of Jews into our life has resulted, in those social circles which have become connected with them, in such destruction of all preservative characteristics, such rebellion against one's own national tradition, such decay in religious feelings and even basic respect for religion . . . that it has in a sense threatened us with barbarisation. If all of society were to succumb to this influence, we would actually lose our capacity for societal life.

Source: R. Dmowski, *Myśli Nowoczesnego Polska* (London: Koło Młodych Stronnictwa Narodowego, 1953, 7th edn), p. 91; R. Dmowski, *Upadek Myśli Konserwatywpej*, in *Pisma* (Czestochowa: Antoni Gmachowski, 1938), pp. 118–19

Document 6

The Polish Socialist Party on anti-Semitism:

Comrades!

The understanding and solidarity of the workers are – without regard to divisions among them or to differences of origin and religion – the best means for ensuring the victory of our cause and for liberating the working masses from all kinds of coercion. The tsarist government is well aware of this, and tries to weaken our unity by inciting racial and religious hatreds . . . This appalling tactic has been applied in Poland for many years. But our proletariat is too experienced to fall for such a trick . . . However, the government's policy is also supported by all those for whom the class struggle is a permanent affront . . . Catholic priests, Jesuits and National Democrats are all spreading hatred of the Jews. It is perfectly understandable, of course, that they should be angry at the role Jews are playing in all revolutionary movements. But it is both naïve and stupid of them to imagine that we also share their hatred. Jewish blood . . . has cemented in a strong bond the various elements of the proletariat. In our ranks, we recognise neither Jew nor German nor Russian, but only workers attacking the tsarist monster for freedom and human happiness.

Long live international workers' solidarity! Shame on the dark forces of Reaction!

Source: Declaration by a cell of the Polish Socialist Party in Łódź, July 1905

Document 7

Józef Piłsudski's proclamation to his fellow-Poles at the start of the First World War:

The decisive hour has struck. Poland ceases being a slave and will alone determine her fate. She will build her future by throwing the weight of her armed forces into the balance. Detachments of the Polish army have already crossed the territory of the Kingdom of Poland, restoring it to its real owner – the Polish people – who caused it to become fruitful and rich. They take possession of it in the name of the supreme authority of the National Government. To the entire nation we bring release from its chains, and to every class the right to develop in freedom. The entire nation should now rally behind the National Government. Only traitors will stand aside, and for them we will have no mercy.

Source: J. Piłsudski, commander-in-chief of the Polish army, 6 August 1914. Cited in K. W. Kumaniecki, *Odbudowanie Państwa* (Warsaw: Biblioteka Polska, 1924), p. 12

Document 8

Proclamation of the Grand Duke Nicholas (1856–1929), commander-in-chief of the Russian Army, 14 August 1914:

Poles! The time has come when the dream of your fathers and forefathers will at last be realised. A century and a half ago, the living body of Poland was torn into pieces, but her soul has not perished. She lives in the hope that the time will come for the resurrection of the Polish nation and its fraternal union with all Russia. The Russian armies bring you glad tidings of this union. May the barriers which have divided the Polish people be united under the sceptre of the Russian emperor. Under this sceptre, Poland will come together, free in faith, in language, and in self-government. From you Russia expects an equal consideration of the rights of those nations with which history has linked you. With open heart and with hand fraternally outstretched, great Russia comes to you . . . The morning star of a new life is rising for Poland.

Source: J. Holzer and J. Molenda, *Polska w Pierwszej Wojnie Światowej* (Warsaw: Wiedza Powszechna, 1963), pp. 48ff.

Document 9

The response to the outbreak of war of several Polish political parties, including the National Democrats, and of many prominent Poles, was:

[We] welcome the proclamation of His Imperial Highness to the Poles . . . as an act of momentous historical importance, and believe firmly that after the end of the war the promises expressed therein will be realised . . . that the body of Poland, torn to pieces a century and a half ago, will be reunited . . . The blood of her sons shed in the common struggle against Germany will constitute in equal measure a sacrifice offered on the altar of the resurrected fatherland.

Deeply moved by the proclamation of Your Imperial Highness, who declares to us that the valiant Russian Army, unsheathing its sword in defence of all Slavs, fights also for the holy cause of our nation, the restoration of a united Poland, the unity of all her disjointed parts under the sceptre of His Imperial Majesty, [we] representatives of Polish political parties and social groups strongly believe that the blood of Poland's sons, shed together with the blood of Russia's sons in the struggle with the common enemy, will constitute the best guarantee of a new life in peace and friendship for the two Slavonic nations.

On this historic day of the proclamation of such importance for the Polish nation, we are filled with an ardent desire for the victory of the Russian Army, which is under the most illustrious command of Your Imperial Highness, and we await its complete triumph on the battlefield.

We beg Your Imperial Highness to place at the feet of His Majesty the Emperor these wishes and our sentiments of loyalty as Russian subjects.

Source: *Kurier Warszawski*, 15 August and 24 September 1914

Document 10

Resolution of the radical leftist party, the Social Democracy of the Kingdom of Poland and Lithuania, January 1916:

The development of the war has proved that the epoch of national states is over . . . the Polish proletariat has never made national independence one of its aims. The proletariat has sought to destroy not the existing state boundaries but the character of the state as an instrument of class and national oppression. In view of what has happened in the war, the advancement of the slogan of independence as a means of struggle against national oppression would not only be a harmful utopia, but would also constitute a repudiation of the basic principles of socialism. The right of self-determination is impracticable in capitalist society and unnecessary under socialism. Under socialism, cultural autonomy would be wholly adequate. The working class of Poland rejects all pleas for the 'defence of the Fatherland'. The proletariat of Poland will fight neither for the unification of Poland nor for independence . . . The Polish workers will struggle, in solidarity with the international proletariat, for a social revolution, which is the only possible solution to social and national problems.

Source: *Gazeta robotnicza*, No. 25, January 1916

Document 11

Józef Piłsudski on the Polish fighting spirit, 1916:

In 1914, I was not concerned with settling the details of the military question in Poland, but simply with this: was the Polish soldier to remain a mystical entity deprived of flesh and blood? In a great war fought on Polish soil, when a soldier with his bayonet and uniform would penetrate to every cottage and farm of our countryside, I wanted the Polish soldier to be something more than a pretty picture often looked at secretly in corners by well-brought-up children. I wanted Poland, which had forgotten the sword so entirely since 1863, to see it flashing in the air in the hands of her own soldier.

Source: J. Piłsudski, *The Memoirs of a Polish Revolutionary and Soldier*, ed. D. Gillie (London: Faber & Faber, 1931), p. 186

Document 12

The Two Emperors' Proclamation to Poland, 5 November 1916:

His Majesty the German emperor, and His Majesty the Austrian emperor and apostolic king of Hungary, sustained by their firm confidence in the final victory of their arms, and guided by the wish to lead to a happy future the Polish districts which by their brave armies were snatched with heavy sacrifices from Russian power, have agreed to form from these districts

21

an independent state with an hereditary monarchy and a constitution. The more precise regulation of the frontiers of the Kingdom of Poland remains reserved. In union with both the Allied Powers, the new kingdom will find the guarantees which it desires for the free development of its strength. In its own army, the glorious traditions of the Polish Army of former times and the memory of our brave Polish fellow-combatants in the great war of the present time will continue to live. Its organisation, training and command will be regulated by mutual agreement.

Giving due consideration to the general political conditions prevailing in Europe and to the welfare and safety of their own countries and nations, the Allied monarchs express the confident hope that Polish wishes for the evolution of a Polish state and for the national development of a Polish kingdom will now be fulfilled.

The great realm which the western neighbours of the Kingdom of Poland will have on their eastern frontier will be a free and happy state, enjoying its own national life. And they will welcome with joy the birth and prosperous development of the state.

Source: *Schulthess' Europäischer Geschichtskalender*
(Nördlingen: Beck, 1916), II, p. 441

Document 13

From Roman Dmowski's 'Memorandum on the Territory of the Polish State', 26 March 1917:

As the war progressed, the chances of a Russian solution of the Polish problem gradually vanished. The chief reason lay in . . . the character and limitations of Russian policy itself . . . Her Polish policy . . . became simply incomprehensible, and showed a lack of consistency . . . Russia has treated the Polish problem exclusively as her own domestic matter. Now, nobody in Poland and only a small minority in Russia believes in the settlement of Poland's future by Russia.

As the German solution of the Polish problem is unacceptable as far as the Allies are concerned, for it would mean the most important step in the conquest of the whole of Central Europe by Germany, only the establishment of an Independent Polish State remains. That state must be sufficiently large and strong, it must be able to be economically independent of Germany, which means having an outlet to the sea and the rich coalfields of Silesia, and it must be a sovereign state with its own foreign policy . . .

The territory of the future state cannot be defined either on a strictly historical or purely linguistic basis. A re-creation of Poland in its historical frontiers of 1772 would hardly be possible today, and would not produce a very strong state. The basis of the strength of Poland is the territory where the mass of the population speaks Polish, is conscious of its Polish nationality, and is attached to the Polish cause. This territory is not restricted to the limits of the Poland of 1772. There are Polish provinces in Germany and Austria which did not belong to Poland at the time of the Partition, but where the mass of the population not only speaks Polish but is Polish in its ideas and feelings. These are: Upper Silesia, the southern part of East Prussia . . . and part of Austrian Silesia (Principality of Teschen) . . . On the other hand, in the Russian Empire, to the east of the Polish-speaking country, there is a large territory with a population of 25 million which belonged to old Poland and where the Poles are in a minority . . . It is true that the Polish minority represents culture and wealth, that Polish civilisation in spite of the antagonism of the Russian government is predominant there . . . None the less, the masses of that territory would present a field for anti-Polish agitation, and might become . . . a great danger to the solidity of the Polish State.

. . . the most desirable territory of the future Polish State would comprise: Austrian Poland (Galicia and half of Austrian Silesia [Teschen]); Russian Poland (the Kingdom of Poland and the governments of Kovno, Wilno, Grodno, parts of Minsk and Volhynia); and German Poland (. . . Poznania and West Prussia with Danzig . . . Upper Silesia and the southern area of East Prussia). Perhaps the most difficult task is to wrest from Germany her part of Poland . . . for it would mean for her the destruction of the great historical work founded by Frederick the Great, the real author of the destruction of Poland.

Source: Public Record Office, Kew: FO371/3000–63741

Document 14

The Petrograd Soviet issues a declaration to the Polish people, 28 March 1917:

The Tsarist regime, which in the course of the last one and a half centuries has been oppressing the Polish and the Russian people at the same time, has been overthrown by the combined forces of the proletariat and the army.

Notifying the Polish people of this victory of freedom . . . the Petrograd Soviet of Workers' and Soldiers' Deputies declares that Russian democracy stands for the recognition of the national political self-determination of peoples, and proclaims that Poland has the right to complete independence as a sovereign state in national and international affairs.

We send our fraternal greetings to the Polish people, and wish it success in the forthcoming struggle for the establishment of a democratic, republican order in independent Poland.

Source: J. Pajewski, *Historia powszechna 1871–1918* (Warsaw: Państwowe Wydawnictwo Naukowe, 1967), pp. 420–1

Document 15

Proclamation of the Russian Provisional Government to the Poles, 30 March 1917:

Poles! The old regime of Russia, the source of your and our enslavement and disunity, has now been overthrown for good. Liberated Russia, represented by its Provisional Government . . . hastens to extend its fraternal greetings and invites you to a new life, to freedom.

The old regime made hypocritical promises to you which it could, but did not wish to, fulfil. The Central Powers took advantage of its mistakes in order to occupy and devastate your territory. With the sole aim of fighting against Russia and her allies, they gave you chimerical state rights . . . Brother Poles! . . . Free Russia calls on you to join the ranks of those fighting for peoples' freedom . . . the Russian people recognise the full right of the fraternal Polish people to determine their own fate . . . the Provisional Government considers that the creation of an independent Polish State, comprising all the lands where the Polish people constitute the majority of the population, would be a reliable guarantee for lasting peace in the new Europe of the future. United with Russia by a free military alliance, the Polish State will become a firm bulwark of Slavdom against the pressures of the Central Powers . . . The Russian Constituent Assembly will give binding strength to the new fraternal alliance and agree to those territorial changes of the Russian State which are necessary for the creation of a free Poland out of her three, now separated, areas.

Accept the fraternal hand, brother Poles, which free Russia extends to you . . . stand up now to meet the bright new day in your history, the day of the resurrection of Poland . . . forward, to the struggle, shoulder to shoulder and arm in arm, for your freedom and ours!

Source: J. Pajewski, *Historia powszechna 1871–1918* (Warsaw: Państwowe Wydawnictwo Naukowe, 1967), pp. 422 ff.

Document 16

President Woodrow Wilson's 'Peace without Victory' Senate speech on 22 January 1917, and from his Fourteen Points, 8 January 1918, Point Thirteen:

No peace can last, or ought to last, which does not recognise and accept the principle that governments derive all their just powers from the consent of the governed, and that no right anywhere exists to hand peoples about from sovereignty to sovereignty as if they were property . . . statesmen everywhere are agreed that there should be a united, independent and autonomous Poland.

Point Thirteen:
An independent Polish state should be erected which should include the territories inhabited by indisputably Polish populations, which should be assured a free and secure access to the sea, and whose political and economic independence and territorial integrity should be guaranteed by international covenant.

Source: *The Papers of Woodrow Wilson*, edited by A. S. Link *et al.* (Princeton, NJ: Princeton University Press, 1966–98), Volume 40, pp. 535–8; and Volume 48, p. 254

Document 17

Statement issued by the Polish National Committee, Paris, 12 August 1918:

Our aim is to create an independent Polish State composed of all Polish territories including those which provide Polish access to the sea; a strong state which would be able to keep in check its western neighbours, the Teutonic empires, and would be a bulwark against their expansion in Central Europe and the east. We fully appreciate the fact that it is only with the assistance of the great free nations, in conflict with the Central

Powers, that we shall be in a position to achieve the unification as well as the independence of Poland; and firmly trusting in their ultimate victory, which will mean at the same time the triumph of liberty and justice, we consider ourselves as their ally, not only for the duration of the war, but also after the conclusion of peace. We feel ourselves bound to those nations by unity of thought and struggle against the common enemy in order to safeguard the solemn rights of nations which are the basis of humanity's peaceful development.

The Polish State must have a democratic constitution. It must govern according to the principles of liberty and justice, together with principles of order. Without such principles, no effort towards civilisation or progress is attainable. No privileged classes should exist in the new Poland: Polish citizens without distinction of origin, race or creed must stand equal before the law

> **Source: W.Stankiewicz and A. Piber (eds), *Archiwum Polityczne Ignacego Paderewskiego*, Volume 1, *1890–1918*, (Wrocław: Ossolineum, 1973), pp. 483 ff.**

Document 18

Louis Marshall, chairman of the American Jewish Committee, in a letter to President Woodrow Wilson, 7 November 1918:

It is generally recognised that one of the most important subjects to come before the Conference of Nations to be held at the close of the war is the restoration of Poland. It necessarily affects the future of all of the inhabitants within the area of the re-created Polish State . . . approximately four million Jews . . . will be directly concerned. Hence, whatever the geographical extent of the new State or its form of government, the civil, political and religious rights of these Jews must be safeguarded.

The American Jewish Committee has long sympathised with the aspirations of the Polish people for independence and the right of self-government. It heartily approves of the establishment of a [Polish] State . . . Unfortunately, however, in 1912, there was inaugurated by the leaders of the Polish National Committee, and has ever since been carried out in that country, a policy looking to the practical destruction of the Jews of Poland through the medium of a most virulent economic boycott, which is still in full operation and has grown in intensity from year to year . . . an intolerable condition [exists] and bodes unspeakable evil unless immediate remedial action is taken by those who are seeking the recognition of an independent Polish State to end this policy of extermination . . .

Source: Archives of the YIVO Institute for Jewish Research, New York, correspondence Louis Marshall– Ignacy J. Paderewski, 1918

2

CONSOLIDATION

Józef Piłsudski, the personality most intimately associated with the cause of Polish independence in the public mind, arrived in Warsaw on 10 November 1918, following his release from Madgeburg Castle, where he had been interned since July 1917 for having refused to co-operate fully with the German occupation authorities over the creation of a sponsored Polish army, the *Polnische Wehrmacht*. Piłsudski found a chaotic political situation, whose principal ingredients were: the German-installed Regency Council led by Prince Zdzisław Lubomirski (1865–1943) was still in office; a revolutionary provisional government of the 'Polish People's Republic' had been set up on 7 November in Lublin under the veteran socialist Ignacy Daszyński (1866–1936); and the Polish National Committee led by Roman Dmowski in Paris continued to be recognised as the official Polish Government by the Western Allies. As a first step towards establishing at least a semblance of order, the Regency Council appointed Piłsudski commander-in-chief of the Polish armed forces on 11 November and asked him to form a national government. On the same day, and amidst widespread patriotic euphoria, Poland's independence was proclaimed, thus symbolically if not yet formally terminating the partitionist era. Foreign governments were notified of Poland's new status on 16 November, though reaction was not entirely favourable. On 14 November, Piłsudski's hand had been further strengthened with his appointment as provisional head of state, a position he retained until surrendering his extensive power to the Constituent *Sejm* early the following year. When his first choice as Prime Minister, Daszyński, was unable to form a coalition cabinet because of the opposition of the National Democrats, he was more successful with the moderate socialist, Jędrzej Moraczewski (1870–1944), and then sought to co-opt to it the Polish National Committee.

While problems of political, governmental and social stability were obviously of the highest priority for Poland in these turbulent early days, of even greater importance was her national security in a Europe which was convulsed by the dissolution of states, revolution and counter-revolution and vicious disputes over borders. For Poland to survive these extreme dangers, Piłsudski was determined to organise without delay a unified, coherent Polish army from the disparate military units scattered around the country and abroad. These were the Polish armed forces which had been controlled by the now defunct Regency Council, the Polish Corps in Russia, the 50,000-strong Polish Military Organisation, the legionnaires' brigades, and General Józef Haller's (1873–1960) 'Blue Army' in France. Piłsudski's task became all the more imperative in view of the numerous conflicts into which Poland was soon dragged in order to establish and defend her territory: against the Ukrainians over Lwów and Eastern Galicia, the Lithuanians over Wilno, the Czechoslovaks over Cieszyn (Teschen) and, above all, against the Germans in Upper Silesia and the Soviet Bolsheviks over the eastern area. Regardless of how these wars were decided on the ground, a lasting resolution could be provided only within the framework of international diplomacy.

The statesmen attending the Paris Peace Conference beginning in January 1919 were confronted by problems of unprecedented magnitude in international affairs. Proceedings were dominated inevitably by the Great Powers, each of whom was guided in large part by national interests, and they also had to contend with the demands of many well-organised 'lobbies'. How to reconcile all the divergent interests in a way that would be widely regarded as satisfactory was a virtually impossible challenge, and when the terms agreed were published in June in the Treaty of Versailles some countries and groups were pleased, others disappointed, and others still responded with mixed emotions. The commitment of the Western Allies to Polish independence was honoured, though President Woodrow Wilson revised to some extent his original plans for the shape of Poland's territory. This was due partly to pressure from the British Prime Minister, David Lloyd George (1863–1945), who was, in general, unfavourably disposed towards Poland, and to the President's concern at what he saw as the unpleasantly nationalistic tone of some statements from Polish politicians such as Dmowski, and reports of rising anti-Semitic violence in Poland. Consequently, rather than agreeing to give Danzig and Upper Silesia to Poland, Wilson finally agreed with his colleagues that the important Baltic port should be designated a Free City under the auspices of the League of Nations, and that the future of Upper Silesia should be resolved by an internationally supervised plebiscite.

Although the Poles were not best pleased by this turn of events, they were far more exercised by the imposition of the Minorities' Treaty as an integral and compulsory part of the peace settlement for them. More importantly, as the Treaty of Versailles had not definitively pronounced on Poland's borders, it was left to the Poles themselves to fill this lacuna. Thus, at a time in these early postwar years when the country was having to wrestle with a plethora of social, economic, political, constitutional and institutional matters of fundamental importance to her future, to have any future at all, Poland was compelled to confront the substantial threat to her very existence from the two principal anti-Versailles revisionist powers, Germany and Soviet Russia.

Germany's defeat in the First World War, the collapse of the Hohenzollern monarchy, the November Revolution and the introduction at the Allies' insistence of a parliamentary democracy, the Weimar Republic, might have suggested the possibility of a fresh era in her relations with a Poland that also had just experienced a dramatic change in fortune. It was perhaps not unreasonable to think that the bitter historical legacy between them, including prejudiced stereotyping, could be put aside as a constructive contribution to the making of a new and better Europe. From the German side, the liberal and socialist movements might have been expected to take the initiative, particularly as many of their followers had openly supported the cause of Polish independence in the nineteenth century. In 1918–19, political parties representing these ideologies, the German Democratic Party (DDP), the German People's Party (DVP), the Social Democratic Party (SPD) and the Independent Social Democratic Party (USPD), were at the centre of power, and liberal leaders, in particular, such as Erich Koch-Weser (1875–1944) and Carl Petersen (1868–1933), intimated their desire for a friendly attitude towards Poland. Other influential groups, including the German Peace Society, some parts of the trade unions, businessmen, and some officials in the German Foreign Office, endorsed this outlook, to one degree or another.

On the other hand, it is certainly true that the nationalist Right, composed of the German National People's Party (DNVP), the army (*Reichswehr*), the Evangelical (Protestant) Church, and a multitude of paramilitary and smaller political organisations, continued to articulate intransigently the traditional polonophobia of the middle and upper classes. These circles could only ever see Poland, in whatever guise, as a '*Saisonstaat*', an ephemeral, feckless entity. On the Polish side, the fiercely anti-Russian Piłsudski and a number of government ministers gave a cautious welcome to the prospect of better relations. They co-operated in the evacuation of German troops from Poland, and in May 1919 concluded a commercial treaty with Germany. At the same time, the *Endecja* remained hostile to Germany.

It quickly transpired that the forces of liberalism and socialism in Germany were not strong or determined enough to forge a new relationship with Poland. The divisions and inherent weaknesses in both camps undermined their political effectiveness and too many liberals and socialists were unable ultimately to overcome their nationalism. Several socialist leaders, such as Otto Braun (1872–1955) and Otto Landsberg (1869–1957), had a powerful emotional attachment to the Reich's eastern provinces – soon to be at the centre of renewed armed conflict with the Poles – which transcended their otherwise sound democratic credentials. Likewise, the Centre Party, the main representative of Catholic political interests in Weimar, which might have been expected to show some affinity with co-religionists in Poland, was unwilling to become involved in improving relations. Indeed, many in that party, including Joseph Wirth (1879–1956), Reich Chancellor in 1921, were passionately anti-Polish.

The overriding factor in German–Polish relations was, of course, the Treaty of Versailles, by which Germany had to cede West Prussia and other parts of her eastern provinces to independent Poland. The ensuing disputes over Upper Silesia, involving right-wing paramilitary groups (*Freikorps*), three Polish risings and a plebiscite, only exacerbated the situation. Almost all German political parties became revisionist, demanding the return of these 'lost' territories and thus an end to what nationalists called 'the bleeding frontier' with Poland. Such was the anti-Polish animus that there was virtually universal support in Germany for the Soviet Bolsheviks in the war with Poland.

While Polish forces had secured Lwów and Eastern Galicia by July 1919, the danger to Poland from the Bolsheviks increased as they were gaining the upper hand in the Russian Civil War, and there is no doubt that the Polish–Soviet War was the pivotal event in the early history of the Second Republic. It began in a somewhat desultory fashion in early 1919 in the wake of the withdrawal of German troops from the Eastern Front at the end of the First World War. Both Polish and Bolshevik forces then sought to fill the vacuum and assert their territorial claims, and by the end of that year the momentum of conflict had picked up considerably.

The old Soviet claim that the war was caused by an imperialist, bourgeois Poland as the spearhead of a Western-inspired crusade against Bolshevism is fallacious. Piłsudski would never allow himself or Poland to be manipulated in such a way, not least because of his well-founded distrust of the Western Powers. Rather, he pursued an independent policy that served the best interests of Poland, as he understood them. More to the point was his plan to re-create in eastern Europe an edifice akin to the old Polish–Lithuanian Commonwealth, which he believed had shown how harmoniously different national and ethnic elements could be integrated under Poland's leadership into a single state for the benefit of all. The aim was also to construct an effective barrier against both Russian and German expansionism in eastern Europe. In the event, the nationalism of smaller states in the region after 1918 militated against the successful realisation of Piłsudski's federalist concept. Just as important, however, was his resolve to establish as quickly as possible what the Treaty of Versailles had not done, namely, Poland's borders in the east. He saw no alternative than to employ Polish arms in order to safeguard her newly won independence.

Overriding these considerations, however, was one essential factor: the conviction of Lenin (1870–1924) and his fellow-Bolsheviks that the extension of the revolution into the heart of Europe was critical to its long-term survival and success. Germany, with its large, well-organised and active Communist Party (KPD), had been earmarked as the strategic centre of this ambitious enterprise: Poland stood in the way. For the Poles, Lenin's plan was simply the latest manifestation of tsarist imperialism, dressed up in the class rhetoric of revolutionary Bolshevism, claiming Poland as part of the Russian, now Soviet, Empire. Unlike the early pronouncements on the recognition of Poland's right to independence by the Provisional Government and Petrograd Soviet in 1917, the Bolsheviks in 1919–20 had reverted to the tsarist position of not accepting any notion of Polish independence.

Following some early successes in limited engagements, Poland, appreciating the strategic importance of the Ukraine, and in alliance with the anti-Russian Ukrainian nationalists under Seymon Petliura (1879–1926), mounted a pre-emptive strike which brought them as far as Kiev in May 1920. But as the Bolsheviks were less and less distracted by their 'White' opponents in the civil war, they were able more forcefully to address the Polish front. Within a few months, their counter-offensive had expelled the Polish forces from the Ukraine altogether; by the beginning of August 1920, twenty of their divisions, well-equipped, battle-hardened and well-motivated, were converging under the command of General Mikhail Nikolayevich Tukhachevsky (1893–1937) on Warsaw. Not far behind was a Provisional Revolutionary Committee led by two renegade Poles, Feliks Dzierżyński (1877–1926), the head of the notorious Cheka (secret police), and Julian Marchlewski (1866–1925), whose objective was to set up a Soviet Poland in the wake of the Red Army's anticipated victory.

The outcome of the Battle of Warsaw would determine whether Poland remained a free and sovereign state or, in defeat, was transformed into a Soviet satellite, and thus relegated to something like her one-time partitionist situation, only now a lot worse. The stakes, therefore, could hardly have been any higher, and the odds on a Polish victory any lower. After all, there was virtually no help given to Poland from the international community.

The United States had retreated into isolationism. Britain, a belated and rather lukewarm convert to Polish independence who tended to view Poland as an over-ambitious upstart of the natural balance of power in central and eastern Europe, witnessed a vigorous propaganda campaign with the slogan, 'Hands off Russia', backed by left-wing members of the Labour Party, many trade unions, Communists and their sympathisers in the press and academia. The British Government proposed as a way of ending the conflict a Polish–Soviet border, the so-called 'Curzon Line', which both sides rejected. France, deeply fearful and suspicious of Germany and having to face plenty of her own domestic problems, certainly assisted Poland in Upper Silesia, but provided merely a token military mission under General Maxime Weygand (1867–1965) to Warsaw as the Bolsheviks advanced. German and Soviet representatives tentatively discussed an alliance and a new partition of Poland. The Czechs, like British dockers, blocked the shipment of armaments to the Poles. Consequently, Poland fought alone, but rose magnificently to the occasion under Commander-in-Chief Piłsudski and the hastily introduced Council for the Defence of the State, from which emerged an emergency coalition government under the premiership of the Peasant Party leader, Wincenty Witos (1874–1945).

The Polish Army, which had been reformed into a cohesive unit by Piłsudski, was bolstered by compulsory conscription and by a flood of volunteers. Harsh measures were implemented against left-wing agitators and disloyal citizens, almost all of whom came from the ranks of Poland's ethnic minorities, especially the Jews, who, like the industrial working class and peasantry, were singled out by Bolshevik propaganda. Otherwise, and more decisively, the Red threat evoked only a sense of national unity and patriotism throughout ethnic Polish society as earlier social and political differences were set aside in readiness for battle. The British Ambassador, for one, was most impressed.

The Battle of Warsaw was won thanks to a daring counter-offensive conceived by Piłsudski and executed with the aid of his top commanders in the field, including generals Kazimierz Sosnkowski (1885–1969), Tadeusz Rozwadowski (1866–1928) and Władysław Sikorski (1881–1943). In a short period of time, three Soviet armies had been split, encircled, then destroyed. Another fled into internment in East Prussia, while a fifth, which included the *Konarmiya*, the élite cavalry, was roundly defeated several weeks later at Komarów, near Zamość. In early September, the Polish victory at the Battle of the Niemen completed the rout and ended the war. Bolshevik casualties were catastrophic, and thousands more fled in total disarray back to Russia. Lenin, his grand strategy in tatters, was compelled to sue for peace. Despite agreeing terms in the Treaty of Riga in March 1921, however, neither he nor his cohorts ever forgot or forgave this stunning and momentous Polish victory.

The Bolsheviks and their apologists down the years have sought to explain the Red Army's defeat with reference to divisions between it and the party, tactical errors, and poor leadership, thus disparaging the merits of the Polish Army. Piłsudski's political opponents, especially the *Endecja*, attributed the victory to a combination of Divine Providence, hence the 'Miracle on the Vistula', and French help. All of these tendentious arguments miss the point. The Poles won because of their superior skill, boundless courage, sheer determination, inspirational leadership and superb fighting qualities, which were all wrapped up in an impressively intense patriotism.

Poland's victory was not only a telling commentary on the resilient character of the fledgling republic, it also proved to be a most significant factor in its subsequent development. It injected a remarkable degree of self-confidence and self-belief into ethnic Polish society. It taught the overwhelming majority of Poles that Bolshevism meant only repression not freedom, and thus consigned the Communists to marginal status throughout the interwar period. Polish workers and peasants had demonstrated unequivocally in 1920 that country came well before class. Ominously, however, the close association of Jews with Bolshevism (*Żydokomuna*) was confirmed in popular imagination and mercilessly propagated by the nationalist camp and its allies. On the other hand, victory did not bring permanent political harmony to Poland, with the *Endecja* and the Piłsudski camp, in particular, soon at each other's throats again. None the less, Piłsudski's personal reputation was manifestly enhanced in the eyes of most Poles, who approved of the formal conferment on him in November 1920 of the title, 'First Marshal of Poland'. Moreover, he was able, in the longer term at least, to swing the balance of political power in his favour at the expense of his great rival, Dmowski, paving the way for his *coup d'état* in May 1926 and the creation of the *Sanacja* regime. Finally, the victory emphasised the crucial importance of the army to Poland. It epitomised the nation's indomitable will to defend its independence and freedom, it forged as no other institution a sense of national unity, and was rightly accorded after 1920 a status and prestige second to none in the country which allowed it to develop into a most influential political force.

In commemoration of this victory, and in remembrance of the 48,000 who laid down their lives for Poland, the 15 August, the date given to the Battle of Warsaw and also the Feast of the Assumption in the Catholic Church, was designated 'Polish Soldiers' Day'. This patriotic annual event was celebrated with much military and religious pomp until 1939, but because of the Second World War and the Soviet-dominated Communist era, was not revived until the early 1990s, when Poland was once again free and independent. Whatever assessments are made of his political views and actions, Marshal Piłsudski, the conqueror of the Soviet Bolsheviks, rightly has a secure place in the pantheon of Polish military heroes, thereby underlining the importance of this victory for all time, not only for Poland, but also for the whole of Europe, which was spared the nightmare of Soviet Bolshevism for at least another quarter of a century. From these vital perspectives, it was not only Poles who had good reason to be grateful to Piłsudski and the Polish Army for their heroic triumph.

Understandably exhilarated and emboldened by this success, Polish forces were able to emerge victorious from the conflict with the Lithuanians in October 1920, thus securing for the republic Wilno, the city so close to Piłsudski's heart, and in 1921, following a disputed plebiscite and a third Polish rising, against the Germans in Upper Silesia. Only the dispute over the overwhelmingly Polish enclave of Cieszyn with Czechoslovakia had to wait until October 1938 for a just and satisfactory solution. Otherwise, by 1922/3, all of Poland's borders had been settled, and they received formal recognition from the Ambassadors' Conference in early 1923. Poland had been finally consolidated, but only after having been compelled to experience a veritable baptism of fire.

Document 19

Decree by Józef Piłsudski, commander-in-chief, 18 November 1918:

As commander-in-chief of the Polish Army, I wish to notify the former belligerent and neutral governments and nations of the existence of an independent Polish state in all territories of unified Poland.

Hitherto, the political situation in Poland and the constraints of Occupation have made it impossible for the Polish nation to freely decide its own destiny. As a result of the changes brought about by the splendid triumphs of the Allied armies, Poland's re-established independence and sovereignty have now become an accomplished fact.

The Polish State rests on the will of the entire nation and on democracy. A Polish government will now replace the rule of violence which has weighed heavily on Poland's destiny during the last 140 years. This will be achieved by a political system of order and justice. Relying on the Polish Army under my command, I trust that no foreign army will from now on ever enter the territory of Poland unless expressly invited to do so. I am convinced that the powerful Western democracies will give their aid and fraternal support to the reborn and Independent Republic of Poland.

Source: *Monitor Polski*, 1918, No. 206

Document 20

General Hans von Seeckt (1866–1936), head of the German Army Command, on Poland, 1920:

To save Poland from Bolshevism – Poland, this mortal enemy of Germany, this creature and ally of France, this thief of German soil, this destroyer of German culture – for that, not a single German arm should move. And should Poland go to the devil, we should help her go. Our future lies in alliance with Russia . . . no other way is open to us . . . We must count on the probability that Russia will sooner or later, probably this summer, attack Poland. To this attack Poland will succumb. As happened in the Ukraine and Siberia, Bolshevism precedes its military plans with propaganda. There is no doubt that Bolshevik sentiment has recently grown strong in former Russian Poland and has also penetrated the army . . . Poland's internal capacity for resistance is insignificant. Poland cannot count on effective support from the *Entente*. It is certain that neither France nor England or America is in a position to send troops to support the Poles against a Soviet attack, and nor do they want to. Only support by officers, equipment and money remains. If such support does not come very soon, it will be too late, particularly if Germany denies to Poland the passage of such help . . . It should be unquestionably established that Germany deny Poland any help against Russia.

In this regard, German policy must steadfastly and without qualification ignore all offers from England and all threats from France. Regardless of our need to seek an understanding with Russia, we still have the compelling duty to encourage every sign that promises damage or even destruction of this most unbearable neighbour of ours . . .

If we cannot bring it about ourselves at this moment in time, we must in any case regard with gratitude the destruction of Poland.

And in 1922:

Her existence is intolerable and incompatible with the vital needs of Germany. Poland must and will disappear through her own internal weakness and through Russia's action – with our assistance. For Russia,

Poland is even more intolerable than for us; no Russia can allow Poland to exist.

Source: Institut für Zeitgeschichte, Munich, Nachlass Seeckt, memoranda of 5 February 1920 and 11 September 1922

Document 21

Sir Horace Rumbold (1869–1941), the British Minister in Warsaw, to the government in London, February 1920:

The Polish Government are confronted with a situation of extreme difficulty. They consider that the Soviet Government is . . . devoid of any honour or scruples and that its policy is determined solely by questions of expediency. They realise that their geographical situation exposes them in an especial degree to Bolshevik propaganda, and that if they make peace with the Bolsheviks any representative accredited by the latter to Poland will not hesitate to conduct Bolshevik propaganda to the utmost extent in his power, whatever engagements he may have given to the contrary.

Source: Public Record Office, Kew: FO 417/8, Document 16, p. 22

Document 22

Prince Eustachy Sapieha (1881–1963), Polish Minister of Foreign Affairs, in a letter to Sir Horace Rumbold, the British Ambassador in Warsaw, 25 April 1920:

Jews have acted openly against the Polish State, going so far in some cases as to take arms. This is especially true of the adherents of such Jewish organisations as the Bund and the Poale Sion [both radical left-wing], which went openly with the Bolsheviks . . . Jews loyal to Poland should realise that they must openly repudiate those of the elements among them which, like the Bund or the Poale Sion, prove to be enemies of the state.

Source: Archive of the Polish Institute and Sikorski Museum, A.12. P49/4d

Document 23

Józef Piłsudski 's 'Proclamation to the Citizens of the Ukraine', 26 April 1920:

On my orders, troops of the Republic of Poland have advanced far into the lands of the Ukraine. I want the inhabitants of this country to know that Polish forces will expel from your lands the foreign invaders, against whom the Ukrainian people have risen up in arms to defend their homes from violence, banditry and pillage. Polish forces will remain in the Ukraine only for as long as it takes to allow a legitimate Ukrainian government to assume power.

As soon as a national government of the Ukrainian Republic has established its authority and its troops have secured its borders from a new invasion, and the free nation is strong enough to decide its own destiny, the Polish soldiers will return home, having fulfilled their honourable task of fighting for the liberty of nations . . . The Polish forces will provide care and protection to all inhabitants of the Ukraine, regardless of class, nationality, or religion. I appeal to the Ukrainian people and to all inhabitants of these lands . . . to assist with every means the Polish Army in its bloody struggle for their life and freedom.

Source: T. Kutrzeba, *Wyprawa Kijowska* (Warsaw: Gebethner i Wolff, 1937), p. 107

Document 24

From a Polish Communist propaganda leaflet, June 1920:

Soldiers of the Polish Army! Revolution in Poland will succeed only when you stop obeying your traitorous leaders, when instead of fighting your brothers, the workers and peasants of Russia and the Ukraine, you turn your arms against your own officers, the bourgeoisie and the landowners . . . He who fights against Soviet Russia, fights against the working class of the whole world and is an enemy of the people.

Source: *K.P.P. Obronie Niepodległości Polski* (Warsaw: 1954), p. 59

Document 25

The Communist International sought to aid the Red Army with this appeal, July 1920:

Workers of Poland! . . . you will organise demonstrations and strikes on behalf of peace with Soviet Russia. The International is convinced that you will now exert your utmost efforts to strike White Poland in the rear, so that together with the workers of Russia you will win victory over the Polish landlords and capitalists. You know that Soviet Russia brings Poland not oppression, but national freedom, freedom from the chains of Allied capital; help in the fight against your own capitalists. The victory of workers' and peasants' Russia will be the victory of the Polish proletariat, brothers and allies of the Russian workers and peasants. To the attack, Polish workers!

Source: *The Communist International, 1917–1943*,
ed. J. Degras, Volume I (London: Cass, 1971), pp. 91–2

Document 26

M. Tukhachevsky, commander-in-chief of the Red Army on the Western Front, in his Order of the Day, 2 July 1920:

Soldiers of the Red Army! The time of reckoning has come. The army of the Red Flag and the army of the predatory White Eagle confront each other in mortal combat. Over the dead body of White Poland shines the road to world-wide conflagration. On our bayonets we shall bring happiness and peace to toiling humanity. To the west! March!

Source: Public Record Office, Kew: FO 371 3919/213076

Document 27

The following appeal was made by the Council for the Defence of the State, Warsaw, 3 July 1920:

The Fatherland is in need! All men of good will and capable of carrying arms are called to the colours. The entire nation must resist like a solid, immovable barrier. It is on our breasts that the flood of Bolshevism will be broken. May unity, amity and undying toil bring us all together for the common cause. All for victory! To arms!

Source: W. Pobóg-Malinowski, *Najnowsza Historia Polityczna Polski*, Volume II (London: Gryf, 1957), pp. 450–1

Document 28

Proclamation of the Provisional Polish Revolutionary Committee, 30 July 1920:

On Polish lands freed from the capitalist yoke, a Provisional Polish Revolutionary Committee comprising comrades Julian Marchlewski, Feliks Dzierżyński, Feliks Kon, Edward Prochniak and Józef Unszlicht, has been established. The Provisional Committee . . . has set itself the task, pending the formation in Poland of a permanent Peasants' and Workers' Government, of laying the basis of the future Polish Soviet Socialist Republic. To this end, the Provisional Committee

(a)   has removed the previous gentry-bourgeois government
(b)   is forming factory and farm committees
(c)   is setting up municipal revolutionary committees
(d)   is declaring all factories, land and forests to be national property run by municipal and rural workers' committees
(e)   guarantees the inviolability of peasant holdings
(f)   is creating agencies for security, supply and economic control
(g)   assures complete safety to all citizens who loyally observe the dispositions and orders of the revolutionary authorities.

Source: Polska Akademia Nauk, *Dokumenty Materiały do Historii Stosunków Polsko-Radzieckich,* Volume III (Warsaw: 1964) Document 126

Document 29

Józef Piłsudski, commander-in-chief, issues his Order of the Day, 18 October 1920:

Soldiers! You have spent two long years amidst arduous toil and bloody strife. You end the war with a magnificent victory. Soldiers! . . . from the first moments of its existence, envious hands were grasping for the New Poland. There were numerous attempts to reduce Poland to a state of impotence, and to make it a plaything for others. The nation placed the heavy burden of protecting Poland's existence, of establishing general respect, of giving her the freedom to fully chart her destiny, on my shoulders as commander-in-chief and into your hands, as defenders of the Fatherland.

Soldiers! You have made Poland strong, confident and free. You can be pleased at having fulfilled your duty. A country which has produced in only two years soldiers such as you can regard its future with tranquillity.

Source: J. Piłsudski, *Pisma*, Volume III (Warsaw: Instytut Józefa Piłsudskiego, 1937–8), pp. 174 f.

Document 30

Extracts from the Peace Treaty of Riga, 18 March 1921:

Article 3: Both Soviet Russia and Soviet Ukraine abandon all rights and claims to the territories situated west of the agreed border. Similarly, Poland abandons in favour of Soviet Ukraine and Soviet Belarus all rights and claims to the territory situated east of the border . . .

Article 5: Both parties pledge to respect each other's political sovereignty, to abstain from interference in each other's internal affairs, and not to support or create armed detachments with the objective of encouraging armed conflict against the other party so as to undermine its territorial integrity or subvert its political or social institutions . . .

Article 7: Russia and Ukraine pledge that persons of Polish nationality in Russia, Ukraine and Belarus shall enjoy free intellectual development, the use of their national language, and the exercise of their religion. Similarly, Poland recognises the same rights for persons of Russian, Ukrainian, and Byelorussian nationality in Poland . . .

Article 11: Russia and Ukraine shall restore to Poland all war trophies, libraries, archives, works of art, and other objects of historical, ethnographic, artistic, scholarly, and archaeological value that have been removed from the territory of Poland by Russia since 1772 . . .

Article 13: Russia and Ukraine agree to pay to Poland within one year after ratification of the present treaty the sum of 30 million gold roubles in specie and in bars, based on the active participation of the territory of Poland in the economic life of the former Russian state.

Source: Republic of Poland, Ministry for Foreign Affairs,
*Official Documents concerning Polish–German
and Polish–Soviet Relations, 1933–1939.
The Polish White Book* (London: 1942), pp. 162–5

Document 31

Feliks Dzierżyński on the Bolshevik defeat to his comrade Adolf Warszawski (Warski) (1868–1937), November 1921:

Our mistake was to reject the independence of Poland, for which Lenin always chided us. We thought that there could not be a transitional period between capitalism and socialism, and consequently, that there was no need for independent states . . . We did not appreciate that there would be a rather long transitional period between capitalism and socialism, during which, under the dictatorship of the proletariat, classes as well as a proletarian state backed by the peasantry will exist alongside . . . As a result of rejecting every independence, we lost our struggle for an independent, Soviet Poland.

Source: J. Warski, *Z pola walki*, 1929, no. 5–6

Document 32

General Maxime Weygand (1867–1965) in a letter to Marshal Ferdinand Foch (1851–1919) regarding the Battle of Warsaw:

. . . there were so many intrigues around my activities, which the [Polish] opposition parties wanted to exploit against the head of state and of the Polish Command, that I was obliged . . . to give an interview in which I declared that the victory was Polish, the plan was Polish, and the army was Polish . . . I beg you to properly inform French opinion about that important point. This was an entirely Polish triumph. The preliminary operations were carried out in accordance with Polish plans and by Polish generals.

Source: M. Weygand, *Mémoires*, Volume II:
Mirages et Realité (Paris: Flammarion, 1957), p. 166

Document 33

Lord Edgar D'Abernon (1857–1941), one-time British Ambassador to Poland, on the significance of Poland's victory over the Bolsheviks:

The history of contemporary civilisation knows no event of greater importance than the Battle of Warsaw in 1920, and none of which the significance is less appreciated . . . Had the battle resulted in a Bolshevik victory, it would have been a turning-point in European history, for there is no doubt at all that the whole of Central Europe would have been opened at that moment to the influence of Communist propaganda and a Soviet invasion . . . The events of 1920 also merit attention for another reason: victory was secured, above all, because of the strategic genius of one man . . . It should be the task of political writers to explain to European opinion that Poland saved Europe in 1920, and that it is necessary to keep Poland powerful . . . for Poland is the barrier to the perennial danger of an invasion from the east.

Source: Article in *Gazeta Polska*, 17 August 1930

Document 34

The decision of the Conference of Ambassadors on Poland's Frontiers, 15 March 1923:

The British Empire, France, Italy and Japan, signatories with the United States of America, as the principal Allied and associated Powers, of the Versailles Treaty of Peace:

Considering that by the terms of Article 87, paragraph 3, of the said Treaty, it is for them to fix the frontiers of Poland which have not been specified by that Treaty;

Considering that it is recognised by Poland that in so far as the Eastern part of Galicia is concerned, the ethnographical conditions necessitate an autonomous regime;

Considering that the Treaty concluded between the principal Allied and associated Powers and Poland on 28 June 1919,has provided for special guarantees in favour of racial, language and religious minorities in all the territories placed under Polish sovereignty;

Considering that so far as the frontier between Poland and Russia is concerned, Poland has entered into direct relations with that state with a view to determining the line;

Have charged the Conference of Ambassadors with the regulation of this question.

In consequence, the Conference of Ambassadors:

1   decides to recognise as the frontiers of Poland [those agreed] with Russia, Lithuania, Latvia . . .
2   decides to recognise to Poland the [specified] territory of the former Austro-Hungarian monarchy . . .'.

Source: Republic of Poland, Ministry for Foreign Affairs,
*Official Documents concerning Polish–German and
Polish–Soviet Relations, 1933–1939.
The Polish White Book* (London: 1942), pp. 165–8

3

SOCIETY AND THE
ECONOMY

Any objective assessment of the state of Polish society and of the economy
in 1918 could hardly fail to point out the magnitude and complexity of the
tasks confronting both spheres. A common language, culture and religion
had sustained ethnic Poles throughout the lengthy partitionist era, but it
was immediately doubtful whether this basis would be sufficient to promote
a new, integrated society now that Poland was again an independent state.
It was not simply that the inevitable differences in the administration, laws,
conventions and other practices of the three former partitioned areas would
need to be smoothed out, remodelled and eventually made uniformly and
widely acceptable. A further complication was that when Poland's borders
were finally established and internationally recognised by 1923, the population included non-Polish ethnic groups who accounted for approximately
one-third of the total at any time throughout the interwar period.

According to the national censuses of 1921 and 1931, about 14 per cent
of the population were Ukrainian, 4 per cent Byelorussian, 2 per cent
German, 10 per cent Jewish, and a further 1 per cent composed of much
smaller numbers of Russians, Czechs, Lithuanians and so-called 'locals'
of no determinate nationality. In confessional terms, this meant that the
predominantly Roman Catholic Poles were joined by some five million
Orthodox Ukrainians, three million of the Jewish faith, and three-quarters
of a million Protestant Germans. The Polish State, although lacking the
relevant experience, had somehow to find the means of integrating these
minorities so that a cohesive, viable society could develop. In this respect,
it may have appeared to be an advantage that the population as a whole
enjoyed an equal gender balance, and that, as in many other contemporary
European countries, a large majority of both sexes were in 1931 aged under
39 years. Against this was the incontrovertible fact that Poland was very
much a male-dominated society.

Otherwise, the Polish society that emerged after 1918 was overwhelmingly rural and agrarian, so that the largest social group was by far the

peasantry. About 65 per cent of the population of 27.1 million in 1921 and 31.9 million in 1931 was composed of the small holding peasantry and landless labourers. As late as 1939, when the population had risen to 35.1 million, the former groups still constituted well over 60 per cent of the total. There was a small intelligentsia and professional middle class of gentry (*Szlachta*) origin in the cities and small towns who none the less were instrumental in maintaining and propagating the values, traditions, social attitudes and conventions of the gentry. At the top of the social ladder were the aristocratic landowning families, who were particularly evident in western and eastern Poland, while at the bottom was a small but expanding, mainly Polish, industrial proletariat: in 1933, it constituted 16 per cent of the total workforce. Emphasising the essentially rural character of the country was the statistic that the 1931 census recorded only 636 towns, of which a mere 14 had a population of 100,000 or more: the large majority had fewer than 10,000 inhabitants.

As regards the economy, the Second Republic had to wrestle from the outset with many severe handicaps. Although she possessed substantial natural reserves of energy, notably coal (in Silesia after 1921 and the Dąbrowa basin), timber, lignite and crude oil (in the south-east around Drohobycz, Jasło and Stanisławów), large deposits of rock salt and much smaller deposits of iron ore, zinc and lead, only the coal, textile (in Łódź), iron ore and crude oil industries had been developed in any way satisfactorily before 1918, and then primarily for the benefit of the Russian economy. Consequently, Poland had not experienced anything like an industrial revolution on the scale of the advanced western countries. On the other hand, a strong anti-industrial and anti-urban outlook pervaded ethnic Polish society which the hugely influential Catholic Church and other conservative groups and institutions energetically encouraged. For them, industrialisation was a cosmopolitan, 'un-Polish' phenomenon that had to be kept at bay. One direct and important consequence of this antipathy was that Poland lacked throughout the interwar years a substantial indigeneous entrepreneurial class: industry and commerce, as well as the artisanal and handicrafts sectors of the economy, were dominated by Jews as owners, managers and shareholders, while Germans retained a significant presence in factory and coal-mine ownership.

The relative absence of a Polish business class resulted in large-scale state intervention ('étatism') becoming a salient feature of the economy, the most outstanding example of which was the creation in 1936 of the Central Industrial Region, a high-priority enterprise covering the under-developed Kraków–Kielce–Lwów triangle. Under the energetic direction of Eugeniusz Kwiatkowski (1888–1974), the Minister of Finances and Deputy Prime Minister, the region soon had chemical plants, factories of various kinds, hydroelectrical power stations, and a large industrial centre specifically geared to modernising the army. It was a reflection of Poland's continuing anxiety about the threat of external aggression that throughout the interwar period an average of 35 per cent of the state budget was allotted to this, the most revered of Polish institutions. But, of course, such a scale of expenditure was a considerable burden on a country of relatively limited resources.

Another major impediment to economic growth was the dire shortage of investment capital. Foreign businessmen were generally either uninterested altogether in Poland, or, if they did become involved, demanded quick returns and excessive, if not exorbitant, rates of interest for loans. Hence, Poland was unable to attract the foreign (mainly American) investment that Germany did following the introduction in 1924 of the Dawes Plan, which devised a more manageable way of making reparation payments to the Allies. France, Poland's main ally, was burdened with her own financial and economic problems after the First World War and was not really in a position, therefore, to lend meaningful assistance. Furthermore, the widespread devastation inflicted on the Polish lands by the ferocious battles and rapacious Occupation policies of the First World War were compounded by woefully inadequate transportation, communications, postal and banking systems as well as a chaotic currency situation: in the early 1920s, no fewer than six different currencies were in circulation. Finally, the important pre-war Russian market for Polish goods had now all but collapsed, and was not to revive as the Soviet state began to pursue introspective and largely autarchic policies associated with the doctrine of 'Socialism in One Country', and in response to her defeat by the Poles in the 1919–20 war. In 1918, therefore, Poland faced an overall economic situation akin to a veritable 'Year Zero'. The essence of the challenge facing her was to put the economy on to a new footing, in a way that would at last securely serve Polish national interests instead of those of the former partitioning powers.

The fundamental key to economic rejuvenation was without doubt wide-ranging reform of the extensive agricultural sector, the main activity of the population and the principal source of Poland's modest volume of wealth. Polish agriculture produced mainly wheat, rye, barley, oats, potatoes and sugar-beet, and there was considerable dairy farming: cows, horses and pigs. Although before 1914 in the German Partition progressive methods of cultivation and a degree of mechanisation had been success-fully introduced, the rest of the sector was backward and inefficient, and had an overall retardative impact on the economy as a whole. A market-oriented attitude was conspicuously absent among all rural classes, and there was a basic imbalance already in 1918, in so far as a small number of very large estates existed, mainly in western and eastern Poland, alongside a multitude of small peasant holdings, most of which operated on or below a modest subsistence level. Throughout the sector, horses and hand-tools rather than tractors and labour-saving heavy machinery were the norm.

The problem was exacerbated when an already over-populated sector bore the brunt of the considerable increase in the Polish population before 1939. Smallholdings were then liable to be divided among several family members, thus creating further obstacles to efficiency and innovation. Far too much labour and far too many resources were tied up unproductively in agriculture, resulting not only in underemployment and so-called 'invisible' or disguised unemployment, but also in low rates of productivity and extreme poverty, especially in the Eastern Provinces. For many observers, this state of affairs confirmed the existence in reality of an economic Poland A, a relatively developed area to the west of an imaginary line from Warsaw to Kraków, and a Poland B, still anchored in the previous century, to the east of that line.

In addition to the provision by the government of modest subsidies to some small farmers and the imposition of tariffs on selected imported goods to protect domestic producers, the principal contribution of government was the introduction of land reform legislation. The first Act, in 1920, gave the state the power of compulsory expropriation of large estates and the parcellation of land to the small peasantry, in the expectation that this would promote productivity in the medium to long term. Legislation was enacted again, in 1925, because of the general ineffectiveness of the first Act. Following more smaller-scale legislation in the late 1930s, the amount of land finally distributed in total was insufficient to provide anything close to a satisfactory solution to the countryside's problems. Periodic rioting by peasants, noticeably in 1936-7, accentuated the disappointment at the lack of real progress. But not everyone subscribed by any means to the premise that the large estates were the main problem anyway. Some of them at least appear to have been managed quite carefully and efficiently, so that in most circles a certain amount of confusion and uncertainty inevitably clouded the issue. An obvious exception was provided by the poorly supported Communists and their radical leftist confrères, who advocated the wholesale expropriation without compensation and the redistribution of the large estates and nationalisation of the land.

The most important reasons for the lack of effective reform, however, were of a financial, economic, ideological, constitutional and political nature. The state simply did not have the financial means, especially in relation to the legislation of 1920 and 1925, to offer large landowners adequate compensation for loss of parts of their estates. In any case, most of these estate owners had no wish to have land which had been in the family for generations and which had miraculously survived Russian confiscation, particularly after the 1830–1 and 1863–4 risings, handed out to the peasantry or anyone else. Moreover, the Constitution of 1921 afforded them protection by enshrining the rights of private property and, in any event, such was the political turbulence in Poland until the mid-1920s that not one of the numerous governments during those years had the requisite authority and perspicacity to effectively implement the legislation.

In their opposition, the landowners were firmly supported by conservative political forces, above all, the Catholic Church, itself a large landowner, and its close ally, the *Endecja*, the most powerful influence in government from 1918 to the Piłsudski *coup* in 1926. Both tended to view the reform legislation as 'socialist' or 'bolshevik' and hence detrimental to the 'natural' conservative social order and the national interest, which they believed demanded, in particular, the maintenance of a strong Polish presence in the Eastern Provinces, where non-Polish minorities predominated. Even after the 1926 *coup*, the landed magnates were at pains to reach an understanding with Piłsudski, himself from a landowning family in the environs of Wilno, in north-eastern Poland. The celebrated meeting in October 1926 between him and the magnates on the Nieświęz estate established the desired understanding. Allied to the debilitating weaknesses and divisions in the political parties representing the peasantry and the stultifying impact of the Depression in the early 1930s, the unsurprising outcome was that during the Piłsudski era in government (1926–35), the status quo in the countryside was largely maintained. The overall consequence was that agriculture was unable to provide the kick-start to the other sectors of the economy which had been the pattern of industrialisation and growth in, for example, Britain in the eighteenth century, and in Germany in the second half of the nineteenth century.

The general context within which Poland was being obliged to meet these formidable social and economic challenges must not be overlooked: that is, amidst the most unpropitious economic circumstances – not only the 'Year Zero' scenario in 1918–19, but also the unprecedented problems that resulted from the hyperinflation of 1922–3. In the absence of appropriate levels of taxation and its efficient collection, the state resorted to over-printing note currency in order to meet high government expenditure at a time of extreme domestic and external instability. In addition, of course, there were the unprecedented problems created by the Depression. More calm and productive periods of economic development were admittedly interspersed between these major economic landmarks.

Thus, the general turbulence of the early 1920s gave way in 1924, if only for a year or so, to a series of reforms introduced by the right-wing government of Władysław Grabski (1874–1938): the stabilisation of the currency under the newly introduced *złoty*, the establishment of the Bank of Poland and the Bank of National Economy, reductions in state expenditure, increased and more efficient collection of taxes, and sales of some public-owned industrial and commercial enterprises. Moreover, Poland's foreign trade was boosted by the construction in the mid-1920s of a new port on the Baltic, Gdynia, which soon began to rival and then overtake neighbouring Danzig as an international commercial centre.

The beginning of a tariff war with Germany in 1925 – the latest episode in the Weimar Republic's relentless anti-Polish campaign – and some financial complications, however, undermined these reforms and initiatives to a degree, until the General Strike in Britain in 1926 gave a considerable boost to Polish coal exports, which was reinforced by a general upturn in the European economy, of which Poland was a beneficiary. The successful negotiation of a so-called 'Stabilisation Loan' of 62 million US dollars with American bankers the following year indicated a welcome measure of international confidence in the Polish economy, which then proceeded to develop reasonably well until the Depression struck in 1930. Even so, by 1929, industrial output was reckoned to be only 91 per cent of the 1913 level. On the other hand, the late 1920s had witnessed the most buoyant economic situation in Poland since the end of the war, with unemployment showing a sharp fall, stable prices and rising wages. Major centres of industrial activity were by then well established in and around the cities of Warsaw, Łódź (the 'Manchester of Poland'), Poznań, Katowice, Radom, and, in the east, Wilno and Lwów.

In response to the changes taking place in society as a result of economic developments, including a drift of population from rural to urban areas and the associated privations, such as unemployment, homelessness, poverty and destitution, the state had embarked upon an ambitious programme of social insurance, welfare and housing provision, albeit within tough budgetary constraints, on the model of the path-breaking Weimar *Sozialstaat*. Social insurance was made compulsory for all salaried and wage-earning workers, with the exception of civil servants and some categories of agricultural workers. Unemployment benefit was restricted to those engaged in workshops/businesses with a minimum of five employees. A vigorous co-operative movement, especially in the Eastern Provinces, helped fill the gaps the state was unable to cover. Public and private contractors were involved in the house-building programme, with the Society for the Construction of Workers' Dwellings a noted success. None the less, overcrowding in small flats in the larger towns and cities remained an all too common feature throughout the period and, of course, the Depression brought many initiatives to at least a temporary, if prolonged, halt.

Indeed, the Depression hit all sections of Polish society hard, especially as the government pursued doggedly a deflationary strategy whose primary objective was to defend the currency in international markets. Although that was achieved to a large extent, it meant that there was little state assistance to alleviate the profound social consequences, while the public social welfare system, though impressive-looking on paper, was overwhelmed by demand and buckled alarmingly under the strain. Weimar Germany endured a similar experience. Unemployment rose quickly to around 500,000, which was a not inconsiderable percentage of the industrial workforce, and consumption, even of staple items, fell markedly. Immiseration produced serious tensions throughout society, but they were especially acute in the countryside and in terms of inter-ethnic relations.

The Depression only began to lift in Poland around 1935/6, but the last years before the outbreak of the Second World War saw a decided upturn in the economy, with increases in industrial production and productivity (except in chemicals and crude oil). Foreign trade was reviving, though it struggled to reach pre-Depression levels in terms of quantity and value; the national income rose so that there was a budget surplus in 1938; prices were generally stable and real wages started to increase again. Also, improvements were becoming more apparent in the public provision of roads, railways and bridge-building as well as in domestic and industrial electrification. The social insurance and welfare systems showed tentative signs of recovery. Altogether, a quiet feeling of optimism began to reappear, particularly as more and more sections of the population started to enjoy once again a higher standard of living, in effect, picking up from the point that had been reached in the late 1920s.

Although Warsaw emerged as a vibrant and rather stylish capital city, and as such came to personify the spirit of the new Poland, it stands to reason that the twenty years before the Second World War were insufficient for Polish society and its economy to reach anywhere near the point of development already attained in the major industrial western countries such as Britain, Germany and France, with whom Poland always compared herself. Although her progress was thus relatively modest from that perspective, and Poland was still in 1939 a rather poor and backward country, perhaps the fairest and most objective way to assess her overall performance is to use the dire situation in 1918 as the overriding benchmark. This approach has led one economic historian to describe Poland's progress as 'outstanding'. Although there may be more than a tinge of hyperbole in this judgement, it should at least be taken as an acknowledgement of real progress in the face of the most inauspicious domestic and external circumstances in which the Second Republic was compelled to function.

Document 35

Wincenty Witos (1874–1945), the peasant political leader and Prime Minister of Poland on three occasions in the 1920s, eulogises in the Sejm, *June 1919:*

I firmly maintain that the Polish State can be founded in the future on the common people alone . . . I admit that other classes have the same rights, but we know that the marrow of the state is and must be the Polish people – the peasant and the worker! In Poland, if anywhere, the soil is the basis for our national existence.

The village was and is the most substantial foundation of the country . . . Poland has survived only when the Polish peasant has put down roots. During the worst times, the peasant stuck to his land, his faith and his nationality. These three values have provided the basis for creating the state, and without them we should never have achieved it . . . The future of Poland cannot be built on towns that are mainly Jewish, that are undermined by Socialism, which is the gateway to Communism. For such a task, even an ocean of idealism and goodwill . . . is not enough. The foundation of the future can only be the countryside, only the Polish peasantry.

Source: W. Witos, *Moje Wspomnienia*, Volume 2
(Paris: Instytut Literacki, 1963), pp. 236–8

Document 36

The national censuses of 1921 and 1931 recorded the Polish population, as follows:

	1921	1931
	(by declared nationality)	*(by main language used)*
Polish	18, 814, 239 (69.2 %)	21, 993, 444 (68.9%)
Ukrainian	3, 898, 431 (14.3%)	4, 441, 622 (13.9%) *
Byelorussian	1, 060, 237 (3.9%)	989, 852 (3.1%)
Jewish	2, 110, 448 (7.8%)	2, 732, 584 (8.6%) *

German	1, 059, 194 (3.9%)	740, 992 (2.3%)
Lithuanian	68, 667 (0.3%)	83, 116 (0.3%)
Russian	56, 239 (0.2%)	138, 713 (0.4%)
Czech	30, 628 (0.1%)	38, 097 (0.2%)
Local	49, 441 (0.2%)	707, 088 (2.2%)

Total: 27, 176, 717   Total: 31, 915, 779

Note: *generally considered to be underestimates

Source: Compiled from E. Szturm de Sztrem (ed.), Statistical Atlas of Poland (London: Polish Ministry of Information, n.d. [1942]), pp. 19–31

Document 37

Count Aleksander Skrzyński (1882–1931), diplomat and one-time Foreign Minister, expressed his views on land reform:

Soviet Russia solved its agrarian problem by the complete elimination and expropriation of the large landowners . . . [and] agrarian reform was carried out by the new Baltic countries . . . A clear-minded social politician must recognise that the agrarian developments in Russia and the benefits thereby accruing to the peasantry could hardly fail to impact on the Polish village. Such are the factors which today make the agrarian question the heart of all the political, social and economic problems in Poland . . . Because of the deep conservatism of the large empires which divided and oppressed Poland over a century and a half, agrarian conditions changed the least and remained much as they had been at the end of the eighteenth century . . . more or less feudal.

There is no doubt of the need for land reform in Poland, from both a social and a political perspective. Anyone who wishes to govern the country must accept that land reform is inevitable, and no one can deny its importance. In discussing this question, it has to be concluded that it cannot be solved unless the agricultural colonisation of Poland is directed towards the east, where there still exist some very extensive landed estates. But here the Polish colonist runs up against the claims of the native population, which is also land-hungry and can justify its claims by indicating that these lands were always worked by their hands.

Source: A. Skrzyński, Poland and Peace (London: Allen & Unwin, 1923), pp. 67–74

Document 38

A contemporary observer on the passing of the 1925 Land Reform Act:

While the Bill was under consideration by the Senate [the Polish upper house], a great congress of landlords met in Warsaw and, under the auspices of Prince Casimir Lubormirski . . . passed resolutions against all land reform. The results of their lobbying and influence in the upper house were particularly noticeable in the land exemption provisions and numerous restrictive and reactionary clauses. Under the Bill as passed by the Senate, lands scheduled for parcellation but not actually distributed within a given year would not thereafter be subject to distribution; all forced partitioning was postponed until 1927; land alone was to be valued at a computable rate, while buildings and movable property were to be paid for at their 'real' worth. In short, the effort made by the Senate was to complicate the reform as much as possible and to increase the profits accruing to the proprietors.

On the return of the demanded Bill, the *Sejm* accepted most of the Senate amendments and added new ones exempting forests and historic estates from compulsory partitioning and further taking the sting out of its provisions. As finally passed, 28 December 1925, the Bill was, in the opinion of the Christian Nationalist press, 'no longer contrary to the constitution or economic life'. This tribute from the arch-representatives of a clerical, monarchist, feudal, landholding aristocracy was indeed significant!

Source: M. W. Graham, *New Governments of Eastern Europe*
(New York: H. Holt & Co., 1928), pp. 514–15

Document 39

A description of the gathering inflation of the early 1920s in the countryside:

For money, we continued to use the Austrian paper crowns . . . The price of things remained for the time what it had been, and only began to rise by slow degrees . . . But at the beginning of 1920 the Austrian crowns were changed over into Polish marks . . . This did not suffice, however, to stabilise the currency, and the value of the mark began to go down far below the crown. As a result, prices went up with meteoric rapidity . . .

The paper marks were issued without restraint, and their worth degenerated. If anyone sold something and did not at once buy something else with the money, he would lose heavily. There were many who sold house or field, or part of their cattle, only to keep the money either at home or in some bank. These lost all they had and became beggars. On the other hand, those who borrowed money and bought things with it made fortunes.

There were endless heaps of money, one had to carry it in briefcases or baskets. Purses and the like were useless. For things for the house one paid in thousands, then millions, and finally in billions. Officials were paid fortnightly, for the amount received had a far different value in the first half of the month from it did later . . . Then, early in 1924, the Polish złoty was introduced . . . [and] the economic status of the country improved.

Source: J. Słomka, *From Serfdom to Self-Government.*
Memoirs of a Polish Village Mayor, 1842–1927
(London: Minerva, 1941), p. 262

Document 40

A factory inspector describes conditions in the Łódź textile industry in 1926:

Łódź gives the impression of being a huge factory settlement rather than a town. The factories dominate the town, they overwhelm it, not only by their quantity, but the entire pulse of its life and temperament is subordinated to the interests of industry. At night, when the life of the town dies down and the streets become quiet and empty, the louder is the noise of the motors, the clearer the language of work expressed by lighted windows and whole floors of factory buildings. The work of the night drums through the air . . . Łódź cancelled the 8-hour day and the 46-hour working week [introduced by legislation in November 1918], so the 24 hours . . . is divided into two shifts of 12 hours each, usually without any break . . . In many factories in Łódź, the staff work a 16-hour day . . . There are factories where the workers are told when they are hired that the shift lasts 12 hours and that they are employed only on this condition. There are factories where management publishes the extension of the working day in writing; the tone of such notices is peremptory, and the workers are not consulted.

Source: H. Krahelska, *Report on Łódź Industry and Labour Legislation*
(Warsaw: the Institute of Social Economy, 1927), pp. 15–20

Document 41

A description of economic revival in Eastern Galicia before the Depression:

During the Austrian regime industry was not favoured among us, and stood very low. In our county there was almost nothing. But now [post-1918] it began to grow. Different enterprises arose, which provided work for people and paid taxes to the new state. Among the first were the distilleries . . . that had been destroyed by the war. So, too, the Dzikov brewery was restored. Further, the brick factory in Chmielov was refitted . . . As for new ventures, we got a tile factory in Chmielov, and a furniture factory that at times engaged several hundred workers. Then, many sawmills were rebuilt. In Chmielov there was built a large factory for treating agricultural products. Steam flourmills appeared, which were unknown heretofore. One of them, situated in a neighbouring county to ours . . . was built on the newest American lines, and opened in 1927. Its capacity is 15 tons [15.24 tonnes] of rye daily, and twelve workmen are employed in each of three eight-hour shifts. Last year we got a soda-water factory, founded in Dzikov.

Basket-making has become a business. Workshops have grown up in Dzikov and two other villages. They have here good prospects . . . The older branches of production by Polish artisans held their own, and new ones were added unknown before, e.g., the good bookbindery and the watchmaker's . . . Every year more houses are going up . . .

The volume of business in Christian hands has undoubtedly grown. In Tarnobrzeg . . . there have appeared many firms with Polish owners. Even the fruit business, which was entirely in Jewish hands before the war, is now changing . . . On every market day one sees more and more how the farmers sell their products direct to the consumer . . . The number of Polish booths on the square gets larger each time.

Source: J. Słomka, *From Serfdom to Self-Government.*
Memoirs of a Polish Village Mayor, 1842–1927
(London: Minerva, 1941), pp. 263–5

Document 42

An unemployed young worker on his situation, 1932:

Tomorrow will be another day, a day on which I shall find work. Every day I cling to this thought as to a lifebuoy. Sometimes, indeed, I think that it is my last link with life, this mysterious faith in a tomorrow which will bring me the glad news of work. Work! I want to work. The will to work is all I have left . . . Tomorrow creates the illusion that things will be better. Today I am a pauper, but tomorrow? Tomorrow I may find work. Not may, but must, tomorrow I must find work. I must be able to eat my fill, and so must also my father, my mother, and my brothers . . . Always the same things to eat: potatoes, pickled cabbage, rye flour, barley meal . . . no meat, no sugar, no butter; even bread is looked upon as a luxury. On such a diet the worker rapidly loses his strength. His clothes become ragged, obliging him to pass more and more of his time at home . . . These conditions inevitably have an evil effect on family life. The crowding of several people into a single room where soon there is not enough furniture for them to sit down, eat or sleep, and where there is less and less food to be divided, and the atmosphere becomes more and more hopeless and depressing – all this cannot but lead to constant quarrelling . . . The break-up of family life is accelerated and the road lies open to a life of vagrancy or prostitution.

Source: *International Labour Review*, Geneva, March, 1933, p. 37

Document 43

From an official report on unemployment and the unemployed in Poland, 1935:

There has been an increase since 1931 in the spread of typhus . . . The figures began to rise in 1931 and have been augmented each year since . . . the figures for Poland were 3,490 for the first half of 1934, compared with 1,820 and 2,132 in the corresponding period of the two previous years . . . Part of the increase in suicide has been attributed to unemployment – in Warsaw, for instance, 5.2 per cent of deaths by suicide were ascribed to unemployment in 1928, and 18.3 per cent in 1931 . . . Inquiries by the Institute of Social Problems in Poland showed that most families were in arrears with rent for ten years . . . The greater part of the coal used by unemployed persons was obtained by theft. The inquiries showed that marked increases in cases of suicide and in prostitution were among the direct effects of unemployment.

Source: *Unemployment* (London: Royal Institute of
International Affairs, 1936), pp. 20–5

Document 44

The Depression's devastating impact on the countryside was recounted by a contemporary observer, 1935:

Sugar no longer is to be had in the villages. Most children . . . have seen it only in the form of sugar-cakes. Now, the grey type of salt is used and sometimes even the red type intended for the cattle. In spring, before the harvest, even this worst kind is used over and over again because of the lack of ready money; salted water is saved from one meal to cook the next meal's potatoes.

The average peasant goes around today wearing the same boots, repaired and repaired many times, the same shirt . . . the children have one piece of clothing each. It is easier in summertime, but in winter one comes across children huddled up in huts and swathed up to the neck in bags filled with chaff, because without this clothing they would freeze in the cold, unheated dwelling . . . .Life has become so wretched for all.

Source: J. Michałowski, *Wieś nie ma pracy* (Warsaw: Towarzystwo Naukowe, 1935), pp. 49–50

4

POLITICS

The Second Polish Republic was created as a parliamentary democracy with a broad range of political parties able to compete in elections, a parliament (*Sejm*), an upper house (Senate), and a head of state with the title in due course of President. Of equal importance to, if not more importance than, these overt manifestations of a political system, was the need for generally inexperienced politicians and an inchoate electorate to quickly accept and understand how a parliamentary democracy could and should operate. As in other spheres, Poland faced the challenge of devising a coherent and sustainable political life from the disparate remnants of the partitionist legacy and from the variegated character of her population. A sense of proportion and responsibility, maturity and a willingness to compromise and reach agreement – the essence of any properly functioning democracy – would have to be displayed, particularly by those representing and supporting the most prominent political organisations. This meant, for instance, that the factionalism and exaggerated individualism for which the Poles had become notorious throughout Europe since the eighteenth century – the 'Republic of Anarchy' – would have to be abandoned and replaced by a consensus about what constituted the 'national interest'.

It was inevitable that the principal political movements of the pre-independence era, the nationalists (*Endecja*), socialists (in the Polish Socialist Party, or PPS, and smaller, splinter groups), and the populists (initially in five parties), representing the peasantry, should exercise a dominant influence on political developments. To these are to be added smaller but by no means obscure parties drawing support from ethnic Poles, such as the Christian Democrats (*Chadecja*), National Workers' Party, Party of Labour and Democratic Party, and others representing the non-Polish minorities, especially the Ukrainians, Germans and Jews. In addition, radical left-wing parties, above all, the Communists (KPP from

1925), lurked on the periphery. The Polish party-political scene was, therefore, highly fragmented and diversified.

The nationalist camp, which constituted the largest and single most powerful party in government prior to the 1926 Piłsudski *coup*, and continued thereafter in similar mode in the country at large albeit outside government, underwent various name changes. For example, it was renamed the Popular National Union (ZLN) from 1919 for a few years, but was always popularly referred to as the *Endecja*, and was led throughout the interwar period until his death in January 1939 by Roman Dmowski. In 1919, the *Endecja* reaffirmed the principal tenets of his ideology as the basis for its role in the new state, emphasising its devotion to patriotic, conservative, middle-class, Catholic and anti-Jewish values in domestic politics, and its opposition above all to Germany and its friendship with France in foreign affairs. It adopted a hardline attitude towards Poland's other ethnic minorities in keeping with its intrinsic belief in a 'Poland for the Poles', and rejected the Piłsudski notion of federalism as both undesirable and impracticable. The *Endecja*, which had an extensive press network throughout the country, with its main organ being *Gazeta Warszawska,* drew most of its support from the professional middle classes and better-off peasantry, especially in former Prussian Poland and Eastern Galicia, though its influence was more widely apparent. In the 1930s, the mainstream nationalist movement suffered breakaways by some of its more radically minded members, leading to the setting-up of quasi-fascist organisations, such as the National Radical Camp (ONR) and Bolesław Piesecki's *Falanga*.

Dmowski's greatest rival and opponent remained, as before the First World War, Józef Piłsudski, who none the less ended his formal affiliation to the PPS as soon as independence had been achieved in order to underline his non-party position above politics and his sole identification with the national interest, as he interpreted it. The PPS was, in fact, a very broad church, encompassing not only mainstream socialists, but also many highly patriotic former military followers of Piłsudski, anti-clericals, and a relatively large number of assimilated Jews. Its core following was supplied by industrial workers, the lower peasantry, trade unionists, some liberal intellectuals and some members of the ethnic minorities. The party demanded the separation of church and state, considerable autonomy for the ethnic minorities, and the nationalisation of some parts of industry and agriculture, including the large estates, forests and waterways, as well as progressive policies for education, workers' rights and public welfare: it was strongly anti-Communist. In foreign affairs, it identified Russia as Poland's main enemy, but generally sought to pursue an independent policy among the Great Powers.

The peasant movement, split into three main parties until they united in 1931, had in Wincenty Witos (1874–1945), its best-known personality, who regarded the peasantry as the essential foundation for the new state after 1918. As leader of the right-wing Piast Peasant Party in the 1920s, Witos was Prime Minister on three occasions before being marginalised as a political casualty of the 1926 *coup*. He led his party on a platform of land reform, in the shape promised by the legislation of 1920 and 1925, the observance of Christian principles in private and public life, patriotism and equality (at least in theory) for the ethnic minorities. Unsurprisingly, the anti-Socialist and anti-Communist Piasts frequently allied with the *Endecja*.

At the beginning of the republic's political life, therefore, there were different, often radically so, visions being articulated as to what shape the new Poland should take. A number of overt incompatibilities were immediately present, the most obvious example being the unbridgeable chasm between the nationalists and the Communists. On the other hand, many other party-political differences, however irreconcilable they might have appeared on paper, had the potential to be brought together, given conducive circumstances, able leadership and the implementation of recognised democratic norms and procedures.

It was to be Poland's great misfortune, however, that few of these elements and qualities became permanent or sufficiently influential characteristics of political life, so that instead of harmony and goodwill, there was invariably for much of the interwar period bitter inter-party strife, instability and poisonous personal feuds, at the heart of which lay the polarisation between the *Endecja* and its right-wing allies and what may be loosely described as the 'Piłsudski camp'. Dmowski and Piłsudski, the two most prominent and significant political leaders of the period, projected their personal animosity for each other and antithetical ideological perspectives on to the wider political stage. Over the longer term, this fact and other failings may be said to have made a by no means inconsequential contribution to the domestic factors which played a part, albeit a minor one, in the catastrophe that befell the republic in September 1939.

The earliest postwar years already gave clear notice that Poland's political development would most likely take a rather excitable, disputatious course. The first government, led by the moderate socialist and Piłsudski's close associate Jędrzej Moraczewski (1870–1944), proclaimed Poland a republic on 22 November 1918 and succeeded in enacting several important social reforms, including the eight-hour working day in industry. But it had barely survived a half-hearted right-wing *coup* when it was replaced in mid-January 1919 by a new, right-wing government under

Ignacy Paderewski, whose arrival in Poznań from abroad a few weeks previously had sparked off an anti-German rising in western Poland. Important events came thick and fast thereafter: the Paris Peace Conference convened a few days after Paderewski assumed office; Czechoslovakia reneged on an agreement with Poland over the future of Cieszyn; elections were held for a Constituent *Sejm* (26 January); the United States formally recognised Poland (30 January); the first session of the Constituent *Sejm* passed a decree on compulsory primary school education, approved a provisional ('Little') constitution (20 February), confirmed Piłsudski as head of state, established the Polish Army (26 February) and introduced conscription (7 March). On top of all this frenetic activity, political parties were being formed and the Paderewski government had to contend in the east with the initial skirmishes in the Polish–Soviet War.

Well-intentioned and patriotic though he was, however, Paderewski was not a natural politician and became increasingly frustrated by the laborious pettiness of political and parliamentary life. Shortly after co-signing (with Dmowski) the Treaty of Versailles on behalf of Poland (28 June) and witnessing the final victory of the Polish Army against the Ukrainian nationalists in Eastern Galicia (20 July), as well as the beginning of the First Polish Rising in Upper Silesia (16 August), he resigned on 27 November. In the following nine months, the most daunting task confronting his right-wing or centre-right successors as Prime Minister, Leopold Skulski (1878–1940), Władysław Grabski and Wincenty Witos, was to address the increasing tempo of the Polish–Soviet War, culminating in the Battle of Warsaw in mid-August 1920, and its consequences for the republic.

While the resounding defeat of the Red Army had given a tremendous boost to the self-confidence of the nation, and ensured that an over-whelming majority of Poles rejected emphatically the blandishments of Bolshevism for the remainder of the interwar era, the political unity that had been belatedly forged by the Government of National Unity under Witos, and which had been an indispensable factor in the victory, very quickly passed amidst bitter recriminations involving, above all, the *Endecja* and the Piłsudski camp. Alarmed by what they regarded as the foolhardy military strategy that had allowed the Bolsheviks to reach the outskirts of Warsaw and threaten the very existence of Poland as an independent state, the nationalists denounced Piłsudski in the most scathing terms and insulted him by claiming that the Polish victory was achieved by a combination of French military assistance (under the leadership of General Maxime Weygand) and Divine Providence – hence their coining of the phrase, 'Miracle on the Vistula', to describe the outcome of the Battle of Warsaw and of the war as a whole. They also strongly criticised the consequent Treaty of Riga as something of a 'sell-out' since historically Polish territory was relinquished and large numbers of ethnic Poles were left stranded, unenviably, on the Russian side of the border. The reaction of Piłsudski and his followers was to loathe the *Endecja* even more than before, thereby adding substantially to a political atmosphere that was already rapidly reverting to pre-war levels of acrimony.

In the short term, this unfortunate fall-out from the war exercised a significant influence on the constitution that was passed by the *Sejm* in March 1921 because the *Endecja*, in a deliberate move against Piłsudski, made it their business to limit the powers of the President while at the same time entrenching executive power for policy in the 444-member *Sejm,* which was to be elected for five-year terms on the basis of proportional representation. The latter allowed a plethora of political parties to appear – no fewer than 92 by 1925, a third of which found seats in parliament. The Senate, which had 111 members, was thus given a subordinate role in the formulation of government policy. The President, chosen for a seven-year term by a vote of both chambers of parliament, was in theory head of state, though, in fact, presidential authority was largely restricted to formal duties. An independent judiciary and a system of decentralised local government for Poland's seventeen administrative provinces (voivodships), each with a governor, was provided for. Other-wise, the constitution, which was modelled partly on that of the Third French Republic, incorporated the wide range of liberal and democratic measures expected of a western-style parliamentary republic, including civil rights, the rule of law, freedom of expression, assembly and religion, and guarantees for the ethnic minorities.

None the less, the snub to Piłsudski in this document could not disguise the fact that in the longer term, it was he, the First Marshal of Poland (formally since November 1920) and not his rival, Dmowski, who enjoyed the balance of political power in the country and who had the status and credibility to seize the political initiative when he deemed the moment appropriate. Before that moment arrived, in May 1926, however, the inherent instability of Polish politics was accentuated by yet more and frequent changes of government, notably in 1921–2, when Witos was replaced as Prime Minister by a succession of rather nondescript and ephemeral personalities lacking substantive authority.

It was widely hoped that the first parliamentary elections under a new electoral law, in November 1922, and the election of the first President of the republic, in early December, would somehow restore at least a semblance of calm to political life. Instead, the very opposite happened. Although the nationalist Right emerged as the largest single block in both the *Sejm* and Senate, with 29.1 per cent and 39.1 per cent of the vote, respectively, it was unable to secure victory for its candidate in the presidential election, Maurycy Zamoyski (1871–1939), who was defeated in the final round by Gabriel Narutowicz (1865–1922), the candidate of the Left and the recently created Bloc of National Minorities, in which the outspoken Zionist leader, Yitshak Gruenbaum (1879–1960), was a leading figure.

The *Endecja* reacted violently, denouncing the hapless Narutowicz as the 'Jewish President' and demanding his immediate resignation. The frenzy resulted in the assassination of Narutowicz by an ultra-nationalist on 16 December in Warsaw, thereby arguably pushing the country to the edge of profound civil discord. And all this barely fifteen months after a country united by a fierce patriotism had helped destroy the invading Red Army! However, the worst was averted when a new government led by General Władysław Sikorski (1881–1943), a hero of the Polish victory over the Bolsheviks, reasserted a measure of control, and when Stanisław Wojciechowski (1869–1953) became President as a compromise candidate. Meanwhile, Piłsudski, disgusted and angered in equal measure by the turn of events, withdrew six months later from active politics and went into a brooding, temporary retirement in his modest country estate.

Over the next few years, Poland experienced many economic tribulations, not least hyperinflation in 1922–3, and further frequent changes of government, which were always broad coalitions of right-wing and centrist parties. There was, therefore, no lasting stability in political life. The economic and financial reforms introduced by the Grabski government were by 1925 running into serious difficulties, prompting a recession the following year. Moreover, the *Sejm* proved incapable of enacting necessary legislation for many areas. Its proceedings all too often degenerated into chaotic tumult which occasionally even spilled over into violent and abusive confrontation. It was brought further into disrepute among the general public by well-founded stories of endemic corruption and graft among the politicians. Too many of them came across as selfish, arrogant opportunists with scant regard for the national interest, however loosely or nebulously that concept was defined. A fundamental crisis in the entire political system became clearer with each passing day, and no one, politician or party, possessed the prestige and authority to restore order, no one, that is, apart from Piłsudski.

The marshal and his followers had never accepted the 1921 Constitution as a legitimate document, even though it had been promulgated by a democratically elected parliament. He blamed it for being the root cause of the political instability and corruption which by 1925 he had come to believe threatened Poland's very independent existence. As the person most intimately associated with the achievement and consolidation of that independence, he was not prepared to stand aside and watch it being squandered, particularly by those whom he regarded with the utmost revulsion and contempt. As a soldier above all, Piłsudski had never had much time for politicians anyway. He put his trust in the Polish Army, an attitude firmly reinforced by its great victory over the Bolsheviks and its subsequent and often decisive intervention to settle Poland's other border disputes in the early 1920s.

The core of the army officer corps was provided by his loyal comrades from the legions of the First World War. He had been affronted by parliamentary moves, initiated in 1923 by his fellow-soldier General Sikorski when Minister for War, but prosecuted subsequently and resolutely by other politicians, to rein in the army and bring it under a large measure of direct parliamentary control. The sight of incompetent, squabbling politicians, which included the hated *Endecja*, interfering with his sacred institution convinced him that he had to act to clean up the political and moral mess, to rid Poland once and for all of such elements. Moreover, he felt that the politicians' behaviour could only encourage Poland's bitter external enemies, especially the Germans and Russians, to threaten more overtly Poland's independence, particularly as he was deeply and justifiably disturbed by the implications of the Locarno Pact (October 1925) and the Treaty of Berlin between Germany and the Soviet Union (April 1926). He had concluded, finally, that parliamentary democracy, as practised hitherto, was inappropriate at that time for Poland, which really required a stronger governing hand. It is also worth stressing that Piłsudski regarded himself as a 'man of destiny', someone chosen from above to provide supreme leadership, especially in moments of crisis, for his beloved Poland. The outcome of his deliberations and convictions was his decision to mount a *coup* in mid-May 1926.

The *coup*, which in triggering the removal of the elected government of Prime Minister Witos and President Wojciechowski inaugurated the era of the *Sanacja* (that is, 'purification') government, is rightly seen as another important and highly controversial turning-point in the history of the Second Republic, just as the Polish–Soviet War had been a few years earlier. The *Endecja* and its allies on the right and centre, were outraged and never forgot or forgave this blatant violation of democracy, while the Left, including the outlawed Communists, and many groups representing the ethnic minorities, welcomed the *coup* as a barrier to the Right and as the beginning of a better era in which they, for so long excluded from power, would be allowed to play a part. Piłsudski did not regard himself as representing any particular political persuasion: he was acting, as others had signally failed to do, in the national interest. His only regret was the several hundred killed during the *coup* and the divisions, some of them permanent, that it created in the army.

Piłsudski's key priority, the re-establishment of stable, effective government, led inevitably to the emasculation of parliamentary democracy within an increasingly authoritarian framework, where he was the ultimate source of power, even if his nominees formally occupied the major offices of state: thus, for example, Kazimierz Bartel (1882–1941) was Prime Minister on three separate occasions between 1926 and 1930, while Ignacy Mościcki (1867–1946) was President from 1926 until 1939. Within a few months of assuming power, Piłsudski, whose formal offices were Minister for War, Inspector-General of the Armed Forces, and (from September 1926 until June 1928, and then August–December 1930) Prime Minister, had instigated various constitutional amendments which strengthened the executive at the expense of parliament, a trend that intensified until culminating in a new constitution promulgated in April 1935.

As restrictions of one kind or another were placed on the political opposition, Piłsudski sought to build up support for his regime with key groups, such as the army, of course, and also the large landowners, at a special meeting on the Nieświęz estate in October 1926, and in the country at large, principally and not altogether successfully through the establishment in January 1928 of a new organisation, the Non-Party Bloc for Co-operation with the Government (BBWR). In the parliamentary elections held in March 1928, the BBWR failed to attract the level of support hoped for by the regime (130 of 444 seats in the *Sejm* and 46 of 111 Senate seats), while the opposition, which now included quite a few of Piłsudski's former comrades in the disillusioned PPS, performed quite well.

If the *Sanacja* could claim by the end of the 1920s, when it sponsored an international exhibition in Poznań celebrating Poland's achievements since independence, that the country's political turbulence was a thing of the past, it still could not ignore the existence of a sullen, somewhat restless opposition, which was encouraged not only by its showing in the 1928 elections, despite governmental manipulation and irregularities, but also by the whiff of financial scandal surrounding the Treasury Minister, Gabriel Czechowicz (1876–1938), in March 1929. Piłsudski intervened personally to defend his minister, but damage was done. The beginning of the Depression acted as a further spur to action by the opposition. Consequently, at a specially arranged congress in Kraków in June 1930 of the centre-left opposition parties (the 'Centrolew'), a proclamation was issued denouncing the *Sanacja* and demanding the restoration of full democracy. Piłsudski's immediate response was to arrest and imprison in an old military fortress in Brześć-nad-Bugiem many of the opposition leaders, including former Prime Minister Witos and the hero of the

Polish risings in Upper Silesia in the early 1920s, Wojciech Korfanty (1873–1939).

International condemnation of these rather brutal developments made little impact on the regime, particularly as in parliamentary elections in November the same year, the BBWR dramatically increased its share of seats (247 in the *Sejm* and 76 in the Senate). This result galvanised the divided populist movement, leading to the formation of the united Polish Peasant Party (PSL) in March 1931. But it also emboldened the regime, in which the influence of military personnel became stronger and stronger, to continue its drive against its opponents. Thus, in 1932, for example, it dismissed over fifty university professors known to be supporters of the opposition. The organised right-wing opposition, which could hardly expect to be spared the *Sanacja* rod either, fell increasingly into disarray, and eventually the Camp of Great Poland, formed by Dmowski in 1926 in response to the Piłsudski *coup*, was banned in early 1933 on the grounds of public security. The *Endecja,* especially its younger, more radical members, thereafter split into various groups guided by ultra-nationalism and anti-Semitism. The regime's pressure on all opposition groups was intensified further in July 1934 with the opening of a harsh internment camp at Bereza Kartuska for leading dissident activists. The undeniably progressive authoritarian character of the *Sanacja* was consolidated by the new constitution that was introduced in April 1935.

The constitution relegated substantially the role of the *Sejm* while correspondingly promoting presidential power: the President, according to Article 11, was 'the highest authority in the state', with a veto over legislation passed by parliament, and, according to Article 12, was the supreme head of the armed forces. The constitution thus elevated the executive branch, particularly the presidency, above all other state bodies. Shortly afterwards, a new electoral law reduced the number of *Sejm* deputies from 444 to 208, and abandoned the system of proportional representation in favour of a nomination process. As for the Senate, the President had the power to select one-third of the new number of 96 senators. The individual rights enshrined in the 1921 constitution were largely retained. In sum, the new constitution was a marked departure from its liberal predecessor and was seen by its protagonists as forming the basis of what they described as a 'guided democracy'.

The marshal's premature and unexpected death from cancer on 12 May 1935 shocked and saddened the whole nation, even if, when alive, he had as many detractors as admirers. For all the criticism levelled at him for being a dictator and the destroyer of parliamentary democracy in Poland, his achievements as a patriot and soldier vastly outweigh his faults and errors as a politician. Above all, as the 'Father of Independence' and conqueror of the Bolsheviks in 1920, he is fully entitled to a glittering place in the pantheon of Polish heroes, which is not necessarily to endorse the cult of personality which his loyal followers contrived to build around him. There is a powerful argument to be made in support of his claim to have 'saved' Poland in May 1926. The time after that date is probably where criticism can be justified more convincingly, and not only because of the authoritarian nature of his regime. He perhaps allowed the army, so triumphant in war and emblematic of national pride, too much of a political role.

On the other hand, for those who would castigate him for not doing more to reconcile the ethnic minorities to the state, including the Jews, to whom he was broadly sympathetic and whom the *Endecja* alleged exercised excessive influence in the inner circles of the regime, the answer must be that the majority among the minorities failed to demonstrate an adequate degree of loyalty to Poland. Patriotic loyalty and allegiance to the republic counted more than anything else with Piłsudski. Finally, the *Sanacja*'s financial and economic policies during the Depression are highly questionable, not least for their failure to do more to alleviate the widespread social misery that was painfully evident. On balance, however, Piłsudski, the most charismatic and politically powerful personality of the Second Republic, the epitome of Polish patriotism, and the quintessential modern Polish hero, is surely a figure most worthy of the nation's everlasting gratitude and admiration.

The new, post-Piłsudski phase in the development of the *Sanacja*, usually referred to in derogatory fashion as 'the Colonels' regime', proved to be, despite the lifting of the Depression, highly problematic. Even if the marshal's guiding hand had still been in place, it is extremely doubtful whether the intensifying domestic and external tensions could have been dealt with any more successfully, or indeed differently, by the regime, which was, in any case, soon riven by serious factionalism. The great paradox, however, was that a Piłsudskiite government became more and more susceptible to the ideas, ideals and ambitions of its most radical and intransigent adversaries, the *Endecja*.

As a fervent Polish nationalism rapidly extended through society at large in the late 1930s, the corollary was increasing authoritarianism in government, rising anti-Semitism and tougher moves against the other ethnic minorities. In response, the political opposition only grew more vociferous and better organised, of which the so-called Morges Front was a dramatic example, and most of them boycotted the elections in September 1935. In a rather desperate effort to maintain its grip, the regime not only allowed itself to become associated with various anti-Jewish measures and partially to condone anti-Semitic sentiment and actions, it set up in 1937, in place of the now defunct BBWR, a new organisation, the Camp of National Unity (OZON), whose aim under the somewhat lacklustre leadership of Colonel Adam Koc (1891–1969) was to rally all patriotic support in the country behind the government. It enjoyed only limited appeal, though did play a part in allowing the pro-government parties to achieve a somewhat tainted victory in the November 1938 elections. None the less, there was no disguising the fact that yet another fundamental political crisis in the history of the Second Republic was imminent.

What arguably prevented such a crisis from fully materialising was the realisation across almost all sections and classes of Polish society that the threat from Nazi Germany was of more pressing concern. That threat, increasing swiftly in the aftermath of the Munich Conference and the fate of neighbouring Czechoslovakia, concentrated Polish minds. During the course of 1939, domestic political differences were scaled down, divisions put aside and tempers cooled: the simmering political crisis was effectively put in abeyance, pending a resolution of the external danger. As it transpired, however, the Second Republic was to collapse because of Nazi and Soviet aggression, but certainly not as a consequence of domestic problems, political or otherwise. The Poland of 1939, for all its trials and tribulations, had more successes than failures to its credit, and had achieved undeniable viability as a independent, sovereign state.

Document 45

Józef Piłsudski to members of the Polish Socialist Party, 1918:

Gentlemen, I am no longer your comrade. In the beginning, we followed the same direction and together took a tram painted red. But I left it at the station marked 'Poland's Independence', while you are continuing your journey as far as the station 'Socialism'. My good wishes accompany you, but be so kind as to call me 'sir'.

**Source: G. Humphrey, *Piłsudski: Builder of Poland*
(New York: Scott & More, 1936), p. 189**

Document 46

The preamble to the constitution of 17 March 1921:

In the Name of Almighty God!

We, the people of Poland, thanking Providence for liberating us from one and a half centuries of servitude, recalling with gratitude the bravery, endurance, and unselfish struggles of past generations, which unceasingly devoted all their best energies to the cause of Independence, adhering to the glorious tradition of the immortal Constitution of 3 May [1791], striving for the welfare of the whole, united, and independent motherland, and for her sovereign existence, strength, security, and social order, and desiring to ensure the development of all moral and material powers for the well-being of the whole of regenerated mankind and to ensure the equality of all citizens, respect for labour, all due rights, and particularly the security of state protection, hereby proclaim and vote this Constitutional Statute in the Legislative Assembly of the Republic of Poland.

Source: M. Kridl, J. Wittlin and J. Malinowski (eds), *The Democratic Heritage of Poland* (London: Allen & Unwin, 1944), pp. 143–4

Document 47

Józef Piłsudski on the Endecja, *July 1923:*

This gang, this band, which impugned my honour, was out for blood. Our President was murdered in what was no more than a street brawl by these same people who had once showed similar base hatred towards me as head of state . . . I am a soldier. A soldier is called upon to attend to difficult duties, often in contradiction of his conscience . . . I decided that I could no longer be a soldier. I submitted my resignation from the army. These are the causes and motives behind my departure from the service of the state.

Source: From the pro-Piłsudski newspaper *Kurier Poranny*, 4 July 1923

Document 48

A memorandum from Sir Max Muller of the British Legation in Warsaw to the British Foreign Office, 20 January 1926:

Since my return to Warsaw a fortnight ago, the air has been full of rumours concerning Marshal Piłsudski's political activities . . . Though conscious of the recrudescence of the marshal's influence, due largely to the proved impotence of the *Seym* and the failure of a parliamentary government to deal satisfactorily with the difficulties threatening the country, I am still unwilling to believe that this influence constitutes a danger to the state. So far as the marshal himself is concerned, I make bold to assert that he has no idea of making himself military dictator and would never be a party to any revolutionary act against the interests of the state, but unfortunately among his followers are many individuals of the adventurer class, capable of any act of folly, and there is no saying what they might do if they only got the chance.

Count Skrzyński told me that one of the first things that he did on becoming Prime Minister was to invite Marshal Piłsudski to a consideration of the various questions concerning the army . . . Piłsudski refused to listen to reason or in any way to abandon his view that in time of peace the army should be under the rule of an Inspector-General who was not responsible to anyone, even to parliament . . . Skrzyński pointed out to him that this would be contrary to the constitution . . . Skrzyński went on to say that the faults inherent in Piłsudski's past life of intrigue and conspiracy, his jealousy and distrust of others, his overweening pride and reliance on his own powers and knowledge, his egotism and autocratic spirit had now developed to a point which really rendered him abnormal and made it quite impossible to work with him.

Source: Public Record Office, Kew, FO 371/11760

Document 49

A statement from Prime Minister Wincenty Witos, May 1926:

Let Marshal Piłsudski finally come out of hiding, let him form a new government, let him make use of all creative factors involving the interests of the country. If he fails to do this, he will create the impression that he does not really care about setting things right in the country . . . It is said that Piłsudski has the army behind him; if he does, let him seize power by force . . . I would not hesitate to do so. If Piłsudski does not do so, It would appear that he does not have these forces behind him after all.

Source: Quoted in the newspaper *Nowy Kurier Polski*, 9 May 1926

Document 50

An official of the British Foreign Office, Mr J. D. Gregory, comments on the Piłsudski coup, 21 May 1926:

I had some conversation today with a Polish Socialist whom I have known for many years and who is very much in touch with current events in Poland.

He said that, however regrettable the methods employed for upsetting the existing administration might have been, it was generally considered in Poland that the time had come to put an end to the constant changes of government and the inefficiency of the ordinary Polish politicians and endeavour to obtain some sort of stability. At least 80% of the country welcomed Piłsudski's strong action and were solidly behind him . . . Piłsudski's main effort would be to bring some sort of order into administrative conditions at home, particularly in regard to finance. With this object, he proposed to turn quite definitely to England and to ask us to supply him with technical advisers . . . In general, it was suggested to me that the advent of the Piłsudski regime was the best thing that could possibly have happened for the purposes of the prevailing British policy.

Source: Public Record Office, Kew, N 2322/41/55

Document 51

Roman Dmowski on the Piłsudski coup in a newspaper article, 10 June 1926:

The events which have taken place in the last few weeks may be the climax of the first seven years of Poland's independent life, but they are not the beginning of a new and longer era. We are far from having reached a state of internal equilibrium which would offer, if not the certitude, at least the possibility of a period free of internal friction and of disturbances involving the risk of serious bloodshed. We must be prepared for this and we should spare no efforts to make this transitory period as short as possible and to prevent the state from suffering irreparable loss as a result of permanent internal strife.

In the first place, we must remove from our political life the element most favourable to chaos and representing therefore a considerable danger to the state. This danger is the cowardice of those who are responsible for the welfare of the state and for the internal and foreign policies of the nation. Only men of great courage who remain cool in the face of the greatest danger and who are ready to lay down their lives for their beliefs and aims will not disappoint the confidence placed in them. The cause of our present ruin lies in those who value their own skin more highly than honour and conscience . . . Our nation has an insufficiently developed sense of moral responsibility and in our political struggles . . . courage is seldom found. The authors of the May *coup d'état* fully understood this, and knew that a little cunning and display of terrorism would suffice to make their opponents prepare the ground for the success of an upheaval . . . It is difficult to imagine greater helplessness and greater lack of co-ordination of mind and action than that shown by the government, and particularly by the generals standing around it, at the moment of the *coup d'état* . . . Can anything be expected of people who behave thus at a critical moment of the country's history? There is a lull in the storm, but there is nothing to guarantee that a still greater storm is not approaching.

The political organisation of the people must be refashioned rapidly, a new choice of men must be made and men of strong faith and conscience, who have the courage to defend their beliefs, must be brought to the fore.

Source: Public Record Office, Kew, FO 371/11763: R. Dmowski

Document 52

From the declaration of the congress of centre and left opposition parties ('Centrolew'), Kraków, 29 June 1930:

The representatives of Polish democracy . . . declare the following:

Whereas Poland has been living for more than four years under the power of the actual dictatorship of Józef Piłsudski: the will of the dictator is carried out by changing governments: the President of the republic is subject to the will of the dictator: the nation's confidence in the law of its own state has been undermined . . . and the people have been deprived of any influence over the republic's domestic and foreign policy.

We therefore resolve:

To struggle for the rights and freedom of the people is not merely the struggle of the parliament and Senate, but the struggle of the entire nation.

Without the abolition of dictatorship, it is impossible to control the economic depression or to solve Poland's great domestic problems. The abolition of dictatorship is the indispensable condition for preserving the independence and integrity of the republic.

And we declare:

That the struggle for the abolition of Józef Piłsudski's dictatorship has been undertaken jointly by us all, and will be pursued jointly to victory;

that only a government which has the confidence of parliament and of the nation will have our support;

that any attempt at a *coup d'état* will be met with determined resistance;

that the nation will acknowledge no obligations to a government which seizes power by such a *coup*;

that any attempt at terrorism will be met with physical force.

We declare further that the President of the Republic, Ignacy Mościcki . . . should resign.

Long Live the Independent Polish People's Republic! Down with Dictatorship! Long Live the Government of the Workers' and Peasants' Congress!.

Source: M. Kridl, J. Wittlin and J. Malinowski (eds),
The Democratic Heritage of Poland,
(London: Allen & Unwin, 1944), pp. 161–2

Document 53

A contemporary description of the elections in Poland, November 1930:

There is no doubt whatever that if the Polish elections were being held by fair means they would sweep Piłsudski and his government out of existence by an overwhelming majority . . . to look a little way beneath the surface and to realise the implications of all that is being done is to be filled with a sense of disgust with a dictatorship and of tragic pity for the highly gifted people . . . who are doomed to live beneath it . . . Warsaw looks like a city under martial law. Khaki-clad infantry, cavalry and machine-gun detachments clatter through the streets all day. Even more conspicuous are the blue-uniformed police [who] wear steel helmets and carry rifles and steel shields that make them look like medieval warriors. Besides the soldiers and police are the gangsters. It is chiefly they who commit the innumerable acts of brutal violence that are part of the system. It is they who go about in armed bands tearing down the posters of the opposition parties and beat up the messenger boys of opposition newspapers. It is they who deal with politicians or journalists who are inconvenient to the dictatorship.

Source: *Manchester Guardian*, 14 November 1930

Document 54

The programme of the oppositional Morges Front, 19 April 1936:

1   A peaceful foreign policy whose aim is the defence of the peace treaties . . . firm opposition to the policy of *faits accomplis* pursued by Germany.
2   The strengthening of the alliances with France, Romania and Czechoslovakia, the establishment of proper methods of co-operation between the Polish Army and the armies of its allies, the improvement of relations with other states who also stand on the basis of the defence of the rule of law.
3   The holding of new elections to parliament on the basis of an electoral law similar to that of 1922.
4   The creation of a government based on a clear majority of the nation.
5   The return to state service of all those specialists who have been retired early.
6   The undertaking of an attempt to undo the ill-effects of policies pursued between 1926 and 1935 and, in particular, the holding of new local government elections, a school reform and a tax reform.
7   The confiscation by the state treasury of monies wrongly paid to individuals or institutions, the abolition of unjust settlements, privileges and favours, the punishment of abuses and of the use of force.

8 The pursuit of a policy of heightened economic activity in order to improve the military potential of Poland by raising the standard of living of the poorer classes.

9 The reconstruction of the economic system to improve the position of the masses by (a) land reform, and (b) appropriate industrial reforms.

10 The systematic development of Polish trade and industry; the facilitating of Jewish emigration, while limiting the export of capital; the holding of an economic census on a national basis.

11 The energetic combating of Communism and all subversive movements which demoralise society and lower its religious and moral standards.

Source: H. Przybylski, *Front Morges w okresie II Rzeczypospolitej*
(Warsaw: Książka i Wiedza, 1972), p. 52

Document 55

From the Theses of the Camp of National Unity, February 1937:

We value the level and content of our cultural life – along with order, peace and quiet, without which no state can function – too highly to be able to approve of any arbitrary action and brutal anti-Jewish outbursts, which demean the dignity and majesty of a great nation; but the instinct of cultural self-preservation is understandable, and the desire of the Polish community for economic self-sufficiency is natural. This is also the more comprehensible in the period we have just lived through, a period of economic and social shocks, when only a deep sense of citizenship, self-sacrifice in relation to the state, and an uncompromising bond between one's life and the state can enable it to emerge unweakened from these shocks . . . a sense of national solidarity prevails in all strata and plays endlessly on the strings of an ardent patriotism which embraces the entire nation.

Source: Cited in the pro-government newspaper
Gazeta Polska, 22 February 1937

Document 56

From the speech that Prime Minister Felicjan Sławoj-Składkowski (1885–1962) made before the Sejm in relation to a draft Bill to protect the name of Marshal Piłsudski, 15 March 1938:

The spirit of nations, just like the spirit of individuals, experiences extraordinary, definitive moments of heroic revival. The tension and length of such revivals have had decisive influence on the development of the life and history of the nations so affected.

Józef Piłsudski created a heroic epoch in the life of the Polish people, awakened us from a century of slavery and cast us into the struggle for the independence and future of Poland. Piłsudski's life was the struggle for a powerful Poland. On the day of his death, the idea and effort of his whole life triumphed over the outlook of his enemies and dominated the hearts of Poles. His spirit will be in us for centuries and be carried over from one generation to another, as long as we are worthy to be called sons of Poland. But we must not simply continue his memory and veneration from one generation of Poles to another, but also perpetuate the great work of Jósef Piłsudski. We shall sweep from the battlefield all those evil powers which doubt the greatness of his work . . .

I commend to parliament the government-sponsored 'Law for the Protection of the Name of Jósef Piłsudski, the First Marshal of Poland'.

Source: From the Piłsudskiite journal *Polska Zbrojna*, 16 March 1938

Document 57

A contemporary verdict on Poland, 1938:

It need hardly be doubted that, given another ten years of peace, Poland will gradually return to more democratic forms of government – probably somewhere between the extreme liberalism of 1920–6 and the 'directed democracy' which was Piłsudski's aim. Time may well show that the agonies and disunity (even within the governing regime) of the last three years were merely the birth-pains of a new order which will evolve gradually . . . Both President Mościcki and Marshal Śmigły-Rydz [commander-in-chief], during recent weeks, have disavowed any ideas about totalitarianism: nor was it, indeed, ever seriously thought that they would countenance such ideas in others.

Source: *The Economist*, 6 August 1938

Document 68

From an obituary for Roman Dmowski, who died on 2 January 1939:

His influence on public views, on the psychology of the nation, is enormous. The ideals propagated by Dmowski are believed by a very substantial portion of our entire society, and are particularly adhered to by the great majority of youth. The question which only a future historian can adequately illuminate is why a majority of the younger generation has not found itself in the camp of Piłsudski, surrounded by the aura of legend, but has instead followed the path of the realist politician, Dmowski . . . The greatest ideological triumphs have been Dmowski's in the last years of his life. For all of us who have belonged to the camp of Marshal Piłsudski, the national ideology which Dmowski enunciated has exerted a great influence . . . his heritage has become the treasury of the nation as a whole.

Source: From the conservative Kraków newspaper
***Czas*, 3 January 1939**

5

THE ETHNIC MINORITIES

As a multiethnic and multicultural state, the Second Republic had quickly to address a series of leading questions about how best to establish a positive relationship with those of its citizens, approximately one in three, who did not regard themselves in any meaningful way as being 'Polish'. Were the five or six million Ukrainians, over three million Jews, one and a half million Byelorussians and some 800,000 Germans to be encouraged to assimilate and thus to become wholly 'Polish' over time, or were they to be assimilated only to a certain degree and permitted to retain in some sense a dual national consciousness? The answer was provided from several sources. In the first instance, the concept of the nation-state was almost universally accepted in Europe after 1918 and had been a crucial part of the postwar peace settlement, so that nationalist sentiment was running at historically high levels.

In Poland, specifically, there were in addition political pressures, articulated most vociferously, but by no means exclusively, by the *Endecja*, to construct a strong country in which the non-Polish minorities should not be allowed to constitute an impediment to the realisation of this goal. Dmowski's prescription of an integral Polish-Catholic nationalism was designed to form the basis of a unitary state. For a while, the Piłsudski camp, in trying to resurrect within a democratic framework a modified version of the old Polish-Lithuanian Commonwealth, adopted the softer line of favouring a supranational, federalist Poland. But it soon came unstuck in the face of the early postwar turmoil and powerful manifestations of nationalism from the minorities which now found themselves incorporated into Poland. The other Polish political parties generally formulated variations of what the *Endecja* and Piłsudski camp offered, with a few striking exceptions; for example, the Communists, who did not recognise the validity of the Polish State in the first place. Some parties, including those representing the peasantry, paid at least lip service to the principle of minority rights, and endorsed with varying degrees of enthusiasm the idea of limited territorial autonomy. Whatever proposals were adduced, it is undeniable that the Second Republic did not face any greater challenge than that of devising a policy towards the minorities that would bring harmony and peaceful coexistence rather than bitterness, confrontation and strife.

The historiographical verdict is that Poland signally failed to address this question in a satisfactory manner. Indeed, the vast majority of historians have adopted a highly censorious attitude towards the multitude of policies and attitudes which were pursued towards the minorities by the state. Often influenced by Communist, Marxist, Soviet or liberal political and ideological perspectives, they refer unequivocally to 'oppression', 'persecution', 'terror', 'discrimination', even 'murder', as the salient characteristics of an intrinsically chauvinistic Polish approach that was designed to relegate the minorities to the status of second-class citizens. Such a situation, it is argued, meant that Poland failed repeatedly to respect the formal statutory guarantees which were introduced after 1918, notably through the Minorities' Treaty of 1919, the Treaty of Riga (Article VII) in 1921, and the Polish constitutions of 1921 and 1935.

The problem with this line of interpretation is that it is blatantly tendentious, above all, because it focuses exclusively on what is deemed to be the failings of Polish policy, while completely ignoring the duties and responsibilities which the minorities, as citizens of the Polish State, were meant to carry out. In other words, in formulating such critical assessments, this approach overlooks the other half of a complex equation. For a satisfactory outcome, which would have seen the minorities assume a full and secure place in society, both they and the Polish State had to work together in an atmosphere of tolerance and mutual respect. This applied, in particular, to Poland's relations with the most important of the minorities, the Germans, Ukrainians, Byelorussians and the Jews. An objective analysis of a wide body of pertinent information might well postulate that the long-standing historiographical consensus is ill-founded and unreliable, to put it no more strongly, and in urgent need of radical revision.

Following the alleged 'Diktat' of Versailles in 1919, almost all major political groups in Weimar Germany united in denouncing the border with Poland as the 'bleeding frontier' and in demanding its removal at the earliest possible opportunity. Successive Weimar governments of whatever complexion actively encouraged the Germans in Poland to maintain their own national identity and their ultimate allegiance to the Reich. Towards this end, funds were always found to support the revanchist agendas of political and cultural organisations, such as the *Reichszentrale für Heimatdienst* and the *Deutschtumbund*. Anti-Polish propaganda, which employed every conceivable negative German stereotype about Poles and Poland, was maintained at an intensive level throughout the interwar years, interrupted only briefly and temporarily following the Non-Aggression Pact between the two countries in 1934. For the Polish State, it was abundantly clear from the outset that it was having to contend with an obstreperous and fundamentally disloyal German minority. Only a relatively unimportant number of German socialists ever openly and sincerely declared their loyalty to Poland, and even they, following Hitler's advent to power in 1933, began to backtrack amidst an upsurge of fanatical German nationalism.

From the Polish side, there is no denying the anti-German animus of the *Endecja* and its right-wing allies after 1918, particularly in view of the politically burdensome partitionist legacy and then, more immediately, the violent confrontations in Poznania and Upper Silesia in the early 1920s and the tariff war initiated by Germany in 1925. A number of prominent Polish politicians demanded stern measures against the German minority and talked extravagantly of the need for a wholesale programme of 'de-Germanisation', which was actually confusing, because it directly contradicted the *Endek* view that these Germans were so different from Poles that they could not be assimilated into Polish society. In any case, before 1926, no Polish government was strong enough to successfully implement such a controversial programme, and after his *coup*, Piłsudski had no interest in pursuing such a course of action.

The outcome was an uneasy and unclear stalemate between the German minority and the state. On the one hand, there were Polish government-backed campaigns in the 1920s to confiscate and reclaim some German property, including houses and farms. On the other hand, however, a situation soon settled in which the Germans were able to resist such campaigns, allowing them to hold on to most of their possessions: thus, for example, German ownership of textile factories in Łódź and Bielsko-Biała and of coal-mines in Silesia remained disproportionately high. Moreover, not only did the Germans enjoy a level of income and standard of living that were significantly better than those of the indigeneous population, they were able to develop without too much trouble their own schools, press, banks, co-operatives, sports clubs and cultural groups. They were allowed to practise their Protestant faith in their own churches, and had their own political parties which participated on equal terms in elections and which, in consequence, won seats at every election in the *Sejm* and Senate: for instance, 17 and 5 seats, respectively, in the 1922 national elections, and 19 and 5 seats, respectively, in the 1928 elections. This latitude still did not discourage their elected representatives from frequently criticising government policy or even from calling into question the very existence of the Polish State. Furthermore, German organisations lodged a higher number of formal complaints to the League of Nations in the 1920s than any other minority constituency in Poland.

Instead of suffering persecution, as might have been expected in view of their negative attitudes towards Poland, however, the German minority and its interests were protected and safeguarded in comprehensive judicial and political terms. It is surely extraordinary that while they were the recipients of largely benevolent state policies, the Germans reciprocated by invariably adopting a hostile, provocative and disloyal attitude towards Poland. They had made little effort to conceal their hopes for her defeat in the war against the Bolsheviks in 1920, believing that this would result in the Reich recovering the 'lost' eastern provinces. Even when their hopes were dashed by the Polish victory, the Germans continued to regard the Polish State as a temporary and artificial entity (*Saisonstaat*) which would inevitably fall apart. It comes as no great surprise, therefore, that the overwhelming majority of these Germans became ardent Nazis in the 1930s and a 'fifth column' when Poland was attacked in September 1939.

This regrettable pattern of Polish–German relations was replicated to a large degree in Polish–Ukrainian relations. There were from the very beginning a number of similar combustible ingredients, above all, the bitterness evoked by the Polish–Ukrainian struggle over Lwów and Eastern Galicia in 1918–19 and a thwarted Ukrainian nationalism, which were always going to make it extremely difficult for each side to adopt an enlightened attitude towards the other. To the clash of nationalities was added class warfare, for the Ukrainians, characterised by a huge, poor peasantry and an exiguous intelligentsia, were deeply resentful of the overwhelmingly Polish estate-owners and landlords, who, along with the Polish peasantry, were in a clear minority in Eastern Galicia, Wołyń and southern Polesie, where the Ukrainians were located. Apart from the brief interlude in 1920–1 when Poland allied with the faction of Ukrainian nationalism headed by Semon Petliura against the Bolsheviks, and for a short time following the Piłsudski *coup* in 1926, which all the minorities supported in the hope of a better future free of *Endek* influence, relations between both sides were marked increasingly by mutual suspicion and hatred.

In gestures of defiance against the state, the Ukrainians boycotted the national census of 1921 and the national elections the following year. In-between, in September 1921, a young Ukrainian nationalist attempted to assassinate in Lwów the Polish head of state, Marshal Piłsudski. These developments only served inevitably to stiffen Polish attitudes, evidence for which was furnished, from a Ukrainian point of view, by foot-dragging over land reform, and by restrictions, particularly following the introduction of the 1924 School Law, on Ukrainian schools, as well as on the Ukrainian press and use of the Ukrainian language. The Poles' unwillingness to create a Ukrainian university, the removal of many Ukrainians from local government service on the grounds that they were untrustworthy, and promotion of the resettlement in Eastern Galicia of Polish veterans from the Polish–Soviet and other wars of the early 1920s further exacerbated the atmosphere. Ukrainian public opinion generally gave little credit to the state for allowing the successful growth of the co-operative movement or for the considerable reduction in illiteracy rates, although a moderate section of that opinion decided on a pragmatic approach which included its subsequent participation in elections. Hence, in the 1928 elections, the Ukrainian parties secured 25 *Sejm* and 9 Senate seats, which at least brought a partial degree of Ukrainian recognition of the Polish State.

A crucial difference from the Polish–German situation, however, was that some elements of the Ukrainian population were prepared to take up arms in the cause of independence against the Polish State and organise (with help from Germany, Austria, the Soviet Union and Lithuania) underground terrorist campaigns in which the Ukrainian Military Organisation (UVO) and, later, the Organisation of Ukrainian Nationalists (OUN) were prominent. As a result, a series of assassinations of prominent Polish officials, including the Police Commissioner of Lwów, Emilian Czechowski, in March 1932, and the Minister of the Interior, Bronisław Pieracki (1895–1934), in June 1934, and of moderate Ukrainians, was carried out.

When the Polish Government occasionally took tough action against Ukrainian terrorism, as in the so-called 'pacification' campaigns in 1930, 1934 and 1938–9, and when it suspended the implementation of the Minorities' Treaty in September 1934, any improvement in relations was substantially undermined. The fall-out from the Depression and the rising temper of nationalism were bound to further heighten tension. Polish nationalist attitudes certainly became more militant and were expressed, for instance, in a renewed polonisation drive influenced by the *Endecja* and backed by the newly established Camp of National Unity (OZON) after 1937. The principal Ukrainian response was another bout of terrorism and a demand in late 1938 for territorial autonomy. Fundamental and serious tensions persisted until, in 1939, most Ukrainians, just like their German counterparts in Poland, welcomed the Second Republic's collapse.

From Poland's point of view, the situation regarding its Byelorussian minority, which was located in the eastern provinces of Polesie and Nowogródek, was not nearly as threatening as that regarding the Germans and Ukrainians. For a start, the predominantly Orthodox and peasant Byelorussians had a poorly developed sense and understanding of nationhood, with some regarding themselves, in terms of nationality, as simply 'locals'. Their political consciousness was also far less well advanced than that of the Germans and Ukrainians, and indeed the only political movement to have caused the Poles any real concern was the Hromada, which demanded independence and the confiscation without compensation of the Polish-owned estates. But, in any case, it had all but disappeared by the late 1920s. In the following decade, the Byelorussians were more effectively assimilated through military service, schooling and the proselytising efforts of the Catholic Church, though some of them displayed a little more political awareness, usually in connection with Bolshevism, without posing a serious danger to the state.

However unstable or controversial Poland's relations were with these minorities, the Polish–Jewish situation is of a rather different order, not least because of the implications of the Holocaust in the Second World War. Here, the historiographical debate has allowed few if any concessions to the Polish side, and indeed invariably assumes a virulently polonophobic orientation. The outcome is that the Second Republic has been roundly excoriated for being profoundly and unyieldingly anti-Semitic. The question is, therefore, perfectly unambiguous: does the evidence support such a scathing indictment? The general profile of the Jewish population would be an appropriate place to begin an analysis.

The approximately 3,500,000 Jews by the mid-1930s, representing just over 10 per cent of the total population of Poland, were a richly heterogeneous community in religious, social, economic, political and ideological respects. There were Orthodox and secular Jews, upper-class and proletarian Jews, wealthy and poor Jews, and conservative and radical Jews, with a plethora of sub-strata in all of these broad categories. Their political parties ranged from the *Agudath Yisrael*, which was conservative, Orthodox and patriotically supportive of Poland, to the various Zionists, and then to the Marxist-inclined Bund. Jewish backing for Communism was also not unimportant. Collectively, however, the Jews shared several features.

First, they were overwhelmingly unassimilated: at most, only about 8 per cent spoke and regarded themselves as 'Polish', while the rest kept themselves apart from Polish society as much as possible and spoke Yiddish or, much less often, Hebrew. Second, they were urban-based, with major cities such as Warsaw, Kraków, Łódź, Wilno and Lwów having between 25 and 40 per cent of their inhabitants Jewish, while in small towns (*Shtetlekh*), especially those in the Eastern Provinces, the percentage could be as high as 90. Third, their economic activity was concentrated in the small artisan trades, finance, banking and insurance, and in some liberal professions, notably medicine, publishing and the law. Fourth, they enjoyed, as an overall average, a higher per capita income and thus paid proportionately more taxes than ethnic Poles. Finally, and perhaps most important of all, they had opposed through a well-organised lobby at the Paris Peace Conference in 1919 the re-creation of an independent Polish state. When that endeavour failed, they were instrumental in having the Minorities' Treaty drawn up as a guarantee of legal and constitutional rights with particular reference to Jews and imposed on Poland as a mandatory part of the peace settlement for her.

A large majority of Jews who subsequently and unwillingly found themselves in the Polish State after 1919 maintained a hostile or at best a negligent, apathetic attitude thereafter. Thus, degrees of Jewish anti-Polonism combined with a long-established Polish anti-Semitism, intensified by *Endek* agitation and certain developments involving Jewish opposition to Polish independence and Jewish relations with the German occupation authorities in Poland in 1914–18, to constitute an unpromising basis for longer-term relations. Already at the end of the First World War, therefore, both sides tended to perniciously regard the other as alien, antagonistic and even inferior.

These attitudes were strengthened, unfortunately, by several develop-ments in the early postwar years. Poles resented reports that appeared in the international press about alleged pogroms, such as those reputed to have taken place in Lwów in November 1918 and Pińsk in April 1919. When it emerged from reliable sources, which included American officials in Warsaw and a team of investigators led by Henry Morgenthau (1891–1967), that virtually all these reports were exaggerated, distorted or simply fabricated, Polish anger at the Jews responsible seemed to be justified. There was, as a corollary, a widespread perception among Poles that many Jews, especially those in the Eastern Provinces, welcomed and in some cases actively supported the advance of the Bolsheviks into Poland in 1920, thus reinforcing Polish fears about Jewish disloyalty.

It was also unhelpful, to say the least, that the pro-Soviet Communist Workers' Party of Poland was attracting, especially to its political and ideological leadership cadres, a substantial Jewish following. The influx into Poland by 1921 of some 600,000 Jews – 'Litvaks' – from Russia who had no affinity whatsoever with Poland and her traditions, exacerbated the situation. Furthermore, the Bloc of National Minorities, which was created largely by the efforts of an arch-critic of the Polish State, the General Zionist leader Yitshak Gruenbaum (1879–1960), to contest the national elections in late 1922, was seen as an affront by ethnic Polish opinion, especially on the Right. When Gabriel Narutowicz was elected President of Poland shortly afterwards, thanks to the bloc's votes tipping the balance, the outrage on the Right threatened to plunge Poland into a civil war. The Jews were widely blamed for once again stirring up trouble.

That the history of Polish–Jewish relations was not uniformly negative was underlined by the pioneering agreement (*Ugoda*) reached in July 1925 between the government of Władysław Grabski and leading representatives of the Jewish Parliamentary Club, including Leon Reich (1874–1929) and Ozjasz Thon (1870–1936). Both sides had their own particular reasons for trying to put past differences behind them and forge a more fruitful understanding for the future. As the country settled down after the manifold traumas of the early postwar era, the government, having introduced significant financial reforms in 1924, was eager to attract the goodwill of potential financial investors abroad, particularly from Jewish business circles in the United States, and sought to demonstrate, therefore, that it was indeed possible to put Polish–Jewish relations on a more harmonious footing. For their part, the Jewish leaders in Poland could appreciate the many advantages for their community as a whole which might follow such an agreement.

Concessions to Jews under the *Ugoda* included: Jewish businesses and workshops observing Saturday as the sabbath were to be allowed to operate for longer hours on Sundays, more favourable tax and credit facilities were to be made available, more equitable representation for Jews in governmental financial and other agencies as well as in the junior officer ranks of the army, government help to facilitate Jewish emigration to Palestine, attendance of Jews at religious services in schools and the army was to be easier, and various political restrictions on Jews dating from the partitionist era were to be scrapped.

Certain influential circles in government doubted the value of this agreement and gave it only lukewarm backing, but it was principally sabotaged before long by the Jews themselves, specifically, by those such as Gruenbaum who had been vehemently opposed to talking to the government in the first place and who denounced the agreement as a cynical Polish ploy and for not going far enough, anyway. By the end of the year, the *Ugoda* was effectively a dead letter, and thus the most encouraging opportunity for a Polish–Jewish *rapprochement* was missed. It was never to reappear in the lifetime of the Second Republic, despite the advent to power in 1926 of the philo-semitic Piłsudski and the fulsome support given at first to the *Sanacja* regime by the Jewish community. Although the regime acceded to Jewish demands for the reorganisation of their local self-governing bodies, the legal recognition of Orthodox religious schools (*cheder*) (which led to the *Agudath Yisrael* joining the government's BBWR organisation), and the abolition of discriminatory legislation dating from the tsarist era, relations soon deteriorated: the Jews wanted more concessions, which Piłsudski was unwilling to give because he remained unconvinced of the Jews' loyalty to the state.

The failure of the *Ugoda* and the Jewish–Piłsudski relationship should not disguise the fact, which is conveniently overlooked by critics of the Second Republic, that the Jews enjoyed not only the normal protection afforded by the laws and constitution, but also far-reaching freedoms to express themselves in many important sectors of their daily lives. They had many of their own cultural and academic organisations, an extensive press publishing numerous daily and weekly newspapers and periodicals in Polish, Yiddish and Hebrew throughout the country, and Jewish schools, charities, hospitals, cemeteries, orphanages, senior citizens' residential homes, and sports clubs. Jews worshipped in thousands of synagogues, had their own rabbinical colleges, political parties, parliamentary and Senate deputies, and occupied a substantial, if, from the early 1930s, declining number of places at university and other institutes of higher education; even so, there remained until the introduction in many universities in the mid- to late 1930s of the *numerus clausus* and 'ghetto bench', a disproportionately high number of Jewish students. Assimilated Jews were able to make important and frequently distinguished contributions in their chosen field of expertise, whether in the economy, the arts, sciences, literature and professions. Particular pieces of legislation which aroused Jewish opposition, such as the Sunday Rest Law (1919) and a Bill to outlaw the ritual slaughter of animals (1937), either were implemented in a lax and unthreatening fashion or they failed to reach the statute book altogether. In short, far from suffering murderous discrimination and persecution, as is so often claimed, the Jews of Poland were allowed to develop into the most creative, dynamic and innovative Jewish community in the whole of interwar Europe.

This assertion is not to deny, of course, that anti-Semitism existed in Poland, just as it did in every other European country. Unlike Nazi Germany, Hungary, Fascist Italy and Romania, however, Poland never enacted any specific anti-Jewish legislation, despite the pressures arising from the Depression and the rise of an *Endek*-inspired Polish nationalism in the late 1930s. Anti-Semitism in Poland was invariably of a non-violent type, and based, not on racism, but on traditional Christian attitudes, economic and cultural concerns as, for example, August Cardinal Hlond (1881–1948) pointed out in a widely circulated pastoral letter he issued in 1936. He justifiably condemned those Jews who and those Jewish organisations which promoted atheism, pornography, prostitution, white slavery, freemasonry, usury and Bolshevism. A political dimension to anti-Semitism was indeed furnished by the *Endecja* and its allies, but it should not be forgotten that many Poles and Polish parties and organisations opposed anti-Semitism in any form. They included the radical left-wing parties, the Democratic Party, the radical wing of the Peasants'

Party, some trade unions and many academics and members of the liberal intelligentsia.

Many Jews became impoverished during the Depression, it is true, but so also did millions of Poles, who could not look to international aid of the sort provided by Jewish relief agencies from the United States. On the other hand, the economic crisis threw into sharper focus some of the disadvantages and restrictions that the Jews did undoubtedly suffer, including their ineligibility for public unemployment benefits and their heavy tax burden. They were also virtually excluded from employment in the civil service, state-owned industry, the army (except the medical and legal branches), the school-teaching profession and the administration of public transport; moreover, in the late 1930s, they were increasingly denied entry to professional organisations. The situation convinced some Jews, particularly the Revisionist Zionists led by Vladimir Jabotinsky (1880–1940), that their future lay in a setting-up, with the help of the Polish Government, of a Jewish state in Palestine. But discussions about a scheme of mass voluntary emigration of Jews came to nothing.

For more and more Poles, the brutalising impact of the Depression exposed acutely their resentment of the Jews and the anti-Polish attitudes expressed by many of them. Large parts of the Jewish press, as well as many Jewish political leaders and Jewish groups, became outspokenly critical of Poland. They whined about and usually exaggerated their problems, which they attributed to Poles, and ridiculed the state, patriotism and the cherished beliefs, traditions and values of Poles, who reacted to this onslaught with understandable unease and resentment.

It is difficult to take due account of all the pertinent and complex developments which shaped the Polish–Jewish symbiosis before 1939 and reach a conclusion acceptable to all. However, it is as clear as anything can be that the overall situation of the Jews was far more propitious than is usually credited. Anti-Semitism existed, but it was not nearly as widespread, nor as profound or as significant, as has so frequently been claimed. Both Poles and Jews were caught up in a range of circumstances which was bound to create difficulties for their relationship, particularly as the Polish State was handicapped in so many diverse ways. It may not have fulfilled all its legal and constitutional obligations, but it would only be fair to say that it did as best it could. The same, however, cannot be said of the Jews as a whole. Far too many of them were either stubbornly hostile or sullenly apathetic towards the republic.

Like the German and Ukrainian minorities, the Jews incessantly demanded recognition and fulfilment of their rights and complained bitterly and often about what they did not have, when they should have been devoting at least as much time and energy to thinking about and actually performing their duties and responsibilities as citizens. That they were not compelled to do so was perhaps a failing of the state, for there is much evidence to suggest that it too often adopted a liberal, patient and flexible attitude towards these intransigent minorities when a tougher approach was called for. But even Piłsudski, whose attitude to the minorities was influenced above all by the demand that they show loyalty to the state, declined to pursue a suitably aggressive course of action when they did not. Consequently, those who have criticised Polish policy for not, as a solution to the minorities issue, ceding territory, or granting autonomy, federalism, or more assistance to their cultural aspirations, and so on, miss the point entirely.

No Polish government, regardless of political complexion, before or after the 1926 *coup*, could have seriously contemplated any of these concessions, for they would have, sooner or later, compromised not only the integrity of the state, but also Poland's very independence. Besides, there is no convincing evidence that any of these suggested remedies would have satisfied the minorities because while the Germans and Ukrainians wanted nothing short of outright independence, they and the others kept their distance, physically and emotionally, from a state which they repudiated. The onus lay primarily on the minorities to signal their interest in reconciliation by adopting a constructive, co-operative attitude as loyal, responsible citizens who had the privilege of living in Poland. They all signally failed to do so, and ended up not simply as a gross liability to the Second Republic in the shape of an enemy within, but also, with their gruesome fate in the Second World War in mind, as a liability to themselves.

Document 59

From the Minorities' Treaty of 28 June 1919:

Article 2: Poland undertakes to assure full and complete protection of life and liberty to all inhabitants of Poland without distinction of birth, nationality, language, race or religion.

All inhabitants of Poland shall be entitled to the free exercise, whether public or private, of any creed, religion or belief, whose practices are not inconsistent with public order or public morals.

Article 3: Poland admits and declares to be Polish nationals *ipso facto* and without the requirement of any formality German, Austrian, Hungarian or Russian nationals habitually resident at the date of the coming into force of the present treaty in territory which is or may be recognised as forming part of Poland . . .

Article 7: All Polish nationals shall be equal before the law and shall enjoy the same civil and political rights without distinction as to race, language or religion.

Differences of religion, creed or confession shall not prejudice any Polish national in matters relating to the enjoyment of civil or political rights, as for instance admission to public employment, functions and honours, or exercise of professions and industries.

No restriction shall be imposed on the free use by any Polish national of any language in private intercourse, in commerce, in religion, in the press or in publications of any kind, or at public meetings.

Notwithstanding any establishment by the Polish Government of an official language, adequate facilities shall be given to Polish nationals of non-Polish speech for the use of their language, either orally or in writing before the courts.

Article 8: Polish nationals who belong to racial, religious or linguistic minorities shall enjoy the same treatment and security in law and in fact as the other Polish nationals. In particular they shall have an equal right to establish, manage and control at their own expense charitable, religious and social institutions, schools and other educational establishments, with the right to use their own language and to exercise their religion freely therein.

Article 9: Poland will provide in the public educational system in towns and districts in which a considerable proportion of Polish nationals of other than Polish speech are residents adequate facilities for ensuring that in the primary schools the instruction shall be given to the children of such Polish nationals through the medium of their own language. This provision shall not prevent the Polish Government from making the teaching of the Polish language obligatory in the said schools.

In towns and districts where there is a considerable proportion of Polish nationals belonging to racial, religious or linguistic minorities, these minorities shall be assured an equitable share in the enjoyment and application of the sums which may be provided out of public funds under the state, municipal or other budget, for educational, religious or charitable purposes . . .

Article 11: Jews shall not be compelled to perform any act which constitutes a violation of their Sabbath, nor shall they be placed under any disability by reason of their refusal to attend courts of law or to perform any legal business on their Sabbath. This provision however shall not exempt Jews from such obligations as shall be imposed upon all other Polish citizens for the necessary purposes of military service, national defence or the preservation of public order . . .

Source: J. A. S. Grenville, *The Major International Treaties 1914–1973* (New York: Stein & Day, 1975), pp. 72–3

Document 60

The Jewish leader Lucien Wolf (1857–1930) commented on the Minorities' Treaty on 16 September 1919:

We cannot pretend to have solved the Jewish Question in eastern Europe, but at any rate we have got on paper the best solution that has ever been dreamt of. We have still before us the task of working out this solution in practice. It will be difficult and delicate because we shall be confronted by two kinds of mischief-makers – on the one hand the violent anti-Semites, and on the other the extreme Jewish nationalists. We have, however, in the Minorities Treaty so solid a basis to work upon that I think we can look forward to the future with a great deal of confidence.

Source: Lucien Wolf, *Peace Conference Diary* (London: University College Library)

Document 61

Hugh Gibson, the first American Minister to Poland, on the situation concerning the Jews, 1919:

We are getting telegrams every day from America about alleged massacres of Jews in Poland . . . If there were massacres it would be easier to handle for there would be something to report but it is hard to explain things that do not happen. There were some Jews killed early in April at Pińsk [where] the Jews form more than half of the population. They were outspokenly hostile to the Polish Government and laid themselves open to suspicion. One evening . . . the Jews held a meeting under very suspicious circumstances. After it had been raided a number of men were taken out and shot [by the Polish Army]. It was certainly summary justice such as is likely to be meted out on all fronts . . . Jews all over the world have been excited about the matter ever since. I have never seen a matter concerning which so many versions were issued. I get a new one every day . . . There is no doubt that the Jews were killed; there is also no doubt that their behaviour was such as to invite trouble. It was in no sense a religious matter. However, official reports are powerless to quiet the propaganda artists and they are getting stronger and stronger every day. Now they are manufacturing massacres of Jews at all sorts of places and sending cables about the need for our saving the lives of all sorts of Jews who are very much surprised, when we ask about them, to know that they have been considered in danger. There is a big propaganda bureau at Kowno, not far from Wilno, now in German occupation, and its main function is to send out long reports of the killing of Jews in Poland, regardless of fact. The Berlin papers carry these yarns and they get into the neutral papers and gradually into our own. Of course, it is to the advantage of the Germans to stir up as much dissension in Poland as possible, so as to keep the country weakened. There are other influences with similar interests, and altogether I can see that we are in for a long siege of Jewish atrocities.

Source: *Hugh Gibson Papers* (Stanford, CA: Hoover Institution),
Box 69, Gibson Diary, 29 May 1919

Document 62

Hugh Gibson, American Minister to Poland, on his meeting with Jewish leaders, 1919:

I find that most of these people are over-wrought and have reached that stage where they unconsciously want to believe every exaggerated yarn about excesses against the Jews. They take it as prejudice if you question any story, no matter whether they know where it comes from or not, so long as it makes out a case against the Poles and shows that the Jews are suffering . . . you can't help the patient by treating him for an ailment he does not suffer from. I can see that there will be a tremendous amount of patient-talking to be done among the Jews before they be willing to abandon the idea of curing all their ills by one blast at the Polish Government. They have got to make up their minds to work untiringly with the government and not against it . . .

Source: *Hugh Gibson Papers* (Stanford, CA: Hoover Institution),
Box 70, Gibson Diary, 27 June 1919

Document 63

Hugh Gibson, American Minister to Poland, on American Jews, 1920:

Practically ever since I have been here, we have had a steady stream of American Jews, either in official positions or with official backing and recommendation, coming in here to gather material for anti-Polish intrigue. Most of them have come ostensibly for purely relief work . . . There is hardly an instance of an American Jew coming into Poland on relief work or any of the other 'missions' . . . who has not, after leaving the country, come out with attacks upon Poland . . .

The record of American Jews abusing their passports and the privileges accorded them here is both shameful and embarrassing to us, and I think the time has come when positive action should be taken by our government . . . before the patience of the Polish Government is exhausted and they point out to us the unfriendliness of our action in permitting our people with official support to carry on a concerted effort to undermine this country and its government . . . it is only the unbelievable patience of the Polish Government that has saved us from having several very unpleasant incidents here.

**Source: *Hugh Gibson Papers* (Stanford, CA: Hoover Institution),
Box 43, letter of 14 February 1920**

Document 64

Hugh Gibson, American Minister to Poland, on the Jewish situation in Poland, 1922:

The American Jewish Committee is apparently at some pains to gather all possible reports, without regard to their accuracy, referring to the mistreatment of Jews . . . In general, it can be said that for purposes of agitation, these Jewish leaders have a tendency to accept as proof positive any allegations made by a Jew against the Poles and to accept any newspaper report or anonymous statement, so long as it indicates that a Jew has been unfairly treated . . . they expect me to accept as evidence any unsupported story they bring about the mistreatment of Jews and resent any disposition I may show to examine the evidence and verify the facts. This is not said impetuously, but as the result of several years of daily dealings with these people.

I have carefully studied the Jewish Question in Poland . . . and am convinced that . . . the organised Jews of this country are deliberately and openly anti-Polish. The Jewish press daily hurls abuse at the Polish Government and people and calls down on them every imaginable curse. The daily run of Jewish callers at the [American] Legation . . . are loud in their denunciations of Poland, its government and people, and frequently express annoyance if their sentiments do not elicit approval from American representatives . . .

It must be remembered that the Jews here do not demand equal but exceptional treatment. They demand exemption from military service, exemption from certain taxes, separate courts in which cases are to be tried by Jewish law, and separate schools at government expense controlled entirely by themselves at which all subjects will be taught in Hebrew or Yiddish. In order to obtain these demands they resort to any tactics which will place the Poles in an unfavourable position. There is not only no co-operation on their part to build up a Polish state, but they endeavor to frustrate the settlement of Polish problems by interference, threats and non-participation. It is clear, therefore, that when these Jewish demands are pressed and the intervention of the United States is called for, it is not to prevent cruelties and injustices to an oppressed minority, but to secure the aid of a large power for their selfish ends . . .

Source: *Hugh Gibson Papers* **(Stanford, CA: Hoover Institution),**
Box 100, letter of 10 November 1922

Document 65

An expression of German nationalist fear for the 'lost' eastern territories, 1927:

We shall be able to definitely repulse the Slav danger only if by persistent, long-term effort we strive to strengthen the agricultural areas in the east. The peasants are the future of the nation. That is why the only effective means of repelling the Polish threat is to settle German peasants in these areas. Only a planned colonisation of the border regions can save the German nation there from ruin.

Source: From the journal *Archiv für innere Kolonisation*,
6, 1927, Nos. 1–3, pp. 2–3

Document 66

A typically stereotyped Polish view of Germans, 1928:

Individually, Germans are sober-minded, realistic and positive, but collectively, as a nation, they are guided by illusions and are rapacious, acquisitive and tremendously impulsive, while their perseverance can make them stubborn. In these circumstances, business-like negotiations with Germans are difficult, sometimes even hopeless. Stubbornness, an inability to recognise the other's just requirements, unbridled greed, and the lack of a conciliatory spirit have always characterised the Germans . . .

Source: From the newspaper *Dziennik Poznański*, 8 May 1928

Document 67

A statement by the Ukrainian Military Organisation (UVO), October 1930:

By means of individual assassinations and occasional mass actions, we will attract large numbers of the population to the idea of liberation and into the revolutionary ranks. The broad masses must become involved in the cause of revolution and liberty. Only with continually repeated actions can we sustain and nurture a permanent spirit of protest against the occupier, and maintain hatred of the enemy and the desire for final retribution. The people dare not get used to their chains, they dare not feel comfortable in an enemy state . . . a state of constant revolutionary ferment will lead to the final showdown with the enemy . . .

Source: From the UVO journal *Surma*, 37, 1930, No. 10, October, p. 7

Document 68

A spokesman for the moderate Ukrainian parliamentary group in the Sejm, *5 February 1931:*

. . . one of the splendid chapters in the history of the Ukrainian nation will be that relating to the part played by the Ukrainian population of Poland in the life of the Polish Republic. The presence in the *Sejm* and Senate of representatives from the Ukrainian community, and of other National

Minorities, is sufficient evidence that the Polish State in no way tends to denationalise or to belittle them, but, on the contrary, treats them on the basis of full political and national equality before the law . . . the government of Marshal Piłsudski not only affords them its protection but also desires the National Minorities to take an active and effective part in the consolidation and development of the Polish State, demanding in return only a loyal and honest attitude towards the Republic.

Experience has clearly shown that the policy of indiscriminate opposition to all things Polish, adopted some time ago by various political groups among the Ukrainians, is a policy which produces no good results. It did no more than destroy good feeling between Poles and Ukrainians and postpone an honest solution of the Ukrainian problem in Poland . . . we desire to act in conformity with the opinion of the large mass of the Ukrainian population, who demand from their delegates constructive work and loyalty to the state . . . while we shall continue to cultivate our own national and regional characteristics, we shall strive together with the Polish nation to strengthen and develop the Polish State . . . we consider it our duty and our obligation to co-operate actively with the Polish people, as citizens of a common state, to strengthen the prosperity, the solidity and the power of the Polish Republic . . .

Source: M. Feliński, *The Ukrainians in Poland* (London: privately published by the author, 1931), pp. 62–71

Document 69

A spokesman for the pro-assimilationist Jewish Agudath Yisrael *party, 3 January 1934:*

Regardless of how many demands we have of the present regime, which has not fulfilled our just demands, it remains obvious that any other regime composed of the present opposition would be incomparably worse for the Jews and for the country as a whole. It only remains for us to demand our rights, to express firmly our justified and fundamental beliefs . . . We continue to believe firmly that the current regime, which maintains order in the country with a powerful hand, strongly and steadfastly looks after the security of the Jewish population and prohibits all outbursts of anti-Semitism.

Source: From the Yiddish newspaper *Dos yudishe togblat*, 5 January 1934

Document 70

From Polish Foreign Minister Józef Beck's address to the League of Nations Assembly, 13 September 1934:

The existence of such a system of minority protection as exists today has proved to be a complete failure. The minorities themselves gain nothing from it whilst the system, only too often misused in a manner which is quite incompatible with the spirit of the treaty, has in a great measure become the tool of a slanderous propaganda directed against the states bound by it; it has also become a means of applying political pressure on the countries which freed of all minority protection obligations benefit by the right and prerogative of participation in control . . . Awaiting the entrance into force of a universal and uniform system of minority protection, my government finds itself obliged to refrain as from today from all co-operation with the international organs controlling the application of the minority protection system by Poland.

Quite obviously this decision of the Polish Government is in no event directed against the interests of the minorities. These interests have been and will continue to be defended by the constitution of the Polish Republic which assures the lingual, racial and confessional minorities freedom of development and equality of rights.

Source: S. Skrzypek, *The Problem of Eastern Galicia* (London: Polish Association for the South-Eastern Provinces, 1948), p. 87

Document 71

From August Cardinal Hlond's pastoral letter of 29 February 1936:

The Jewish problem exists and will continue to exist as long as Jews remain Jews. This question varies in intensity from one country to another. It is especially difficult in our country and ought to be the subject of serious consideration . . .

It is a fact that Jews strongly oppose the Catholic Church, that they are freethinkers and that they are in the vanguard of atheism, Bolshevism and revolutionary activity. It is a fact that they exert a pernicious influence on public morality and that their publishing houses spread pornography. It is true that Jews are swindlers and usurers, and that they deal in prostitution. It is true that, from a religious and ethical standpoint, Jewish youth is having a negative effect on Catholic youth in our schools. But let us be fair: not all Jews are like this. There are very many Jews who are believers, who are honest, just, merciful and philanthropic. There is a healthy, edifying sense of family in many Jewish households. We know Jews who are ethically outstanding, noble and honourable.

I warn against the moral stance, imported from abroad, that is fundamentally and ruthlessly anti-Semitic. It is contrary to Catholic ethics. One may love one's nation more, but one may not hate anyone. Not even Jews. It is proper to prefer your own kind when shopping and to avoid Jewish shops and Jewish stalls in the market-place. But it is forbidden to demolish a Jewish shop, damaging its goods, break windows, or even throw things at Jewish homes. One should avoid the harmful moral influence of Jews, avoid their anti-Christian culture, and especially boycott the Jewish press and immoral Jewish publications. But it is forbidden to assault, beat up, maim or slander Jews. One should honour and love Jews as human beings and neighbours . . . When divine mercy enlightens a Jew to sincerely accept his and our Messiah, let us welcome him with joy into our Christian fold. Guard against those who incite anti-Jewish violence. They serve a reprehensible cause . . .

Source: August Cardinal Hlond, *Na Straży Sumienia Narodu* (Ramsey, NJ: Don Bosco, 1951), pp. 164–5

Document 72

The Polish Prime Minister, General Felicjan Sławoj-Składkowski, in the Sejm, 24 January 1938:

The Polish people have to realise that their attitude towards the minorities will determine to a large extent the fate of Poland . . . Therefore, I regard all manifestations of hatred and intolerance against the minorities as blunders for which Poland, sooner or later, will have to pay.

Source: From the journal *Sprawy Narodowościowe*, XII, 1938, Nos. 1–2, p. 97

Document 73

The Jewish Parliamentary Club on the programme of the Camp of National Unity, May 1938:

[It] is obviously only a hypocritical pretext for depriving the Jewish people of their constitutional rights as citizens, for denying the Jews an economic existence, and for degrading them to the role of an expendable element . . . We state that the Jewish population of Poland will not yield before lawlessness; will not resign from its rights as citizens; will not resign from the possibility of a cultural, social and economic existence; will not allow themselves to be reduced to the status of helots or parasites; but rather will, in support of their solid, indestructible forces and in full awareness of their duties to the state, fight without rest for full legal equality, for the strict execution of both the letter and spirit of the constitution as it refers to three and a half million Jews. The Jewish population is fully convinced that the fascist conception of the Jewish Question in Poland will not entice the broader strata of the Polish nation.

Source: From the Jewish newspaper *Nasz Przegląd*, 25 May 1938

Document 74

A statement by the Polish Democratic Party (SD), July 1938:

The Jewish Question, which provides a platform for anti-democratic forces, is above all a social and economic problem, and it is increasingly more difficult to solve because of the flawed professional structure the Jewish population has to work in . . . We condemn as barbaric any propagation of hatred against Jews, either by legal discrimination or forced emigration. In opposing persecution, which prevents assimilation, we demand a policy that will change the occupational structure of the Jewish masses and also acquire territory for those Jews who wish to emigrate of their own free will.

Source: L. Chajn, *Materiały do historii Klubów Demokratycznych, 1937–1939* (Warsaw: Państowe Wydawnictwo Naukowe, 1964), Volume I, Document 357, p. 519

Document 75

A Polish perspective on relations with the Ukrainian minority, December 1938:

We have now definitely concluded that the thread which binds the Ukrainians to our state is very thin indeed. The fact that our ways are parting and that the slogans of co-operation are being replaced by those of conflict represents a definite loss for Poland . . .

The Ukrainians, however, will also be the losers, and they have chosen their path quite deliberately and recklessly, and with a total disregard for the lessons of history.

Source: From the Lwów newspaper *Wiek Nowy*, 9 December 1938)

Document 76

The right-wing German group in Poland, the Jungdeutsche Partei, *January 1939:*

For everyone who wants to bear the name of a true German, the following guidelines are to be observed:

Keep company only with Germans, for in this way you will strengthen the feeling of community and support the weak and vacillating. Give economic support to Germans in the first instance . . . avoid Poles. Employ only Germans in your businesses . . . avoid Poles.

Remember to leave every single penny in German hands, deposit your capital only in German banks and co-operatives . . . if required, always be prepared to sacrifice your work, capital and yourself, for only when every German is imbued with a sacrificial spirit will we achieve victory . . .

Source: From the periodical *Jungdeutsches Wollen*,
20, 1939, No. 1, p. 14

6

CULTURE AND EDUCATION

It might have been reasonably thought that, in view of the enormous problems the Second Republic had to confront at home and abroad, the development of its cultural and educational spheres would have been extremely limited, even rudimentary and well outside the mainstream of trends in Europe as a whole. However, one of the most striking paradoxes of the interwar years in Poland was the remarkable and often brilliant recrudescence in many fields of the arts and sciences, and the determined and relatively successful efforts made to rejuvenate the schools and universities following the manifold constraints of the partitionist era.

A fully satisfactory explanation of this paradox is difficult for an historian to adduce, for a whole team of sociologists, philosophers, psychologists and other specialists would probably have to be consulted before an acceptable conclusion could be reached. But it perhaps seems reasonable to stress the importance Poles traditionally attached to education, especially when opportunities were restricted, as under the Partitions, and also that the regaining of an independent state in 1918 triggered a new sense of national optimism and patriotic pride, at least among the ethnic Polish part of the population, which was channelled into a prolonged burst of creativity. Moreover, it could have been the case that there was a generational dynamic at work, that is, that the generation which had contributed most recently to reclaiming independence was determined after 1918 to make it a worthwhile reality. There was a broad consensus among ethnic Poles that the Polish State had to be built up and made as strong as possible in all aspects of its existence. The resulting momentum did not suddenly appear and then function in a vacuum, of course, but rather emanated from those elements of 'Polishness' that had survived the otherwise stultifying partitionist experience, particularly the language, literature, respect for education and, above all, what many Poles regarded as the perfect combination, an effervescent patriotism and a rejuvenated Catholicism.

The role and influence of Catholicism and of the Catholic Church in the Second Republic was always going to be a matter of considerable debate and controversy. There were those, most obviously on the political Right, who demanded that any concept of Poland was inseparable from Catholicism, and others, principally on the political Left and among the national minorities, who argued passionately that the Catholic Church, which they saw as an essentially reactionary institution and a hindrance to modernisation, should have as little to do as possible with the way Poland developed. In 1918, these diametrically opposing views were principally represented, as so many other divisions were in Poland, by the *Endecja* and the Piłsudski camp, and their respective leaders. Roman Dmowski was a devout Catholic and a leading advocate of a Catholic Poland, while Piłsudski, although born a Catholic, had left the Church to become a Protestant for a time (1899–1916) to marry a divorcee, and even after rejoining it remained somewhat aloof, spiritually as well as politically. He and his comrades in the Polish Socialist Party (PPS) could never quite forget that the Church hierarchy had frequently adopted a collaborationist stance *vis-à-vis* the partitionist powers, especially in Russian and Austrian Poland.

None the less, the fact was that the overwhelming majority of ethnic Poles were Catholic, and it was equally undeniable that what might generically be described as the 'Catholic ethos' had permeated all important areas of national life and consciousness. In the 1930s, in particular, the Church, under the astute leadership of Cardinal Hlond, adopted a more militant posture against Communism, atheism and the non-Catholic religions in Poland through an extensive network of publications and lay organisations, of which the most prominent was Catholic Action. Millions of ordinary Poles of both sexes and all age groups became involved. This fundamental reality of society was bound to inform to a significant degree the way in which Polish culture in the broadest sense, and education at all levels, were to progress after 1918.

It was not at all unexpected that at its second congress in October 1919, the nationalist camp, now calling itself the Popular National Union (ZLN), should include in its programme the demand that the Catholic Church should be allotted a leading position in but independent of the state. However, the relationship between church and state was not formally addressed until the promulgation of the constitution in March 1921, and also the Concordat between Poland and the Vatican in February 1925. The result was that the position of the Church was never precisely defined. An element of ambiguity was deliberately retained which allowed the state, in the guise of the government of the day, to pronounce on the relationship according to prevailing circumstances. The 1921 Constitution had rejected the notion of a complete separation of church and state, but reaffirmed the close ties between them without recognising Catholicism as the official state religion. Instead, Article 114 gave the Church the status of *primus inter pares* ('first among equals') among all other organised religions in Poland.

The new constitution that was passed in April 1935 did not make any substantive changes to this arrangement, as might have been anticipated from a *Sanacja* regime which did not usually disguise its anti-clerical proclivities. On this occasion, the regime was reluctant to risk upsetting the nationalist camp with which it was seeking a *rapprochement*. By that time also, the Church was eager to display a more positive attitude towards the *Sanacja*, though moments of crisis did occur, as when, in 1937, Archbishop Prince Adam Sapieha (1867–1951) of Kraków became embroiled in a dispute with the government over the final resting-place of Piłsudski's remains (the so-called 'Wawel Incident'). Otherwise, and in practical terms, the overall consequence was that during the interwar era, the influence of the Catholic-patriotic ethos was felt, directly or indirectly, in many areas of cultural and educational activity. The obvious exception was, of course, those noteworthy contributions made by persons who were Jewish or of Jewish background.

The principal manifestations of an astonishingly creative and innovative cultural scene, which, in many respects equalled the better-known achievements of the same period in Weimar Germany, included outstanding writers such as Stefan Żeromski (1864–1925), Maria Dąbrowska (1889–1965), Witold Gombrowicz (1904–69) and the Jewish fantasist, Bruno Schulz (1894–1942); the leading poets of the Skamander group, Kazimierz Wierzyński (1894–1969), Antoni Słonimski (1895–1976), Bolesław Leśmian (1877–1938) and Julian Tuwim (1894–1953), and the likes of Tadeusz Peiper (1891–1969) of the avant-garde group in Kraków; the playwright-painter-writer-philosophers Stanisław Ignacy Witkiewicz ('Witkacy') (1885–1939) and Leon Chwistek (1884–1944); and musicians and conductors, of whom Karol Szymanowski (1882–1937) was the most influential. The revival in theatre was epitomised by the *Polski* and *Narodowy* in Warsaw, where the most prominent director was Leon Schiller (1887–1954).

These advances in so many different fields, however, did create a serious dichotomy in Polish society. While artistic and intellectual circles, especially in liberal Warsaw, could readily applaud this changing cultural scene as 'progressive' and 'innovative', its resonance in wider society was not nearly as positive. Indeed, an adverse response was often to be observed. The problem was that much of this cultural endeavour not only ran counter to prevailing conservative social mores but also frequently ridiculed or denigrated to one degree or another traditional Catholic and patriotic attitudes and values. Particularly offensive to many Poles were, for instance, the scathing poetry of the Skamander group, many of whose most prominent members happened to be Jewish, and the deeply pessimistic prognostications about society articulated by Witkacy. These artists were commonly perceived to be rather strange, but, more importantly, to be anti-Catholic and unpatriotic. Thus, two divergent worlds of thought were being created, the one generally mocking the other, which reciprocated with suspicion and resentment. In a longer-term perspective, it may be seen that the latter had a point, for quite a few of these interwar artistic luminaries, notably Gombrowicz, Tuwim and Słominski, turned out to be rather enthusiastic early supporters of the Soviet-imposed Communist regime in Poland after 1945. It may be suggested that this was the logical culmination of their fundamentally unpatriotic mindset.

In academia, there were notable advances in many fields, including physics, chemistry, logic, philosophy (notably Tadeusz Kotarbiński, 1886–1981, and the logician Jan Łukasiewicz, 1878–1956, of the famed Warsaw School of Analytical Philosophy), geography, anthropology, linguistics (where Jan Baudouin De Courtenay, 1845–1929, was a pioneer), medical science, economics (which produced in Michał Kalecki, 1899–1970, the original theorist behind what subsequently became known as 'Keynesian economics'), and mathematics; the latter had in Wacław Sierpiński (1882–1969), Kazimierz Kuratowski (1896–1980), Stanisław Mazur (1905–83) and Stefan Banach (1892–1945), one of the founders of functional analysis, internationally renowned experts.

Within the framework of the social and welfare reforms introduced by the state shortly after the regaining of independence, a courageous statement of intent was also made in education. In early 1919, the statute on compulsory primary schooling for seven years was introduced and then reaffirmed in the 1921 constitution, despite there being available only 25,000 qualified teachers when at least three times that number were required, and a woefully inadequate number of schools. The authorities were well aware of these deficiencies, but were also persuaded by the very high illiteracy rate of approximately 33 per cent of the population to invest resources as overall economic and financial circumstances permitted. As a result of further major reform legislation in 1924 and 1932, progress was indeed recorded. The number of children attending primary school rose from 2.9 million in 1920/1 to 4.9 million in 1938/9, representing a virtually 100 per cent enrolment, while the number of schools increased in the same period from 22,600 to nearly 28,000. A host of new teacher-training colleges ensured that the qualified teacher–pupil ratio became much more favourable than in 1921.

Consequently, and despite the fact that a large majority of these children did not receive the full seven years of instruction, illiteracy rates had fallen dramatically, to 23 per cent of the population in 1931 and then to around 10 per cent by the beginning of the war. By that time, most of the illiteracy was found among the Ukrainian and Byelorussian peasantry in the Eastern Provinces, where educational provision was generally of inferior quality compared with the rest of the country. For example, an overwhelming number of schools were organised on the basis of one teacher, one room, and a composite class.

Alongside the state system, in which the Catholic Church's powerful influence meant that religious instruction became a compulsory and key element of the curriculum, a relatively small number of privately run and financed schools existed within ethnic minority communities, especially the Germans and Jews. One example were the Jewish Cysho (Central Yiddish School Organisation) schools, in which Yiddish was both the language of instruction and the banner of national and cultural ideology. Cysho aimed essentially to create a new, secular Yiddish culture, and was supported politically by the Marxist Bund and Left Poale Zion parties. By the mid-1930s, there were 169 such schools employing over 800 teachers and enrolling 15,500 pupils.

Because of the overall and persistent paucity of resources, provision for special education, that is, for children with learning difficulties, physical and mental disabilities and the like, was either extremely primitive or non-existent across the country. Thus, of 70,000 such children in 1921, fewer than 2,000 were cared for to any extent. The National Institute of Special Education was established in Warsaw in 1922 under the energetic directorship of Professor Maria Grzegorzewska (1888–1967), but since few further steps were able to be taken by the state by 1939, which included a failure to pass specific legislation for this sphere, the gap had to be filled, and then only partially, by Catholic voluntary and other professional care groups. Even so, of 90,000 children in this category in 1938/9, only about 12 per cent were receiving anything that might reasonably be described as appropriate attention.

The interwar era saw also a substantial expansion of secondary school and university-level education, particularly in the 1930s, thanks to reforms introduced by Education Minister Janusz Jędrzejewski (1889–1951) and his successors. By 1936/7, when 200,000 pupils were enrolled in 760 secondary schools, Poland had 28 institutions of higher learning, including highly regarded universities in Warsaw, Kraków, Lwów, Poznań and Wilno, as well as the new Catholic University in Lublin, polytechnics in Warsaw and Lwów, four commercial colleges, academies of fine arts in Warsaw and Kraków, and the Mining Academy in Kraków, created in

1919. The student population increased steadily, and by the mid-1930s, when it stood at 48,000, was attracting a rising number from lower-class backgrounds and women. The 28 institutions employed 2,460 staff, of whom 824 were full professors. Consequently, the international reputation enjoyed by Polish universities and scholarship before the Partitions was being re-established, while the rising numbers of graduates was a major factor in the considerable expansion of the intelligentsia by 1939.

Poland's cultural and educational heritage was further augmented by the creation of many public libraries, theatres, central and regional archives, research bodies, specialist libraries and museums, including the new National Library and National Museum in Warsaw, and the Museum of Modern Art in Łódż. A programme of renovation of former aristocratic and royal palaces, notably the Royal Castle in Warsaw, was implemented, and book-publishing and the press rapidly expanded. A plethora of local and national, daily, weekly and monthly newspapers, magazines and periodicals, attached to political parties or other types of organisations and institutions, were produced. Press freedom was fairly unrestricted, except where the outlawed Communists were concerned, until the Piłsudski *coup* in 1926. Thereafter, government censorship and inter-vention, particularly against the nationalist camp, increased conspicuously, with particular reference to the press laws of June 1927 and, more so, of November 1938.

The capital city had its fair share of slum housing, poverty and other social ills of the modern urban landscape, but it also personified, in fact, the vibrancy and quality of these cultural and educational achievements. Warsaw developed in a remarkably short space of time an international reputation as a dynamic, stylish metropolis and a favourite posting for diplomats from all over the world. Even the British, not known for offering particularly favourable opinions about things Polish, joined in the acco-lades. This status was even more evident in the post-Depression years, when, with the economy reviving, the city and Poland as a whole began to recapture the self-confidence and optimism for the future that had been apparent in the late 1920s.

Document 77

Article 110 of the Polish constitution of March 1921:

Polish citizens belonging to national, confessional or linguistic minorities shall have equal rights with other citizens to establish, supervise, and administer, at their own expense, philanthropic, confessional and social institutions, schools and other educational establishments, likewise freely therein to use their language and to carry out the precepts of their religion.

Source: *Monitor Polski*, 18 March 1921

Document 78

On the improvement of school provision in the rural Eastern Provinces, 1925:

How much our schools have advanced, as indeed in the whole of Poland, can be seen when one compares them with what they were half a century ago. In Tarnobrzeg up to 1865 there was scarce a tiny classroom, carrying on in a rented house. We had one teacher, and never as many as 100 pupils. Now there are two elementary schools, a high school, a training college, and a Continuation school for vocational training. Some of them have their own buildings, and they mount up to 40 classrooms with not less than 1,500 pupils. We have 50 teachers, who are provided with scientific equipment, and are busy preparing for life the young generation of future Poles.

Source: J. Słomka, *From Serfdom to Self-Government. Memoirs of a Polish Village Mayor, 1842–1927* (London: Minerva, 1941), p. 270

Document 79

Memorandum from Kazimierz Bartel, Prime Minister and Acting Minister of Religious Cults and Education, to school principals in north-eastern Poland, June 1926:

Any forceful imposition of outward attributes of Polishness in schools, any attempt at disregarding what a child receives from home and, above all, the language of the home, anything that may bear the features of national oppression, always has the most fatal effect on the souls of the young generation, gives rise to feelings of hatred, and consequently brings about a lack of loyalty to the state and also, within a short time, generates hostility towards it.

Source: From the journal *Sprawy Narodowościowe*, 1927, No. 1, p. 45

Document 80

Roman Dmowski on Catholicism, 1927:

The dominant religion, whose principles govern the legal powers of the state, is the Catholic religion, and the Catholic Church is the executor of the religious aspects of state life.

Source: R. Dmowski, *Kościół, Naród, Państwo*
(Warsaw: Narodowiec, 1927), p. 25

Document 81

*From the new programme of the National Democrats (*Endecja*), 1928:*

The National Democratic Party adopts the principle that Roman Catholicism should occupy the leading role in Poland, that the Roman Catholic Church should be governed by its own laws, and that relations with the state should be regulated by an agreement with the Holy See. The laws and actions of the state, particularly regulations concerning the family and marriage, which are the foundation of society, and concerning education, must conform to the principles of Roman Catholicism, whose principles must also pervade public life in Poland.

Source: From the newspaper *Gazeta Warszawska*, 16 October 1928

Document 82

An official description of the attitude of the Catholic clergy towards the government, May 1937:

Compared with previous years, there is an increase in loyalty to the government among the higher clergy. This clergy is trying to develop a proper relationship with the state authorities. But in relation to government measures in the socio-political sphere . . . it is avoiding any involvement. The lower clergy . . . retains a mood of cultural, political and social hostility. They continue to persist in an outlook characterised by a distrust of all state authority, accompanied at the same time by an encouragement of all disaffected circles of the community. The consequence of this political and social 'liberalism' of a certain section of the Polish clergy is activity that undermines the principle of state authority and provides, in due course, opportunities for subversive elements.

The Catholic Church . . . does not always properly respond to the overtures of co-operation put forward by the state. Among certain members of the clergy . . . a tendency may be discerned of extending its power unilaterally, apart from the government . . .

Source: Archiwum Akt Nowych (Warsaw), Ministry of Foreign Affairs, 122, memorandum to President I. Mościcki, 18 May 1937

Document 83

*From a confidential memorandum dated Warsaw, 29 January 1937, on the anti-*Sanacja *political opposition among students at the Jagiellonian University, Kraków:*

The organisations of oppositional youth, especially *Młodziej Wszechpolska* (that is, the youth of the National Democratic Party, whose political agitation on the university campus is well known), have at the present time launched a campaign to change the political orientation of the *Bratnia Pomoc* student group . . . Given that it is not certain that the National Democratic youth candidates will successfully contest the elections on 14 March, this group has launched a campaign of a special type among the students attending the three seminaries in Kraków, aiming to enlist them in its organisation . . . The elections have a political character. Until now, the seminary students have had the good sense not to become involved. Now, however, some of them are leading a certain group that is participating, which could have serious consequences. The *Młodziej Wszechpolska* organisation has enticed the seminary students into its intrigues, which are purely political, and have accordingly stirred up discontent . . . All of this is designed to bring electoral victory to *Młodziej Wszpechpolska* and to eliminate the influence of *Bratnia Pomoc.*

Source: Archiwum Akt Nowych (Warsaw), 2856/Mościcki, 1937

Document 84

The rector of the Jan Kazimierz University in Lwów, Professor Stanisław Kulczyński, defends the principle of academic freedom in Polish universities by opposing the introduction of the so-called 'ghetto benches' for Jewish students, January 1938:

I have resigned from the office of rector because I did not want to put my signature to an act which . . . is essentially a cheque exacted under terrorist pressure to be cashed by a political party and paid for by the university at the expense of its prestige and its vital interests. . . . rectors and academic senates are at the head of independent and respected institutions which exercise a very important influence, based on the authority of learning, over the nation.

To compel the university authorities to introduce a political party's conception of law is blackmail – it is an abuse of the prestige of the universities and of learning for the benefit of the party. For this blackmail, the universities pay not only with their prestige, but also with their freedom of action, and with the total collapse of their organisation. It will readily be seen that under cover of the beautiful ideals of national solidarity and the defence of the Polish spirit of our culture, the autonomous university authorities are being brutally divested of their dignity, and Polish learning is deprived of the rights of liberty, which alone can ensure its development.

Learning cannot develop under conditions of compulsion . . . because learning is free thought, and thought that is not free is not scientific thought.

**Source: Adapted and translated from a copy of
the original supplied from private sources**

7

FOREIGN POLICY

The stabilisation of the Second Republic's territorial integrity in the aftermath of the victory over the Bolsheviks allowed its independent existence until the combined onslaught of Germany and the Soviet Union in September 1939. However, during the interwar decades, Poland's independence was never entirely secure. Not only was the overall international situation in Europe anxious and unstable, but Poland continued to be the object of hatred for the two principal revisionist powers, Germany and the Soviet Union. Both regarded Poland as living proof of their defeat and subsequent loss of territory, influence and status, and both were determined to destroy her at the earliest possible opportunity within the context of their assault on the Treaty of Versailles itself. In the early 1920s, Germany was still too traumatised and weakened by the First World War and its consequences to be able to do anything effective about her Polish problem, while the nascent Soviet Union regarded her defeat by the Poles in 1920 as a temporary setback that would be avenged in due course. For the Soviets, therefore, the Treaty of Riga was as objectionable as the Treaty of Versailles; both had to be swept aside.

If it was bad enough for Poland to have the Germans and Russians breathing heavily down her neck, her situation was made even more disadvantageous because she lacked reliable allies. For one reason or another, the major powers which had played a prominent role in helping Poland to regain independence in 1918–19 in the first place quickly made it clear that they had more pressing concerns and priorities, leaving her very largely to her own devices. This was poignantly underlined by the unwillingness of any of these powers to lend substantive aid to Poland in her conflict with the Bolsheviks.

The United States had retreated into isolationism, rendering redundant the whole Wilsonian ideology that had been so influential in shaping the peace, while Britain had her imperial interests to oversee and, in any case, where Europe was concerned, she was far more intent on helping to rehabilitate Germany than aiding Poland: Britain's pro-German policies in the dispute over Upper Silesia revealed the orientation her policy on the continent was now taking. France, a haven for Polish exiled revolutionaries in the nineteenth century and generally regarded in Poland and the rest of Europe as being basically sympathetic to the Polish cause, had emerged from the First World War much weakened and rather paranoid about a revival of German militarism. France's policy in Eastern Europe after 1919 was mainly influenced by her desire to construct essentially anti-German alliances with states such as Poland and Czechoslovakia. Even then, France proceeded cautiously, and although she had played a supportive role on Poland's side in the Upper Silesian conflict, it was not until after the Polish–Soviet War that she offered a full alliance.

The Franco-Polish alliance of February 1921 was regarded by many in Poland, particularly by the historically pro-French *Endecja* and its allies, as the cornerstone of Polish foreign policy for most of the interwar years. The Piłsudski camp, on the other hand, was never quite as enthusiastic because it firmly saw the Soviet Union as Poland's principal enemy, so that the French alliance was not rated quite as highly. As time went on, that somewhat sceptical attitude was justified, in so far as France herself became more and more hesitant and ambivalent about the alliance. In part, this may be explained with reference to the mounting economic and political problems of the Third Republic, which a succession of short-lived governments seemed powerless to address in a way that would re-establish genuine stability. As a result of this unsatisfactory domestic state of affairs, France's standing and influence on the wider European stage declined, thus diminishing the value of the alliance with Poland.

While support for France and the alliance none the less remained quite strong in Poland right up to 1939, and was endorsed by significant figures outside of government circles such as General Władysław Sikorski, Piłsudski and his *Sanacja* regime after 1926 were well aware of France's declining value as an alliance partner. Indeed, this dichotomy in attitudes in Poland towards the French alliance crystallised, as in so many other facets of the Second Republic, around the opposing *Endek* and Piłsudski camps. While both subscribed to the rather fanciful and premature notion of Poland as an emerging Great Power, for the Piłsudskiites, in particular, it was more realistic to understand and to conduct Polish foreign policy on the basis of what became known as the 'Doctrine of Two Enemies'.

The doctrine recognised that Poland had to contend with two equally implacable enemies, Germany and the Soviet Union, and that the most prudent response was to try as far as possible to steer an independent course between them, with only supplementary support from her allies, France and, from March 1921, also Romania, and on no account allying with

Germany against the Soviet Union, or vice-versa. As Marshal Edward Śmigły-Rydz (1886–1941) later put it succinctly and perceptively: 'Germany will destroy our body, Russia will destroy our soul.' In essence, in a situation where Poland had a choice only between the devil and the deep blue sea, she chose neither in preference to the other, deciding to deal simultaneously with both. It was always bound to be an extremely risky approach, but was probably the only one that was realistically available when all factors in international diplomacy at that time were taken into account. These included, of course, the Treaty of Rapallo of April 1922, which understandably caused profound disquiet in Europe, but especially in Poland. That two ideologically diametrical states could come together in a fully fledged alliance, which also had military provisions, was a great shock to the Versailles system, while for Poland, it gave another clear indication that her mortal enemies meant business. In a longer-term perspective, of course, Rapallo may be seen as the most important diplomatic provenance of the later, notorious Ribbentrop–Molotov Pact.

Apart from Poland's justifiable *Angst* about Germany and the Soviet Union, she had also to contend with antagonism from Lithuania over the controversial way in which the disputed city of Wilno and surrounding district had finally been incorporated into the Second Republic. Despite a number of attempts by Poland, especially Piłsudski, to reach a settlement over an area with which he had the closest personal ties, the matter was never resolved, so that relations with Lithuania remained very tense right up until the Second World War. Moreover, Poland's relations with Czechoslovakia were badly soured by the equally bitter dispute over Cieszyn (Teschen), which was only resolved satisfactorily, at least from the Polish standpoint, when, in the immediate aftermath of the infamous Munich Conference of September 1938, Polish troops occupied the area and incorporated it into Poland. As regards both Wilno and Cieszyn, Poland, it may be said, was only pursuing her legitimate and rightful national interests, though perhaps the timing of her intervention in Cieszyn could have been more propitious. On the other hand, her relations with the other Baltic states, especially Latvia, and with Hungary were friendly throughout the period.

In the post-Rapallo period, the international situation did not appear, on the surface at least, to be particularly threatening for Poland. The Bolshevik regime in the Soviet Union had retreated into a period of domestic consolidation within the concept of 'Socialism in One Country', and as regards Poland contented itself with allowing marauding bands to harass Polish towns and villages along the Riga border. While these activities did not pose a serious threat, they were sufficiently troublesome and persistent for the Polish Government under General Sikorski to initiate in 1923/4 the creation of the Border Defence Corps (KOP) in the east, which quickly restored order. Of much greater concern was the new direction of German foreign policy under Gustav Stresemann (1878–1929) from 1924 onwards.

Stresemann, who had been a strong supporter of Germany's ultra-nationalist annexationist policy during the First World War, and a staunch monarchist, had come to accept in the early postwar era that the parliamentary Weimar Republic was the only viable option for Germany, while as Foreign Minister, he became convinced that Germany's best long-term interests lay in effecting a *rapprochement* with the Western Allies. His approach culminated in the Locarno Pact of October 1925, by which, *inter alia*, Germany accepted her western borders as defined in the Treaty of Versailles. But although, therefore, the loss of Alsace-Lorraine and other, smaller territories was now accepted without too much fuss by Germany, including the nationalist Right, her eastern border with Poland was, signally, not recognised. Stresemann, the self-styled 'good European' and reborn democrat, was as committed as anyone on the German Right to recover the 'lost' eastern provinces of the Reich, including Upper Silesia, Poznania and West Prussia. The Poles naturally took fright, not only at this latest manifestation of an unreconstructed German nationalism, but also at the alacrity with which her main ally, France, had signed the pact.

The German Foreign Minister had brought off quite a *coup*, for he now believed that, with the tacit approval of Britain and France, he was free to pursue, albeit by exclusively non-military means, his prime objective: revision of the border with Poland, a country for which, like so many other Germans, he had nothing but the utmost contempt and hatred. It was very much at his behest, for example, that Germany began the 'Tariff War' with Poland in 1925 as a means of undermining Poland economically and of ultimately destroying her. When, the following year, Germany and the Soviet Union renewed their formal ties in the Treaty of Berlin (April 1926), and Germany was well on the way to being admitted to a permanent seat at the League of Nations while Poland's application for the same was rejected, Warsaw's consternation reached new heights of intensity. The dramatic, new international configuration certainly also played an important part in helping to persuade Piłsudski to launch his *coup* in May 1926. The restoration of stability at home he saw as the essential prerequisite for dealing with the increasingly fraught situation in foreign affairs. In the event, against the backdrop of a reviving European economy, the late 1920s did not witness any more significant developments that could be said to have further damaged Poland's position. Indeed, she may well have been reassured to some extent by the premature death of her arch-adversary,

Stresemann, in October 1929. He had been successful in relieving some of the Versailles burden on Germany, but had not made any tangible progress in his quest to revise the border with Poland.

The onset of the Depression added its own peculiar strains to international affairs and Germany, under Chancellor Heinrich Brüning (1885–1970), was able to secure more concessions, including a moratorium and then complete cancellation of reparation payments (June 1932). Nationalist agitation against Poland increased, though there was still no sign that the border issue would become a major flashpoint. Indeed, it could be said that Poland's overall international position was strengthened, at least symbolically, by the conclusion of the Polish–Soviet Non-Aggression Pact in July 1932. Piłsudski never abandoned his inveterate anti-Russianism, and regarded both tsarism and Bolshevism as imperialist and anti-Polish, but he would draw some comfort from the pact, even if he was convinced that it would be nothing more than a temporary respite from Soviet hostility. He may have been taking advantage of this more congenial climate when he turned his attention to Germany the following year in the wake of Adolf Hitler's (1889–1945) assumption of power in January 1933.

The new German Chancellor headed a militantly chauvinistic party, the National Socialists (NSDAP), which in elections since 1930 had drawn massive support in the eastern electoral districts (*Wahlkreise*) of the Reich adjacent to Poland. Among all classes in these areas, such as East Prussia, Pomerania, Mecklenburg, Frankfurt/Oder and German Silesia, anti-Polonism was endemic. However, although Nazi propaganda had included attacks on Poland, Hitler himself had not at this stage displayed any particular animosity towards Poland. In fact, just as he had admired Benito Mussolini (1883–1945) for seizing power in Italy in 1922, Hitler had occasionally expressed his admiration for Piłsudski as a strong leader and for the *coup* which had brought him back into power in 1926. In 1933, the Führer was fully aware of Germany's relative military weakness, so that even if he had wanted to, he would not have been in a position to launch an attack aimed at fulfilling the nationalist dream of recovering the 'lost lands' from Poland. For Piłsudski, however, the situation was rather different. Now confident that the Soviet threat had been diminished for the time being by the Non-Aggression Pact, and alert to Germany's weakness, he could appreciate that the idea of a pre-emptive strike against Germany had its merits.

Historians are sharply divided over whether or not Piłsudski advocated a preventive war against Germany in the early months of Hitler's regime. There is certainly an absence of documentary evidence to show conclusively what was in Piłsudski's mind, but there is a fair amount of anecdotal evidence from highly placed diplomatic sources in Poland, Germany and France to indicate that he was serious about this proposition. He raised the issue on two separate occasions with the French, who may, in turn, have informally conferred with the British Government. In any case, Piłsudski, unwilling and unable to act alone, received a negative response from the French, and dropped the matter. It can only be said that if Poland had been able to persuade France to march with her against Hitler, with every chance of a successful campaign, Germany, Europe and the rest of the world would almost certainly have been spared the tragedy of another world war for which the Nazi regime was responsible.

In the event, Piłsudski was now eager, as was his new Foreign Minister (from November 1932), Józef Beck (1894–1944), to put relations with Germany on a formal diplomatic footing similar to that which had been forged with the Soviet Union. Finding that Hitler was keen for his own reasons to reciprocate, the Poles signed a Non-Aggression Pact with Germany in January 1934. Despite the rhetorical extravagances that accompanied the pact, and the subsequent conclusion of several agreements on minority issues, neither side believed that the major problems that had informed German–Polish relations since 1919 had been solved. Their border was as before. Both sides wanted and secured a breathing-space before the showdown which Piłsudski, for one, believed was inevitable. In the meantime, a considerably weakened France as well as francophile, anti-*Sanacja* political elements in Poland were horrified by Poland's new alignment with Germany, but then they all lacked the perspicacity of the marshal.

Piłsudski's death in May 1935 meant that Beck assumed the leading role in the conduct of Polish foreign policy through the rapidly gathering storm clouds in Europe. A rejuvenated Germany increasingly took the initiative in international affairs, beginning with her reoccupation of the Rhineland in early 1936 in blatant violation of the Versailles settlement, without provoking the Western Powers into anything stronger than the policy of appeasement. At the same time, the Soviet Union had become a power to be reckoned with as a result of Stalin's (1879–1953) ruthlessly implemented industrial, agricultural, social, political and military reforms. With two aggressive totalitarian regimes on either flank with deep-seated grudges against her, post-Piłsudski Poland was unavoidably caught up in an increasingly desperate situation. Worse still, it had become clear after the failure to oppose Germany's reoccupation of the Rhineland, and particularly in view of the débâcle of the Munich Conference in September 1938, when Czechoslovakia had been given no support in resisting Hitler's demands over the Sudetenland, that Britain and France could not be relied upon to lend meaningful support to any other country under threat.

Despite this, it is equally clear that the ruling political and military circles in Poland continued to believe that, in the event of a German attack, France and Britain would honour their alliance commitments and aid Poland. It is perhaps only in retrospect that it can be fully appreciated that neither was able or willing to offer anything other than moral and semantic assistance, the 1921 Franco-Polish and 1939 Anglo-Polish treaties notwithstanding. France, debilitated by a multitude of domestic problems which no government of whatever complexion had been able to address successfully, was a pale shadow of a Great Power by 1939, while Britain, eyes as usual on the empire and regarding Eastern Europe as being composed of 'far-away countries', had no intrinsic inclination to become involved in a major war on behalf of Poland or anyone else – until, in 1940, not 1939, it could not be avoided.

Beck's policy, particularly *vis-à-vis* Germany, has been criticised frequently for being wrong-headed and ultimately disastrous for Poland. He himself has attracted criticism for his personality and style of diplomacy, especially from *Endek* circles suspicious of his Frankist (Germano–Jewish) background. In all fairness, however, such criticisms seem largely misplaced. In the first instance, the overtures to Germany were understandable in terms of being simply an attempt to assuage the anger of the Nazi beast and also as a compensation for the relative frailty of the French alliance. But, more importantly, Beck and Poland were having to deal with the two most appalling dictators of the twentieth century. Both Hitler and Stalin had the power and determination to pursue their own particular agendas, and there was nothing in the end, no course of action followed by Poland which would have averted the catastrophe of September 1939. Above all, neither Beck nor any other Polish leader can be blamed for not envisaging the nightmare scenario where Nazi Germany and the Communist Soviet Union, ideological opposites who had been conducting violent propaganda wars against each other since 1933, came together in a formal alliance in August 1939. In that context, there was no Polish foreign policy, military or political strategy that could have prevented or repulsed the combined onslaught that ensued.

In face of the German invasion on 1 September and of the Soviet invasion on 17 September, Poland stood alone. Britain and France declared war on Germany, but confined their action to diplomatic protests and radio broadcasts to Poland – empty, futile gestures. True to historical tradition and the national temperament, the Polish armed forces fought heroically and well against overwhelming odds. The final outcome, however, could never have been in doubt. Warsaw formally surrendered on 29 September and the last regular engagement of the Polish Army, at Kock, ended on 5 October. As the world looked on, Hitler and Stalin proceeded to carve up Poland between them, thus effecting a fourth Partition. The Second Republic had suffered a terrible military defeat, but it was not finished, not by any means. Remnants of the military and political leaderships were able to escape to the West, often through Hungary and Romania, to continue the fight in the name of the republic, whose constitutional seals and symbols of office went with them. The vast majority of Poles who remained trapped under the Nazi and Soviet yoke could hardly have anticipated, however, the horrors that awaited them in the years ahead.

Document 85

Gustav Stresemann, the German Foreign Minister, outlines his principal aims, 1925:

In my opinion, there are three great tasks that confront German foreign policy in the more immediate future:

In the first place, the solution of the Reparations question in a sense tolerable for Germany . . .

Secondly, the protection of Germans abroad, those 10 to 12 million of our kindred who now live under a foreign yoke in foreign lands.

The third great task is the readjustment of our eastern frontiers; the recovery of Danzig, the Polish corridor, and a correction of the frontier in Upper Silesia.

**Source: G. Stresemann, *His Diaries, Letters and Papers*,
ed. E. Sutton (London: Macmillan, 1937), Volume II, pp. 503 ff.**

Document 86

From the Polish–Soviet Non-Aggression Pact, 25 July 1932:

Article 1: The two contracting parties, recording the fact that they have renounced war as an instrument of national policy in their mutual relations, reciprocally undertake to refrain from taking any aggressive action against or invading the territory of the other party, either alone or in conjunction with other Powers.

Any act of violence attacking the integrity and inviolability of the territory or the political independence of the other contracting party shall be regarded as contrary to the undertakings contained in the present Article, even if such acts are committed without declaration of war and avoid all possible warlike manifestations.

Article 2: Should one of the contracting parties be attacked by a third state or by a group of other states, the other contracting party undertakes not to give aid or assistance, either directly or indirectly, to the aggressor state during the whole period of the conflict. If one of the contracting parties commits an act of aggression against a third state, the other contracting party shall have the right to be released from the present treaty without previous denunciation.

Article 3: Each of the contracting parties undertakes not to be a party to any agreement openly hostile to the other party from the point of view of aggression . . .

Article 5: The two contracting parties, desirous of settling and solving, exclusively by peaceful means, any disputes and differences, of whatever nature or origin, which may arise between them, undertake to submit questions at issue, which it has not been possible to settle within a reasonable period by diplomatic channels, to a procedure of conciliation . . .

The pact is concluded for three years . . .

> Source: Republic of Poland: Ministry for Foreign Affairs,
> *Official Documents concerning Polish–German and
> Polish–Soviet Relations, 1933–1939* (London: n.d. [1941]),
> Document No. 151, pp. 170–1

Document 87

From the Polish–German Non-Aggression Pact, 26 January 1934:

The Polish Government and the German Government consider that the time has come to introduce a new phase in the political relations between Germany and Poland by means of a direct understanding between the two states. They have, therefore, decided in the present declaration to lay down the principles for the future development of these relations.

The two governments base their action on the fact that the maintenance and guarantee of a lasting peace between their countries is an essential prerequisite for the general peace of Europe.

Each of the two governments . . . lays it down that the international obligations undertaken by it towards a third party do not hinder the peaceful development of their mutual relations, do not conflict with the present declaration, and are not affected by this declaration. They establish, moreover, that this declaration does not extend to those questions which under international law are to be regarded exclusively as the internal concern of either of the two states.

Both governments announce their intention to settle directly all questions of whatever nature which concern their mutual relations. Should any disputes arise between them and agreement thereon not be reached by direct negotiation, they will, in each particular case, on the basis of mutual agreement, seek a solution by other peaceful means . . . In no circumstances, however, will they proceed to the application of force for the purpose of reaching a decision in such disputes.

The guarantee of peace created by these principles will facilitate the great task of both governments of finding a solution for problems of political, economic and social kinds, based on a just and fair adjustment of the interests of both parties. Both governments are convinced that the relations between their countries will in this manner develop fruitfully, and will lead to the establishment of a neighbourly relationship which will contribute to the well-being not only of both their countries, but of the other peoples of Europe as well.

The declaration is valid for a period of ten years . . .

Source: Republic of Poland: Ministry for Foreign Affairs,
*Official Documents concerning Polish–German and
Polish–Soviet Relations, 1933–1939* (London: n.d. [1941]),
Document No. 10, pp. 20–1

Document 88

Polish Foreign Minister Józef Beck's memoirs on Piłsudski's 'preventive war' notion of 1933:

As the Marshal said to me, he had thoroughly examined the pros and cons, and all the chances of a preventive war, before taking the decision to negotiate with Germany . . . In the military sphere, the Marshal calculated that the weakest point of our armed forces was the higher command. The weakness of our eventual allies in that period made us abandon the idea of a preventive war. Having verified that there existed a possibility of concluding a non-aggression pact which would give us at least a respite for living and working quietly and normally, it was with a sense of relief that we agreed to sign the pact.

Source: J. Beck, *Dernier Rapport: Politique polonnaise, 1926–1939*
(Neuchâtel: Editions de la Baçonniere, 1951), p. 66

Document 89

Former Reich Chancellor Heinrich Brüning on Piłsudski's 'preventive war':

The fact that as soon as Hitler came to power, Marshal Piłsudski proposed to France joint preventive military action indicates how well-grounded our fears were. And the knowledge of this proposal strongly influenced voting in the Reichstag in March and May 1933. In May 1933, the National Socialist Party made a great patriotic sacrifice and voted together with other parties for a resolution that expressed unanimously . . . the wish of the Reichstag to oppose the action proposed to the French by Piłsudski. This voting had undoubtedly influenced the French Government's rejection of the Polish proposal.

Source: H. Brüning, *Deutsche Rundschau*, July 1947; from
Documents on German Foreign Policy, 1918–1945, Series C
(London: HM Stationery Office, 1957), Volume I,
Document Nos. 142, 180, 183, 192

Document 90

From a speech by the Reich Chancellor, Adolf Hitler, to the Reichstag, 30 January 1934:

. . . the Reich Government has made efforts since its first year to arrive at new and better relations with the state of Poland. When I took power in Germany, I had the impression that relations were far from satisfactory.

Divergences existed which had arisen out of the territorial clauses of the Treaty of Versailles, but there was also a mutual irritation which resulted from those clauses, and there was a danger of seeing such hostility . . . transformed into hereditary hatred. Such an evolution would have constituted an eternal obstacle to fruitful collaboration between the two peoples. Germans and Poles must reconcile themselves to the fact of each other's existence. A thousand years of history have not been able to eliminate this state of things, and it will go on existing after us. Therefore it is more rational to give It such a form as will ensure the greatest benefit possible.

No matter what divergences may exist between the two countries in the future, to attempt to settle them by military action would have such mournful results that they could not be compensated by any gain whatsoever . . . The German Government is also ready to organise economic relations with Poland of such a nature as to ensure that a period of sterile abstention shall be followed by an epoch of fruitful collaboration.

Source: Republic of Poland: Ministry for Foreign Affairs,
*Official Documents concerning Polish–German and
Polish–Soviet Relations, 1933–1939* (London: n.d. [1941]),
Document No. 12, pp. 22–3

Document 91

Professor A. J. Toynbee on Polish foreign policy, 1935:

The aristocrats, who still enjoyed considerable power in Poland, together with those Poles of all classes who were under the influence of the 'legionary' spirit of the Piłsudski regime, felt much more in sympathy with the Hungarians than with the Czechs. They were, indeed, inclined to despise the latter as a grasping and bourgeois race, inhabiting a country far inferior in status to their own beloved Poland, whom they believed to be at last about to fulfil her divinely appointed mission as a Great Power. (The Czechs for their part were apt to give way to a corresponding prejudice against the clerical and aristocratic traditions of Poland.) Whether Marshal Piłsudski and his government were actually harbouring any sinister designs against Czechoslovakia, or whether they merely wished to accustom public opinion to their newly established reconciliation with Germany by promoting Czechoslovakia to the position of public enemy . . . the signing of the German–Polish Non-Aggression Pact certainly coincided with the opening of a campaign of propaganda in defence of the Polish minority in Teschen.

Source: A. J. Toynbee, *Survey of International Affairs*
(London: Oxford University Press, 1935), pp. 279 ff.

Document 92

General Władysław Sikorski on possible Polish co-operation with the Soviet Union against German aggression, 1937:

An alliance between Poland and Russia, resulting in the Red Army marching over Polish territory, is unacceptable to us. At least, as long as Communism reigns in Russia. And yet we cannot dismiss out of hand all forms of assistance which would be possible in the event of a war with Germany. The simplest solution would be an understanding with Russia that would provide us with a secure supply of Russian goods. This would be an expression of a provident, far-sighted and truly creative policy. To base our future on the ancient antagonism between Germany and Russia, or on our declaration of neutrality in the event of a conflict between these powers, would be the policy of an ostrich which would have catastrophic consequences for us.

**Source: W. Sikorski, *Diaries 1936–9*, extracts in
Polish Perspectives No. 13 (Warsaw: 1970), pp. 28 ff.**

Document 93

The British Military Attaché in Warsaw, Lieutenant-Colonel Edward Roland Sword, on Poland and her army, January 1939:

. . . it is doubtful whether Poland would count on military support by France other than in war material . . . It is probable, therefore, that the foreign policy of Poland will remain at present based on the maintenance of her independence and neutrality between her powerful neighbours . . . Her comparative poverty is directly responsible for the numerical inferiority of her air force and limits the equipment of land forces, particularly as far as artillery and mechanisation are concerned. Furthermore, the army would be largely dependent on imported war material in the event of prolonged hostilities.

As far as training is concerned, the army possibly suffers from a certain conflict between French and German doctrine, together with a lack of appreciation of the power of modern weapons, and of the administrative problems inseparable from military operations. On the other hand, the Polish Army is designed to fight on Polish soil . . . Polish officers, particularly in the higher ranks, possess an undoubted power of leadership, and the courage and endurance of the rank and file is welded into a composite whole by strict discipline and morale . . . The cohesion of the army is really remarkable . . . almost every activity of the people is, or can be, harnessed to meet the requirements of the armed forces.

Source: *Edward Roland Sword: The Diary and Despatches of a Military Attaché in Warsaw 1938–1939*, ed. E. Turnbull and A. Suchcitz (London: Polish Cultural Foundation, 2001), pp. 77–8

Document 94

From the secret protocol of the Nazi–Soviet Non-Aggression Pact, 23 August 1939:

On the occasion of the Non-Aggression Pact between the German Reich and the Union of Soviet Socialist Republics . . . the two parties discussed in strictly confidential conversations the question of the delimitation of their respective spheres of interest in eastern Europe. These conversations led to the following conclusions . . .

Article 2 referred specifically to Poland:

Article 2: In the event of a territorial and political transformation of the areas belonging to the Polish State, the spheres of interest of both Germany and the USSR shall be bounded approximately by the line of the rivers Narew, Vistula, and San.

The question of whether the interests of both parties make the maintenance of an independent Polish State desirable, and how the borders of such a state should be drawn, can be definitely determined only in the course of further political developments. In any case, both governments will resolve this matter by means of a friendly understanding.

Source: General Sikorski Historical Institute, *Documents on Polish–Soviet Relations, 1939–1945* (London: 1961), Volume 1, pp. 46–7

Document 95

From President Franklin D. Roosevelt of the United States to Ignacy Mościcki, President of Poland, 24 August 1939:

The manifest gravity of the present crisis imposes the urgent obligation upon all to examine every possible means which might prevent the outbreak of a general war . . . It is, I think, well known to you that, speaking on behalf of the United States, I have exerted, and will continue to exert, every influence on behalf of peace. The rank and file of the population of every nation, large and small, want peace. They do not seek military conquest. They recognise that disputes, claims and counter-claims will always arise from time to time between nations, but that all controversies, without exception, can be solved by a peaceful procedure, if the will on both sides exists so to do.

> Source: ***Documents concerning German–Polish Relations and the Outbreak of Hostilities Between Great Britain and Germany on September 3, 1939*** **(London: HM Stationery Office, 1939), Document No. 125, p. 184**

Document 96

From the Agreement of Mutual Assistance between the United Kingdom and Poland, 25 August 1939:

Article 1:
Should one of the contracting parties become engaged in hostilities with a European Power in consequence of aggression by the latter against that contracting party, the other contracting party will at once give the contracting party engaged in hostilities all the support and assistance in its power.

Article 2:
(1) The provision of Article 1 will also apply in the event of any action by a European Power which clearly threatened, directly or indirectly, the independence of one of the contracting parties, and was of such a nature that the party in question considered it vital to resist it with its armed forces.
(2) Should one of the contracting parties become engaged in hostilities with a European Power in consequence of action by that Power which

threatened the independence or neutrality of another European state in such a way as to constitute a clear menace to the security of the contracting party, the provisions of Article 1 will apply, without prejudice, however, to the rights of the other European state concerned.

Article 4:
The methods of applying the undertakings of mutual assistance provided for by the present agreement are established between the competent naval, military and air authorities of the contracting parties.

Secret protocol attached to the Agreement of Mutual Assistance . . .

1(a) By the expression 'a European Power' employed in the agreement is to be understood Germany.

2(a) The two governments will from time to time determine by mutual agreement the hypothetical cases of action by Germany coming within the ambit of Article 2 of the agreement.

Source: *Documents concerning German–Polish Relations and the Outbreak of Hostilities Between Great Britain and Germany on September 3, 1939* (London: HM Stationery Office, 1939), Document No. 19, pp. 37–39

Document 97

A proclamation to the Polish nation by the President of Poland, Ignacy Mościcki, 1 September 1939:

Citizens. During the course of last night, our age-old enemy commenced offensive operations against the Polish State. I affirm this before God and History.

At this historic moment, I appeal to all citizens of the country in the profound conviction that the entire nation will rally around its commander-in-chief and armed forces to defend its liberty, independence and honour, and to give the aggressor a worthy answer, as has happened already more than once in the history of Polish–German relations.

The entire nation, blessed by God in its struggle for a just and sacred cause, and united with its army, will march in serried ranks to the struggle and the final victory.

Source: Republic of Poland: Ministry for Foreign Affairs, *Official Documents concerning Polish–German and Polish–Soviet Relations, 1933–1939* (London: n.d. [1941]), Document No. 120, pp. 119–20

Document 98

The Soviet note to the Polish Ambassador in Moscow, Mr Wacław Grzybowski, 17 September 1939:

The Polish–German War has revealed the internal bankruptcy of the Polish State. During the course of ten days' hostilities, Poland has lost all her industrial areas and cultural centres. Warsaw no longer exists as the capital of Poland. The Polish Government has disintegrated, and no longer shows any sign of life. This means that the Polish State and its government have, in fact, ceased to exist. The agreements concluded between the USSR and Poland have therefore ceased to function. Left to her own devices, and bereft of leadership, Poland has become a suitable area for all kinds of hazards and surprises which may constitute a threat to the USSR. For these reasons, the Soviet Government, which until now has observed neutrality, cannot any longer preserve neutrality in view of these facts.

Furthermore, the Soviet Government cannot regard with indifference the fact that the kindred Ukrainian and White Russian people, who live on Polish territory and who are at the mercy of fate, are now left defenceless.

In these circumstances, the Soviet Government has directed the high command of the Red Army to order the troops to cross the frontier and to take under their protection the life and property of the population of Western Ukraine and Western White Russia.

At the same time, the Soviet Government proposes to take all measures to extricate the Polish people from the unfortunate war into which they were dragged by their unwise leaders, and to enable them to live in peace.

Source: Republic of Poland: Ministry for Foreign Affairs, *Official Documents concerning Polish–German and Polish–Soviet Relations, 1933–1939* (London, n.d. [1941]), Document No. 179, pp. 191–2

Document 99

From a proclamation issued by the Polish President, Ignacy Mościcki, 17 September 1939:

Citizens of the republic! At a time when our army is fighting with incomparable courage, as it has from the first day of the war, against the overwhelming power of the enemy, withstanding the onslaught of almost the whole of the armed might of Germany, our eastern neighbour has invaded our country in violation of solemn agreements and immutable principles of morality.

Not for the first time in our history are we faced with an invasion from both the west and the east. Poland, in alliance with France and Great Britain, is fighting for the rule of law against lawlessness, for faith and civilisation against soulless barbarism, against the reign of evil in the world. From this struggle, Poland, by invincible faith, must and shall emerge victorious.

. . . I am certain that throughout the most difficult ordeals, you will preserve the same strength of spirit, the same dignity and glowing pride by which you have earned the admiration of the world. On every one of you falls the duty of guarding the honour of the nation . . . Almighty providence will do justice to our cause.

Source: Polish Cultural Foundation, *The Crime of Katyń.*
***Facts & Documents* (London: 1965), p. 5**

Document 100

A propagandistic appeal to Polish soldiers by Soviet Marshal S. Timoshenko, commander-in-chief of the Ukrainian front, 24 September 1939:

In the last few days, the Polish Army has been finally defeated. The soldiers of the towns of Tarnopol, Halicz, Równe, Dubno, over 6,000 of them, all voluntarily came over to our side.

Soldiers, what is left to you? What are you fighting for? Against whom are you fighting? Why do you risk your lives? Your resistance is useless. Your officers are light-heartedly driving you to slaughter. They hate you and your families. They shot your negotiators whom you sent to us with a proposal of surrender.

Do not trust your officers! Your officers and generals are your enemies.

They wish your death. Soldiers, turn on your officers and generals! Do not submit to the orders of your officers. Drive them out from your soil. Come to us boldly, to your brothers, to the Red Army. Here you will be cared for, here you will be respected.

Remember that only the Red Army will liberate the Polish people . . . Believe us, the Red Army of the Soviet Union is your only friend.

Source: Polish Cultural Foundation, *The Crime of Katyń.*
Facts & Documents **(London: 1965), pp. 11–12**

Document 101

The final communiqué issued by the Warsaw Defence Command, 29 September 1939:

Having exhausted all the possibilities of continuing resistance, and having in view the desperate plight of the civilian population, as also the lack of food and munitions . . . the Warsaw Defence Command announces that it feels obliged to conclude an armistice.

The Warsaw Defence Command has agreed with the German military authorities as to the conditions of surrender of the city of Warsaw and its garrison today at noon. The German military authorities undertake to assure conditions of honourable captivity to the officers who have participated in the defence of the capital, authorising them to retain their swords. On the other hand, the Germans undertake to demobilise the non-commissioned officers and privates and allow them to return to their homes.

Source: Republic of Poland: Ministry for Foreign Affairs,
Official Documents concerning Polish–German and
Polish–Soviet Relations, 1933–1939 **(London: n.d. [1941]),**
Document No. 145, p. 140

8

OCCUPATION AND
RESISTANCE

The defeat of the Polish armed forces in the September Campaign and the evacuation of the Polish Government abroad, to France until June 1940, then London, cleared the way for the genocidal occupation and subjugation of Poland by the allied invaders, Nazi Germany and the Soviet Union. Britain and France, Poland's official allies, looked on without offering by way of protest anything other than vacuous platitudes. The Soviet invasion a few weeks later prompted the same meaningless reaction, with the British Government issuing what must be considered one of the most spectacular understatements of the war, to the effect that 'the full implication of these events is not yet apparent'. Tellingly, neither Britain nor France ever declared war on the Soviet Union. Even more insulting to the Poles was the extraordinarily tasteless article in the press by the former Prime Minister, David Lloyd George, hailing the invasion and rejoicing in Poland's collapse, which he described as just reward for her supposed misdemeanours. When in office, he had scarcely disguised his disapproval of Polish independence in 1918–19. Following a further agreement between Hitler and Stalin on 28 September regarding their respective spheres of control and administration, the Nazis were now able to implement the racial imperatives of their ideology, according to which the Slavic Poles were not only inferior but also sub-human, while the Soviets pursued equally relentlessly the class and polonophobic aspects of Bolshevism. These were the macabre prescriptions for a veritable nightmare in both parts of Occupied Poland.

After incorporating the western areas of Poland into the Reich and establishing the Generalgouvernement under Hans Frank (1900–46), the Germans initiated a ruthlessly barbaric programme of mass murder, looting, desecration and deportation that was designed to break the spirit of the civilian population and transform it into a subservient tool, indeed, into a slave race, whose sole function was to serve the interests of the Reich. The Polish leadership class in all important areas of public life was singled out for particular brutality: army officers, civil servants, clergy, academics and others, with no concessions to the elderly, women or children. By the time they were forced to leave Poland, in 1944, the Nazis had been responsible for the murder of some three million Christian Poles. The Jewish population also felt, of course, the full brunt of this onslaught, as the racial anti-Semitism which had been a basic feature of the National Socialist movement from the beginning of its history was afforded unbridled expression. The construction in the early years of the Occupation of ghettos in large cities and towns was merely the prelude to the eventual wholesale extermination in Oświęcim (Auschwitz) and many other such camps of about three million Jewish citizens of the Polish Republic. Altogether, therefore, at least 20 per cent of the Polish population in 1939 had perished by the end of the Second World War.

While the enormity of Nazi barbarism in Poland is well documented and widely known, the same cannot be said for Soviet crimes in their part of Poland from 1939 until compelled to withdraw in June 1941 as a result of Germany's declaring war and invading the Soviet Union in 'Operation Barbarossa'. The Soviets were to return, of course, in 1944–5. The Red Army's invasion of Poland on 17 September 1939 had taken the Poles by surprise and military resistance had been rather thin and patchy, despite the heroic efforts of the Border Defence Corps (KOP) and small numbers of regular Polish Army units. Both Polish and Soviet losses were light compared with the Polish–German theatre.

Poland was unique among the countries overrun by the two totalitarian powers in that she did not furnish any quislings or anything that came close to the relatively large-scale, systematic collaboration so often found elsewhere. The only noteworthy exception came as regards the Soviet invasion, which was facilitated by the warm welcome accorded the Red Army by substantial sections of the non-Polish population in the Eastern Provinces, especially by many Jews. Their relief at not falling into the hands of the anti-Semitic Germans is understandable, but that was not the most important reason for their welcoming response. These Jews had felt, wrongly, that they had been persecuted viciously by the Polish State before the war and now took the utmost pleasure in seeing it collapse. The empirical evidence for this interpretation is incontrovertible.

At the same time, while some older Jews and the small percentage of Jews in that part of Poland which had been assimilated looked on with disquiet at, or, more likely, with tacit approval of, the Soviets' presence, younger Jews, who were either committed Communists or had nurtured a sympathetic affinity with the ideology, regarded the invading Red Army as liberators. They saw an unprecedented opportunity to wreak revenge on the Poles. Consequently, they became zealous collaborators with the

Soviet security apparatus and administration, eager to participate fully in the campaign that was unleashed to effectively 'de-polonise' the Eastern Provinces. This meant, in practice, that this substantial Jewish element became conspicuous in the NKVD-directed terror regime that prevailed for the duration of this first period of Soviet Occupation. Ethnic Poles were the primary target group, though much smaller numbers of Ukrainians, Byelorussians and even some Jews also suffered.

The most striking features of the Red terror was analogous to the pattern in Nazi-occupied Poland: the mass murder of Polish 'bourgeois class enemies', including army officers, clergy, civil servants and professionals of all kinds, the desecration and looting of churches, confiscation without compensation of property, and mass deportation (some 1.7 million) in the most inhumane manner imaginable to the Gulag: barely a third of them survived. Soviet law, bureaucracy, schooling and other facets of everyday life were firmly established. In short, the corollary of 'de-polonisation' was the almost total bolshevisation of the Eastern Provinces. It is little wonder that when the Germans arrived in summer 1941, some Poles, in their ignorance of what lay ahead, were quietly grateful that the 'socialist paradise' had departed with the retreating Bolsheviks.

Domestic resistance by Poles to the Occupation assumed various forms, some of which were of the petty, mundane types of sabotage, but by far the most significant was the organised military and political response. At first, such were the severity and constraints of the Occupation that only locally organised military groups appeared, with limited efficacy. The single exception was the 'Service for the Victory of Poland' (SZP) organisation which arose in Warsaw in late September 1939, only to be replaced a few months later by the 'Union for Armed Struggle' (ZWZ). At the same time, an embryonic, clandestine political structure loyal to the exiled Polish Government and working with it as the legitimate heir of the Second Republic, developed. From this basis, the Polish underground authorities, whose primary aim was to liberate Poland, regain her independence, and prepare for her postwar recovery, had succeeded in creating by 1942 not only a comprehensively functioning governmental structure – the 'Underground State' – but also a coherent, well-organised military organisation, the Home Army (*Armia Krajowa*, or AK).

The Underground State had its own parliament, the Council of National Unity, and incorporated the Delegature of the exiled Polish Government. This state, which had departments for many different and specific forms of activity, including finance, the press, culture, education, justice and foreign affairs, operated throughout Occupied Poland through provincial, county and local branches. The Home Army supplied the military muscle. Staffed largely by regular officers from the pre-war army but drawing its rank and file from all sections of Polish society, and imbued by a fierce patriotism, it evolved into a most formidable fighting force, the largest and best-organised in the whole of Occupied Europe. It was dedicated, above all, to the restoration of a free and independent Poland. The Home Army was at its most active in the area of the Generalgouvernement and southern Poland. Also appearing in the course of the war to fight the Germans were the smaller, ultra-nationalist National Armed Forces (NSZ), which often acted in unison with the AK and in 1944 many of its units amalgamated with it. There were also the so-called Peasant Battalions (BCh) in the Eastern Provinces, and much weaker, poorly equipped Communist (the People's Army [AL]) and Jewish resistance groups.

From 1941, in particular, the military situation in Poland became increasingly complex and vicious. It was not simply a matter any longer of these military groups fighting the Germans. There were internecine rivalries which sometimes broke out into armed conflict, and in the Eastern Provinces, inter-ethnic clashes, especially involving Polish formations, Ukrainian fascist-nationalists, and separate Soviet and Jewish partisan units, acquired a ferocious racial, political and ideological intensity that continued, in many instances, even beyond 1945. The Poles, however, were invariably everyone's target. An especially shocking and controversial episode that exemplified the fate of tens of thousands of ethnic Poles in the east occurred in January 1944, when a well-armed Jewish partisan group conducted, on its own authority, a carefully planned assault on the small village of Koniuchy. Every single, defenceless inhabitant was massacred and the entire village burnt to the ground.

Of all the appalling atrocities inflicted on the Polish people during the war, however, two gross episodes stand out, with due respect to the Gulag deportations and the Jewish Ghetto Rising in April–May 1943. These were the Katyń Massacre of 22,000 Polish officers by the NKVD, which was committed in 1940 but not discovered until April 1943, and the Warsaw Rising by the Home Army (AK) in August–October 1944. The officers, the flower of the nation, had been taken prisoner by the Red Army in 1939, held in several internment camps for a period, and then, on Stalin's personal orders, as is now known, shot one by one and buried in mass graves. It was arguably the most heinous and pusillanimous crime of the entire Second World War, compounded by vehement Soviet denials of culpability which continued right up until the Gorbachev era, and had immediately the most serious consequences for Polish–Soviet relations and for the anti-Hitler Allied coalition.

After 1945, Katyń was one of the taboo subjects in Communist Poland, and a veil of silence was thrown over it by successive British and American governments. In Britain, the Establishment, perhaps suffering from a collective bad conscience, but also influenced by pro-Soviet and left-wing circles in the media, academia and the labour movement, instigated a comprehensive and persistent cover-up of the episode. Only in April 2003, two days before the sixtieth anniversary of Katyń, did the Foreign Office finally acknowledge in an in-house publication that the British Government had known all along about Soviet barbarities in Poland's Eastern Provinces in 1939–41 and about Soviet responsibility for Katyń. None the less, the shameful mendacities and denials of half a century have left a permanent stain on the British Government's reputation for honesty and integrity. It should not have been left to the Polish Government-in-Exile in London and Polish émigré organisations in this country to try to keep Katyń in the public eye, which it did with very limited success. Not surprisingly, therefore, Katyń was and remains to this day a potent symbol of Polish distrust, contempt and even hatred of Soviet Communism and its successors in Russia.

The significance and enduring symbolism of the Warsaw Rising are of at least equal stature in modern Polish history. In view of the Red Army's inexorable advance on the Eastern Front in the aftermath of its victories over the *Wehrmacht* at Stalingrad and Kursk in 1943, it was considered imperative by the leadership of the Polish Government in London and the AK that they attempt to seize the initiative as the Germans were being pushed out of Poland, and establish themselves as a credible force, able to take over the running of the country, ahead of the Soviets and their Polish Communist lackeys. There were, in addition, a number of military-strategic factors in the equation pointing to the same conclusion: Free Poland, in defence of its credibility and long-term future, had to stage a national uprising in the capital. There were, therefore, sound and entirely understandable reasons for staging such an event, though it was an obviously high-risk strategy and as such was not fully endorsed by all involved, whether in London or on the ground in Warsaw. Indeed, to this day, vigorous debate about the merits of the decision to proceed continues in many Polish circles.

The order for action was given, none the less, and the upshot was yet another episode of Polish arms being raised against overwhelming odds, beginning on 1 August 1944. The battle raged for two months before the poorly equipped, outnumbered and isolated insurgents had to admit defeat and surrender. By the time the Germans, supported by renegade Russian and Ukrainian fascist auxiliary units, had completed their operations, 200,000 Poles were dead and, on Hitler's explicit decree, Warsaw had been razed to the ground. The defeat spelt the end of the Home Army as an effective, co-ordinated fighting organisation, though a few other, smaller patriotic formations soon appeared to continue the fight against both the retreating Germans and the incoming Soviets.

It is astonishing and wholly unjustified that in recent times the AK should have become the object of criticism and denigration from some quarters in the West, invariably from left-wing historians and Jewish groups. An example is provided by several contributions to Bernhard Chiari's edited volume, *Die polnische Heimatarmee. Geschichte und Mythos der Armia Krajowa seit dem Zweiten Weltkrieg* (Oldenbourg, Munich, 2003). Above all, the AK has been accused of collaboration with the Germans and of murdering innocent Jews as part of some sort of calculated anti-Semitic campaign. Much is made, in particular, of AK Commander Tadeusz Bór-Komorowski's (1895–1966) directive against banditry (usually but incorrectly described by many historians as Order 116) of September 1943, which has been somehow construed as having been directed specifically against Jews. This and other allegations have one distinguishing characteristic: they are not supported by any credible evidence, and indeed fly in the face of the copious documentation already available concerning the history of the Home Army. It may have had, as a 400,000-strong organisation, a few rogue members, but the overwhelming majority fought in the finest and most honourable traditions of Polish arms. In short, the Home Army was an exemplary manifestation of Polish patriotic heroism.

The valiant failure of the rising signalled the end, if any doubt still lingered, of the Polish Government in London as an effective player in the Allied corridors of political power, though it may be plausibly argued (see Chapter 10) that that unhappy and completely undeserved situation had emerged quite some time prior to the rising. For many Poles, the failure of the Western Allies and the Soviets, who had an army camped on the right side of the Vistula outside Warsaw, to provide any more than token help to the insurgents, was a revealing and defining development. Consequently, with no substantive military opposition left in Poland, the onward sweep of the Red Army across the country soon resulted in a second, even more intensive, bout of bolshevisation, only this time it was not simply confined to the Eastern Provinces. The same routine was set in motion, of mass murder, deportations, medieval-like pillage, and so on, as well as the conspicuous role of Jews in the Soviet and Polish Communist security administration, all under the spurious banner of 'liberation'. Before long, this desperate situation led inevitably to the establishment of a Soviet-controlled Communist government over all Poland. In other words, the nightmare that had begun for the Poles in September 1939 did not end in May 1945: it was to continue for nearly the next half-century.

Document 102

Accounts of the reaction of the Jewish population of the Eastern Provinces to the arrival of the Red Army, September 1939:

'When the Bolsheviks entered Polish territory, they were very mistrustful of the Polish population, but fully trusted the Jews. The more influential Poles and those who before the war had held important positions were deported to Russia, while all offices were given mostly to Jews . . . As soon as the Russians arrived, the Jews had shown their contempt for the Poles and often humiliated them. The coming of the Bolsheviks was greeted by Jews with great joy. Now they felt proud and secure . . . and were condescending and arrogant towards the Poles . . . There were many Jews who took every opportunity to tell the Poles, with special pleasure, that their time was over, that now nothing depended on them, and that they had to obey the Soviet authority.'

'The Red Army entered Wilno on 19 September to an enthusiastic welcome by the Jewish residents, in sharp contrast to the Polish population's . . . Particular ardour was displayed by leftist groups and their youthful members, who converged on the Red Army tank columns bearing sincere greetings and flowers . . . Someone shouted, "Long live the Soviet Government!", and everyone cheered. You could hardly find a Gentile in that crowd.'

'When the Jews of Kowel were informed that the Red Army was approaching the town, they celebrated all night. When the Red Army actually entered, the Jews greeted it with indescribable enthusiasm.'

'In Ciechanowiec, a band of Jewish Communists erected a triumphal arch bedecked with posters bearing general greetings and messages such as "Long live the Soviet regime".'

'In Białystok, the Red Army marched into a city decorated with red flags . . . Jewish youths embraced Russian soldiers with great enthusiasm . . . Orthodox Jews packed the synagogues and prayed with renewed fervour.'

Source: Jewish Historical Institute, Warsaw, Underground
Archive of the Warsaw Ghetto; and the Polish Educational
Foundation in North America, *The Story of Two Shtetls,
Brańsk and Ejszyszki* (Toronto: 1998), Part Two, pp. 183–4

Document 103

The Nazi Governor in Poland, Hans Frank, informs his associates that, at Hitler's command, he had to murder potential Polish resistance leaders, 30 May 1940:

If thousands of the best Germans must now be sacrificed every minute and every second in the West, then we National Socialists are required to ensure that the Polish nation does not rise at the expense of these German sacrifices . . . this unique pacification programme is aimed at ridding the world of the mass of rebellious resistance politicians and other politically suspect individuals who are in our hands. I have to admit quite freely that this will cost several thousand Poles their life, especially where the Polish intellectual leadership cadres are concerned. For us all, as National Socialists, the times impose the duty to ensure that the Polish nation will never again be capable of resistance . . . We shall carry out these measures, and – I can tell you this in confidence – we shall do so in response to an order given to me by the Führer himself.

We are not murderers. For the police and SS who are compelled to carry out these executions it is an awful task . . . Every police officer and SS leader who has the hard duty of carrying out these death sentences must be entirely certain that he is simply carrying out a lawful sentence passed by the German people.

Source: Berlin Document Center, Personal File Hans Frank

Document 104

The President of Poland, Władysław Raczkiewicz (1885–1947), on the situation in German-occupied Poland, March 1941:

The Germans have murdered thousands of scholars, professors, artists, social workers, artists, and even priests. The flower of the Polish intellectual class and the finest sons of the nation, as well as young women and girls, are being deported to German concentration camps and prisons, and condemned to a lingering death of martyrdom.

The Germans are systematically starving the population of Poland. With barbaric ruthlessness they are evicting hundreds of thousands of industrious people from their ancestral homes, robbing them of their lands, their houses, their property, throwing them down anywhere, without shelter and without means of sustenance, either to perish, or deporting them as slaves for forced labour in Germany. No one knows how many men, women and helpless children have perished of hunger, cold and torture in consequence of these monstrous practices.

Walled-up ghettos are being established in Polish cities, as during the darkest periods of the Middle Ages, and people are being persecuted for their nationality and creed. Simultaneously with the extermination of the nation, Polish culture is being destroyed. Ancient monuments, temples of learning, museums, national memorials and theatres which escaped destruction by bombing and bombardments are being closed down, pillaged, broken up. The religion of the devout Polish people is being persecuted and their churches destroyed. All higher and secondary schools have been closed, the printing and sale of books prohibited, and newspapers suppressed.

Source: **The Polish Ministry of Information,** *The German New Order in Poland* **(London: n.d. [1942]), p. 6**

Document 105

From a speech by Prime Minister Winston Churchill on Polish National Day, 1941:

All over Europe races and states . . . are now prostrate under the dark, cruel yoke of Hitler and his Nazi gang. Every week, his firing parties are busy in a dozen lands. Monday he shoots Dutchmen, Tuesday Norwegians, Wednesday French or Belgians stand against the wall, while Thursday it is the Czechs . . . and now there are the Serbs and the Greeks to fill his repulsive bill of execution. But always, all the days, there are the Poles. The atrocities committed by Hitler upon the Poles, the ravaging of their country, the scattering of their homes, affronts to their religion, the enslavement of the manpower, exceed in severity and scale the violence perpetrated by Hitler in any other conquered land.

Source: **The Polish Ministry of Information,** *The German New Order in Poland* **(London: n.d. [1942]), pp. 7–8**

Document 106

Winston Churchill on the Katyń Massacre:

Early in April 1943, Sikorski told me that he had proofs that the Soviet Government had murdered the 15,000 Polish officers and other prisoners in their hands, and that they had been buried in vast graves in the forests, mainly around Katyń. He had a wealth of evidence. I said, 'If they are dead, nothing you can do will bring them back'. He said he could not hold his people, and that they had already released all their news to the press. Without informing the British Government of its intention, the Polish Cabinet in London issued a communiqué on 17 April stating that an approach had been made to the International Red Cross in Switzerland to send a delegation to Katyń to conduct an inquiry on the spot.

Source: *The Crime of Katyń. Facts and Documents* (London: The Polish Cultural Foundation, 1965), Appendix 12, p. 295

Document 107

The directive against banditry issued by the commander of the Home Army, General Tadeusz Bór-Komorowski, on 15 September 1943:

Instructions Regarding the Preservation of Security in Local Areas:

I   Security and order do not prevail in all regions or do not prevail to a satisfactory extent. The local population is subject to theft, intimidation, violence and, quite often, loss of life at the hands of gangs of various origin. The occupying power has failed to address this situation. In general, the occupying power represses the innocent local population, which is tormented by bandits. This situation threatens our interests and plans. The Home Army must take measures to improve the state of public security in the provinces.

II   I instruct all regional and district commanders to take action where necessary against plundering or subversive bandit elements.

III Each action must be decisive and aimed at suppressing lawlessness. Action should be taken only against groups which are particularly causing trouble for the local population and the Home Army Command, that is, those who murder, rape and rob.

IV   Action should be taken that will eliminate gang leaders and agitators, rather than entire gangs. Every action must be organised and carried out in complete secrecy . . .

V   Regional and District Home Army commanders will secure the support and co-operation of the local population in the fight against banditry . . .

Source: T. Żenczykowski *et al.* (eds), *Armia Krajowa w Dokumentach*, Volume VI (London: the Polish Underground Study Trust, 1989), pp. 347–8

Document 108

A description from Jewish sources of the destruction of the Polish village of Koniuchy by a Jewish partisan unit on 29 January 1944:

The Brigade Headquarters decided to raze Koniuchy to the ground to set an example to others. One evening, 120 of the best partisans from all the camps, armed with the best weapons they had, set out in the direction of the village . . . The order was not to leave anyone alive. Even livestock was to be killed and all property was to be destroyed . . . The signal was given just before dawn . . . With torches prepared in advance, the partisans burned down the houses, stables, and granaries, while opening fire on the houses . . . half-naked peasants jumped out of windows and sought escape. But everywhere fatal bullets awaited them. Many jumped into the river and swam towards the other side, but they too met the same end. The mission was completed within a short while. Sixty households, numbering about 300 people, were destroyed with no survivors.

When later we had to go through Koniuchy . . . it was like crossing through a cemetery.

Source: M. J. Chodakiewicz (ed.), *Ejszyszki. Kulisy zajść w Ejszyszkach* (Warsaw: Fronda, 2002), pp. 119–21

Document 109

The commander-in-chief of the Home Army, General Tadeusz Bór-Komorowski, makes the case for the Warsaw Rising, 1944:

Inaction on the part of the Home Army at the moment of Soviet entry [to Warsaw] is likely to mean general passivity on the home front. The initiative for fighting the Germans is liable then to be taken by the PPR [Polish Communists], and a considerable fraction of the less-informed citizens might join them. In that case, the country is liable to move in the direction of collaboration with the Soviets and no one will be able to stop it. Also, in that case, the Soviet Army would not be received by the Home Army, loyal to the government and the commander-in-chief [in London], but by their own adherents – with open arms. The participation of the Home Army in the battle for Warsaw would definitely silence the lies of Soviet propaganda about the passivity of our country and our sympathies towards the Germans, and the liberation of the capital by our own soldiers should testify with unquestionable strength to the nation's will to safeguard the sovereignty of the Polish State.

Source: T. Bór-Komorowski, *The Secret Army*
(London: Victor Gollancz, 1953), pp. 201 ff.

Document 110

Reichsführer SS Heinrich Himmler (1900–45) to Hitler on the first day of the Warsaw Rising, 1944:

In historical perspective, what the Poles are now doing is a blessing for us. After five or six weeks, Warsaw will vanish, Warsaw the capital, the head of some 16–17 million Poles, a people who blocked the East to us for 700 years . . . will be no more. Then, historically speaking, the Polish Question will no longer present a problem for us, our children, and for all those who will succeed us.

Source: Bundesarchiv Koblenz, Hauptarchiv der
NSDAP, Sammlung Himmler, 16

Document 111

A typically cynical Soviet exhortation for the Poles to continue fighting in Warsaw, 14 September 1944:

To fighting Warsaw: The hour of liberation for heroic Warsaw is near. Your sufferings and martyrdom will soon be over. The Germans will pay dearly for the ruins and blood of Warsaw. The First Polish Division Kościuszko [under overall Red Army command] has entered Praga [a working-class suburb of Warsaw]. It is fighting side by side with the heroic Red Army. Relief is coming. Keep fighting! I he entire Polish nation is with you in your self-sacrificing struggle against the German invaders. A decisive struggle is now being waged on the banks of the Vistula. Help is coming. Victory is near. Keep fighting!

Source: A. Pomian, The Warsaw Rising. A Selection of Documents
(London: Keliher, Hudson & Kearns, 1945), p. 270

Document 112

General Tadeusz Bór-Komorowski, commander-in-chief of the Home Army, to the Polish Government in London, 17 September 1944:

The long and exhausting fight in Warsaw, the political bargaining in the international arena as well as reports of the internal disputes in the Polish Government-in-Exile has a great and continuing influence on the civilian and military morale and political opinion. Our fight is taking place amidst the most difficult conditions . . . but everyone is determined to persevere. This is all the more reason why both soldiers and civilians are not only waiting for some concrete decision concerning help for Warsaw, but also are demanding indications as to how an independent and sovereign existence is to be regained in the face of Russia's negative attitude towards Poland. There are increasingly frequent accusations about the impotence and inactivity of the political and military bodies here and of the Polish authorities in London. This is due to the lack of information from the government about our international situation just as the Soviets are about to enter Warsaw, as well as the lack of tangible assistance and care from our Western Allies, and increasingly effective Soviet propaganda.

The absence of adequate help from the West, and the numerous disillusionments and disappointments which this has caused us, is forcing the community here, including some commanders, to look to the East for salvation . . . A strengthening of such attitudes and inclinations may push us into the Soviet sphere of influence, and consequently totally cut Poland off . . . The soldiers and civilians have stopped believing in the long and patiently awaited help from the West, and consequently have become angry with and distrustful of the émigré authorities.

It is foreseeable that when Soviet units enter Warsaw, public opinion, affected by Soviet propaganda, will turn against our highest authorities in London and the Western Allies.

Source: Archive of the Polish Institute and Sikorski Museum, PRM.44

Document 113

The Home Army is dissolved by order of its new commander, General Leopold Okulicki (1898–1946), 19 January 1945:

Officers and men of the Home Army!

This is the last order I shall issue to you. From now on, your activity and energies are to be devoted to the restoration of the full independence of the Polish State, and the protection of its population from annihilation.

You must strive to be the leaders of the nation and to bring about the independence of the Polish State. In this endeavour, each and every one of you must be his own commander.

In the belief that you will carry out this order and remain eternally loyal to Poland . . . I hereby, with the authority of the President of the Republic, release you from your oath and disband the Home Army.

I thank you in the name of the Service for the devotion you have shown until this moment. I profoundly believe that our sacred cause will triumph, and that we shall meet once more in a truly free, independent Poland . . .

Source: T. Bór-Komorowski, *The Secret Army*
(London: Victor Gollancz, 1953), p. 242

9

THE JEWISH HOLOCAUST
AND THE POLES

Of the numerous controversies thrown up by the Second World War none is more bitterly contentious than that concerning relations between the majority Catholic population and the Jewish community in Poland. At the heart of the debate is what has come to be known as 'The Holocaust', a descriptive term nowadays applied almost exclusively to the systematically organised extermination by the Nazis in Occupied Poland of some five to six million Jews, half of whom were Polish citizens. Many critics of Poland and the Poles have argued, in the first instance, that pre-war anti-Semitism in Poland somehow prepared the ground for the Holocaust, that it had brought the Jews to the 'edge of destruction'.

Furthermore, it has been persistently alleged by the same critics that Poles and various Polish organisations and institutions, such as the Home Army and the Catholic Church, did not make a sufficient effort to help their Jewish neighbours as they were confronted by the Nazis' genocidal policy. For some critics, the fact that the Holocaust took place in Poland, albeit in death camps set up and administered by the Nazis, has been cited as evidence of Polish guilt, even partial culpability for the appalling fate suffered by the Jews. There have also been claims of voluntary Polish collaboration with the Nazis as regards the 'Jewish Problem', with the corollary that the Poles were just as eager as the Nazis to have the Jews 'dealt with' once and for all. Finally, it has been strongly alleged that Poles in general, in the Communist era and since the re-establishment in 1989/90 of Poland as an independent state, are unwilling to re-examine in a meaningful way their past relations with Jews, that they are indeed indifferent to the whole story of the Holocaust.

Accusations of this type have been met with a variety of responses from the non-Jewish side in the controversy, ranging from admission of a degree of guilt to outright and emphatic repudiation of any responsibility. It is yet another unfortunate consequence of the sensitivities at play that anyone who seeks to explain or to defend the Poles, or to take issue with even an aspect of the Jewish standpoint, is liable to be immediately condemned as an anti-Semite. Such a reaction is, of course, as absurd as it is unhistorical, and does nothing to promote constructive discussion whose objective is simply to gather and examine relevant evidence, and then to endeavour to determine the truth of this complex matter. Altogether, and regardless of the merits of the cases adduced by those involved in this debate, it is surely itself a tragedy that two peoples, Poles and Jews, who both suffered so much and for so long during the war, should have used their experiences not to unite in mutual sorrow and support as victims of Nazism but to criticise and point-score against each other. How pleased Hitler would have been!

For a long time after the end of the war, public debate in Poland about the Holocaust and indeed other highly sensitive topics, especially those relating to the conduct of the Soviet Union, was successfully stifled by the Communist authorities. In relation to Jews, notorious episodes, including the alleged pogrom in Kielce in July 1946 and the anti-Semitic campaign instigated by a so-called 'nationalist' faction of the Polish Communist Party (PZPR) in 1967–8, were studiously ignored or downplayed. For over 40 years, therefore, the questions of the role of the Jews in Poland, anti-Semitism, and the Holocaust were airbrushed out of the historical record and left for debate among interested Western historians and observers. In Poland, this debate was kept out of the public domain until the publication in January 1987, in the liberal Catholic weekly periodical *Tygodnik Powszechny*, of an article, 'The Poor Poles Look at the Ghetto', by Professor Jan Błoński, who held the Chair in the History of Polish Literature at the Jagiellonian University, Kraków. What gave the article added poignancy was not just that he was the first Polish academic to break decisively with the official silence on this issue, but also the fact that he had been a long-standing sympathiser of the Communist regime.

Błoński excoriated the attitude of Poles in general towards the persecuted Jews in wartime Poland, emphasising in particular the culpability of the influential Catholic Church for promoting and helping to sustain anti-Semitism in the country throughout the modern epoch. He agreed with those critics who have argued that anti-Semitism in pre-war Poland was so virulent and widespread that it did indeed prepare the way for the Holocaust, and added for good measure that a majority of Poles had displayed apathy, if not, he seemed to imply, a little *Schadenfreude*, about the treatment meted out by the Nazis to the Jews. These accusations would have been bad enough, but Błoński went further by sensationally averring that more Poles would have become actively involved in the wartime murder of the Jews had it not been for what he referred to as the restraining 'hand of God'. A shocked Polish public took this to mean that some unseen, divine force had intervened just in time to prevent the Poles from doing their worst. The unmistakable insinuation was that an unspecified number of Poles were Nazis in all but name.

The major problem with Błoński's article is that it was full of opinions but scarcely any hard evidence, and from this important perspective, therefore, it arguably does not deserve the serious consideration accorded it. It is also marred by hyperbole. Thus, it is unjustified and unhelpful to suggest, however obliquely, that some Poles were no better than Nazis, because before 1939 only a handful of right-wing fanatics well outside the mainstream of the traditionally anti-German *Endecja* had any time for National Socialism, while during the war the rapacious nature of the Nazi Occupation was hardly calculated to commend National Socialism to Poles. Błoński's article made an impact because it addressed, in an especially provocative manner, a subject which had been hitherto taboo in Poland, and it did certainly trigger a fresh wave of historical inquiry. For all that was subsequently written about Polish–Jewish relations during and after the war – and there has been a plethora of publications of varying value and quality – it took yet another bold and path-breaking publication to re-ignite and extend the controversy to new boundaries.

A respected American historian of Polish-Jewish background, Jan T. Gross, whose Communist parents had been forced to flee the anti-Semitic campaign of 1967–8 in Poland, published, first in Polish and then in English, a brief account of a massacre in July 1941 of Jews in the small north-eastern Polish town of Jedwabne. His claim in *Neighbors: The Destruction of the Jewish Community in Jedwabne, Poland* (2001) that some 1,600 Jewish inhabitants of the town, including women and children, had been murdered in the most barbaric fashion by their Catholic neighbours, provoked one of the most heated and agonising national debates in Poland since the end of the war, reaching the highest echelons of government and the Catholic Church. The book's publication should also be seen in the context of a reviving interest in Poland's Jewish heritage during the late 1970s and 1980s, especially among the younger generation.

In view of what seemed to be compelling evidence, or for some other undeclared reason, the President of Poland, Aleksander Kwaśniewski (1954–), ironically a former Communist Party *apparatchik* and rumoured in some quarters to be himself of part-Jewish origin (father's name Stolzman?), apologised, somewhat egregiously, it might be thought, 'on behalf of the nation' to the world-wide Jewish community for the massacre. However, a number of Polish historians, notably Tomasz Strzembosz, Marek Chodakiewicz and Tomasz Szarota, disputed the validity of at least some of Gross's investigative techniques, evidence and conclusions. For example, he was accused of over-reliance on tendentious or incomplete sources in support of his argument, and of misinterpreting or exaggerating his findings. Other relevant documentation was unearthed by his critics, and amidst claim and counter-claim the whole matter was referred for detailed analysis to the Institute of National Remembrance in Warsaw in the hope that definitive answers could be provided to the satisfaction of all concerned.

In July 2002, the institute reported that Poles had indeed been responsible for the murder of an unverified number of Jews in Jedwabne. However, this conclusion has not, after all, been universally accepted, not least because the institute's report left unanswered several important and highly pertinent questions, which included: what was the precise role of the German authorities who had expelled the Soviets and occupied Jedwabne only a day or two prior to the massacre, and what was the political orientation of the Jews of Jedwabne? How many Jews had assisted, either actively or passively, the 'Red terror' imposed by the Soviets during their occupation of the town from September 1939 until July 1941? Moreover, not all relevant documentation appears to have been examined fully by the institute. Instead of bringing the controversy to an end, therefore, the work of the institute has served only to pose even more questions and to stoke up further debate and argument. It may be suggested, however, that the circumspect posture adopted throughout the controversy by the hierarchy of the Catholic Church in Poland is a faithful reflection of majority opinion in the country.

If nothing else, the Błoński and more recently the Jedwabne controversies have highlighted in dramatic fashion the ultra-sensitive and bitterly divisive subject of Polish–Jewish relations in the first half of the twentieth century, particularly during the Second World War. One man's truth is another man's heresy in this situation, and any claim to present a 'balanced assessment' is unlikely to convince all participants. On the other hand, if, as seems to be the case, all sides accept the proposition that Polish–Jewish relations reached unprecedented levels of mutual hostility in 1939–45, an attempt has to be made to ascertain the reasons for this.

The basic premise and the logical starting-point for such an exercise is that anti-Semitism in pre-war Poland was not as extensive or as serious a political, economic, social or cultural issue as has frequently been alleged (see Chapter 5). Consequently, the charge that the Holocaust was the logical or inevitable result of pre-war Polish anti-Semitism is untenable. The Holocaust has to be explained and understood from more credible perspectives. In addition, it is valid to bear in mind that Polish–Jewish relations were also informed, before and after 1939, and to one degree or another, by the invariably ignored but complementary theme of Jewish polonophobia, which was undoubtedly present in the outlook, for instance, of many Zionist and left-wing Jewish circles, notably political parties such as the Bund and Poale Zion. In sum, how does the balance-sheet look to the impartial observer from the standpoint of the early twenty-first century?

It may be properly argued that the most significant and fundamental influence on Polish–Jewish relations during the war was provided by the sheer brutality and uncompromising character of the racial anti-Semitism and slavophobia which lay at the heart of the Nazi 'New Order' in Occupied Poland. To attribute blame to the Poles for the Holocaust, the ghastly culmination of Nazi racism, is surely to diminish somehow the unique horror of Nazism, and to come close to the morally and ethically dubious practice of 'relativising' it and the entire experience of the Third Reich. To end up shifting the blame from Hitler and his cohorts, even to the slightest degree, would be tantamount to historical revisionism of the very worst kind, a denial of overwhelming, unequivocal evidence to the contrary.

The ideological and political genesis of the Holocaust can be credibly traced back at least to the latter decades of the nineteenth century in Germany, with particular reference to the emergence of influential writers such as Wilhelm Heinrich Riehl, Paul de Lagarde and Julius Langbehn and to the *völkisch* (racist-nationalist) movement, for whom Jews were Germany's principal enemy. These were the essential foundations, strengthened by the traumatic impact of the First World War and Germany's defeat in 1918, of an extreme right-wing political culture whose leading proponent became the Nazi Party during the turbulent course of the Weimar Republic. Racial anti-Semitism, which was articulated most forcefully by Hitler in numerous public speeches, in his autobiography *Mein Kampf* and in the 1920 Nazi Party programme, was the most consistent element in the Nazi *Weltanschauung*. Hitler's personal hatred of Jews has usually been described as pathological.

It was entirely predictable, therefore, that once installed in power as Reich Chancellor in 1933, the Führer and his regime would initiate a punitive programme of action against the relatively small number of Germany's citizens who happened to be Jewish. An economic boycott of Jewish businesses, the dismissal from official posts of Jewish professional employees and petty acts of violence against individual Jews and property were simply the introduction to increasingly harsh and degrading treatment of the Jewish community as a whole: the discriminatory legislation passed at the Nazi Party rally (*Reichsparteitag*) in Nuremberg in September 1935, officially sponsored campaigns promoting emigration, and the wholesale attack on Jews, synagogues and other property in the infamous 'Night of Broken Glass' (*Reichskristallnacht*) in November 1938. The following year, Hitler made his notorious declaration in the

Reichstag, that in the event of a war in Europe the Jews would be annihilated. The Nazis' 'New Order' in Occupied Poland furnished already in its early years ample indications of how atrociously the Poles and Jews were to be treated. But the anti-Semitic animus, in particular, escalated to new heights after the launch of Hitler's invasion of the Soviet Union in summer 1941. 'Operation Barbarossa' was a military campaign of imperialist conquest whose overarching ideological imperative was to destroy what was alleged to be 'Jewish Bolshevism' once and for all.

This pronounced radicalisation of the war was also manifested, of course, in the equally genocidal Nazi Occupation of Poland, when Christian Poles suffered massive extermination and deportation alongside their Jewish fellow-citizens. It must be concluded, therefore, on the basis of the most copious and compelling evidence, that responsibility for the Holocaust of the Jews lies totally and exclusively with the criminal Third Reich. The limited anti-Semitism that existed in Poland before the war and even the ideological outlook of the *Endecja* or that of any other political, social, cultural or religious group or organisation, can in no way be regarded as a kind of preparatory stage of the Holocaust which, it must be emphasised in the interests of historical truth, was Nazi in origin, design and implementation. Moreover, there were no Poles present at the Wannsee Conference in January 1942, when the decision was finally taken by the Nazis to exterminate the Jews of Poland and of the rest of Europe.

With regard to the criticism made by some historians that the Poles could have afforded more help to the persecuted Jews, it should be recalled that, in view of the ubiquitous power of the Nazi terror regime, there was little if any scope for this to be a realistic option, particularly as the Poles themselves were being subjected to much the same barbaric treatment. For example, the first inmates of Auschwitz (Oświęcim), in June 1940, were Christian Poles, and anyone caught helping Jews escape the clutches of the Nazis was killed, according to a decree promulgated by Governor Hans Frank on 21 October 1941. It is also pertinent, if rather painful, to record in this context that Poles could hardly have been expected to lend assistance on a large scale when the vast majority of Jews themselves offered very little active resistance to the horrors engulfing their community.

With the notable exception of the brave but futile Ghetto Uprising in Warsaw in April 1943 and one or two other isolated episodes of protest, the Jews invariably adopted an air of fatalistic resignation as they were being rounded up, ghettoised, then transported to the extermination camps. The Jewish resistance movements, of which the Jewish Combat Organisation (ŻOB) and Jewish Military Union (ŻZW) were the most conspicuous, attracted relatively few members, while a minority of Jews in the Nazi-controlled Jewish councils (*Judenräte*) often adopted, albeit under considerable duress, a co-operative or indeed collaborationist attitude.

In such dire circumstances, which cannot be fully appreciated by those who were not actually ensnared in them, it was surely impossible for Poles to undertake anything other than small-scale, local and usually individualistic acts of succour on behalf of the Jews, or to support the necessarily limited efforts of organisations such as the clandestine Council for Aid to the Jews (*Żegota*), which was established in Warsaw and other major cities in December 1942 by the Delegature of the Polish Government in London. Despite all the constraints and obstacles, however, it has been estimated that as many as 200,000 Jews were saved from the gas chambers by Poles, some 2,500 of whom paid with their lives at the hands of the Gestapo and SS. By any standard, that was a remarkable achievement, which also testifies to the Poles' unbroken sense of decency and humanity in the face of the most nefarious barbarism.

At the same time, there is scant evidence of anything other than sporadic and the most restricted involvement of Poles in denouncing Jews in hiding to the Nazis and, with due respect to the Jedwabne episode, even less compelling evidence of Poles being actively implicated in the murder of Jews. Even if a few local examples are eventually 'proved', they cannot possibly be seen as representative of the country as a whole. A clear distinction has also to be made between the undoubted anti-Semitic rhetoric of the publications of several right-wing Polish underground organisations and actual killing. Only during the last year of the war, as the Red Army swarmed into Poland and began setting up a tyrannical puppet Communist regime with the help of, among others, some Jews, did certain units of the Home Army (AK) and the National Armed Forces (NSZ) specifically target Jews. But then they did so only because those targeted were Communists or agents, informers or in some other ways advocates of the new, Soviet-imposed regime that was anathema to these fiercely patriotic units of the anti-Communist and anti-Soviet resistance in Poland. They were not killed simply for being Jews.

In any case, the 400–700 Jews who were killed in Poland between 1944 and 1947 were just as likely to have been the victims of common criminal bands, Soviet and Ukrainian partisans, itinerant deserters of various armies, fellow-Jews (as a result of personal disputes or vendettas), and even of Polish Communists. An important perspective on this matter is also provided by convincing recent evidence that during roughly the same period, Jewish Communists were directly responsible for the murder of some 7,000 Christian Poles, thereby intimating that at least part of the Polish response was motivated by legitimate self-defence against a ruthless adversary. In the final analysis, on the other hand, for evidence of large-scale collaboration with the Nazis in the murder of Jews during the war it is necessary to examine the record, not of Poles, but of the indigeneous populations of countries and regions such as Lithuania, Romania, the Ukraine and even France, once they had been occupied or brought under the heavy influence of the Nazis.

To refute the criticisms that have been made of Polish conduct towards the Jews during the war is not to deny that Polish attitudes towards them generally hardened: anti-Semitism did intensify as the radicalising impact of the conflict widened. This regrettable development had much to do, in the first instance, with Polish perceptions of the joyfully enthusiastic manner in which a significant proportion of Jews in the Eastern Provinces had reacted to the Soviet invasion of 1939 and the collapse of the Second Polish Republic, and of the role of some Jews in the quintessentially anti-Polish regime subsequently installed there until June 1941.

There is substantial and irrefutable evidence that Jews were prominent in various organs of the Soviet administration, particularly in those branches of the security apparatus directly involved in the murder, deportation and pillage of hundreds of thousands of Poles and their property. Former officials of the Polish State, army officers, landowners and the intelligentsia were marked out for the most punitive measures. As Soviet Bolshevik commissars, these Jews, now convinced, erroneously, as it transpired in due course, that the day of their national and class liberation had finally arrived, often turned out to be the most fanatically committed to the new Bolshevik order, and zealously pursued a campaign aimed at the effective de-polonisation of the area of Poland under Soviet control. Polish memories and accounts of this situation inevitably shaped in a decidedly negative way attitudes in the country as a whole towards the Jews, especially in the desperate turmoil of 1944–5.

An important role in the overall equation of Polish–Jewish relations was played by the Polish Government-in-Exile, based in London since June 1940 and led until his premature death in July 1943 by General Władysław Sikorski (1881–1943). From the outset, the Polish Government had gone to considerable lengths to demonstrate to the wider world, especially the Allied camp, that it represented a clean break from the pre-war *Sanacja* and that anti-Semitism formed no part of its official outlook or plans for a postwar Polish state. Jews, and other minorities, were to enjoy full and unfettered rights as citizens. Sikorski himself had been unfairly called an anti-Semite by some Jewish sources in the early 1920s when he was Prime Minister, and he was determined that such a charge would be equally groundless twenty years later. To underline his sincerity and good faith, he appointed several Jews as ministers and other officials in his government, and ensured that Jewish representatives formed part of the advisory Polish National Council in London. Thus, the likes of Ignacy Schwarcbart (Polish National Council), Herman Lieberman (Minister of Justice, 1941), Szmul Zygielbojm (Polish National Council), Henryk Strasburger (Minister of Finance, 1940–3), Adam Pragier (Minister of Information, 1944–5) and Ludwik Grosfeld (Minister of Finance, 1943–4), were given every opportunity to express their views and to articulate to the government matters of particular concern to the Jewish community.

In turn, the government, on receiving reports of the mass murder of Jews in Poland by the Nazis, sought as much as it could to convey this dreadful news to its allies, and it tried to organise support for the Ghetto Rising from the Home Army. Through a variety of other secret channels, the government tried also to alleviate the suffering of the Jews by lending material and other forms of help. But, with the limited influence and resources available to him, Sikorski's efforts, and those of his well-meaning successors, Stanisław Mikołajczyk (1900–66) and Tomasz Arciszewski (1877–1955), were bound to lack meaningful impact. This drew increasingly bitter criticism from Jewish leaders, who perhaps did not fully understand that the onus was on the much more powerful British and American governments to intervene on behalf of their persecuted kith and kin. In their desperation, some Jewish leaders did not help their cause by resorting to further allegations of anti-Semitism on the Polish side; for instance, in the Second Corps under General Władysław Anders (1892–1970) in Italy, when no substantive supporting evidence was to hand. Such a gratuitous slur against the heroic victors of Monte Cassino (May 1944), of all people, could not fail to exacerbate Polish–Jewish relations.

By the end of the war, despite the honest endeavours of the Polish Government in London, the underground authorities in Poland and some Jewish leaders, there is no denying that Polish–Jewish relations had reached a nadir. The awful suffering of both communities had resulted, not in peace and harmony, but in mutual recrimination, resentment and polarisation. A series of particular developments in the closing stages of the war and immediately afterwards ensured that this bad feeling would remain, if not intensify. First, and at an everyday level, Poles who had acquired Jewish property, possessions and jobs, frequently in compensation for their own material losses during the war, were usually unwilling to surrender them to the 300,000 or so Jews who returned to live in Poland, even if only temporarily. The disputes that arose could not be easily or quickly resolved amidst the detritus of war, the breakdown of public order, and in the absence of normal legal conventions and agencies.

Of far greater importance, however, was the intense and widespread Polish anger at the political outcome of the war which rapidly focused on the Jews. The defeat of the Warsaw Rising in autumn 1944 had been a military and political catastrophe for both the Home Army and the Polish Government in London to which it owed allegiance. It meant, for a start, that the Red Army and Soviet security forces (primarily the NKVD) encountered thereafter, notwithstanding the valiant efforts of several anti-Communist, patriotic military organisations such as Freedom and Independence (WiN), little effective resistance or opposition to the implementation of Stalin's plans for a political settlement in Poland – in other words, to transform Poland into a Communist satellite state of the Soviet Union.

Stalin's preparations for a settlement in Poland had been in the making for a number of years, of course, while Britain and the United States, allies of both the Soviet Union and Poland, had given him virtually a free hand at the Tehran Conference in late 1943, and had then confirmed their abject acquiescence to his demands at the Yalta Conference in February 1945. For the Poles, Yalta represented the final sell-out of the cause of a free and independent Poland for which they had fought courageously and well in battlefields across Europe from the first until the last day of the war. For them, military victory at the side of the Allies over Nazi Germany had now brought only total political defeat: the loss to the Soviet Union of almost half of the pre-war territory of the Second Republic, and subservience to Moscow through a puppet Communist regime in Warsaw.

For an overwhelming majority of Poles at home and abroad, these gross, undeserved and unexpected misfortunes were blamed, not only on the Allies, but also on the Jews. The spectre of '*Żydokomuna*', or a Jewish–Bolshevik conspiracy, which had haunted Polish political life throughout the interwar era, particularly following the Polish–Soviet Bolshevik War of 1919–20 when many Jewish citizens of Poland had been suspected of disloyalty, had now become, it appeared to many, a nightmarish reality. This perception of how the political vacuum in 1944–5 had been filled was also based on an awareness of the radical left-wing and pro-Communist statements which had been issued by sections of the Jewish underground during the war.

Transcending these factors, however, was the incontrovertible point that Jews were disproportionately represented in important leadership posts in the incoming Communist regime, especially in its organs of power, the party, army, secret police, militia, central and local administration, foreign affairs, judiciary and media. The spearhead was provided by prominent figures such as Hilary Minc (1905–74), Stanisław Radkiewicz (1903–), Roman Zambrowski (1909–), Jerzy Borejsza (1906–52), Wiktor Grosz (1907–56), Eugeniusz Szyr (1915–), Adam Schaff (1913–) and Zygmunt Modzelewski (1900–54), and many others.

An additional source of consternation for Poles was that it was frequently the case that Jews of this type, many of whom had arrived in Poland with the Red Army and NKVD, either 'polonised' their name or adopted a new, Polish-sounding one, in a rather pathetic and unsuccessful attempt to make them more 'acceptable' to the public at large. For example, Józef Goldberg became Jacek Różański as a high-ranking officer in the Polish secret police (UB), and Jerzy Reisler became Jerzy Sawicki, the leading Communist state prosecutor. Among those who did not bother to hide their Jewish origin was the *éminence grise* of the new regime, the Stalinist protégé, Jakub Berman (1901–84), who epitomised the breathtaking deceit and treachery that passed for political life in Poland at that unhappy time. The cynical show trial in Moscow in June 1945 of Home Army leaders, and the Allies' equally cynical decision the following month to withdraw their recognition of the Polish Government in London, were the last straws for a vast majority of Poles.

Consequently, the Poles could hardly resist coming to the conclusion that their beloved country had been forcibly taken over, manipulated and betrayed under Soviet protection by a shameless, vindictive cohort of Jewish Communists whose fundamental, longer-term objective was to change the character of Poland wholly and permanently according to the Stalinist model. Ultimately, therefore, it may be postulated that Polish anti-Semitism and Jewish anti-polonism had come full circle in an atmosphere more pernicious and poisonous than at any time previously in Poland's history. Poles and Jews had become entangled in a vortex of retribution and counter-retribution, accusation and counter-accusation, to the patent detriment of both.

Document 114

A declaration on the status of the Jews in a postwar Poland issued on behalf of the Polish Government-in-Exile by Jan Stańczyk (1886–1953), Minister of Labour and Social Welfare, December 1941:

A new world order, based on the principles of liberty and social justice, will emerge from the present war . . . old prejudices and conflicts must rapidly disappear. In the future Poland . . . there will be no place for racial discrimination, and none of the social wrongs of pre-war Polish life. The war has . . . created a strong bond between Gentile and Jew. In the ranks of the Polish Army they fought, and still fight, side by side. The Jewish underground movement is part of the great Polish underground army waging the struggle for the common cause of liberation.

Future relations between Gentiles and Jews in liberated Poland will be built on entirely new foundations. Poland will guarantee all her citizens, including the Jews, full legal equality. Poland will be a true democracy, and every one of her citizens will enjoy equal rights, irrespective of race, creed or origin. The psychological and social changes taking place in Poland today are the best guarantee that this pledge will become a valid fact. The democratic forces of Poland . . . will decide the future of the country.

Jewish cultural life in Poland was rich and manifold. Poland has always been one of the centres of Jewish culture, and the Polish Jews have created a literature, an educational system, and a press of their own. The right of the Jews to possess and to develop a culture of their own will be fully recognised. The system of cultural autonomy seems to be the best method for the realisation of full and unhindered development of Jewish cultural life.

The question is often raised whether Polish Jews who are not at present in Poland will be permitted to return to a liberated Poland. There must be no doubt whatever that every Polish citizen, irrespective of creed, race or nationality, will be free to return to his country. The Polish Government has clearly stated its position with regard to the political rights of the citizens of the future Poland. The constitutional guarantee of legal equality and equal responsibility excludes any possibility of exceptions. The Polish Jew, like any other Polish citizen, will be able to return to Poland . . .

Democratic Poland, freed of the Nazi yoke, will give the Polish Jews, as well as other national minorities, a home and an opportunity for constructive activity for their own good, for the sake of Poland, and of mankind.

Source: M. Kridl, J. Wittlin and W. Malinowski (eds), *The Democratic Heritage of Poland* (London: Allen & Unwin, 1944), pp. 197–9

Document 115

The Home Army condemns the German killing of the Jews in Poland, August 1942:

The persecution of millions of people for no reason other than on racist grounds reveals in an appalling light the ideology which lies behind these murders . . . Thus, after two thousand years of the victorious development of the Christian teaching of loving one's neighbour, and after an even longer period during which all religions of the world have issued the commandment, 'Thou shall not kill', a nation which is located in the heart of Europe, calling itself Christian, acting in the name of Christianity, and supposedly combating Bolshevik atheism, sinks to committing such barbarities. In order to find similar, brutal tendencies, one would have to return to . . . the early Middle Ages, or even further back, to the cave-dwellers.

Source: From the official AK publication, *Wiadomości Polskie*,
14 August 1942

Document 116

A declaration by the Polish Government-in-Exile on the tragic situation of the Jews in German-occupied Poland issued on 27 November 1942:

The Polish Government, fully aware of its responsibility, has made a point of informing the world about the mass murders and atrocities committed by the Germans in Poland and, at the same time, has done everything possible to counteract this terror . . .

A special page in Poland's martyrology is provided by the persecution of the Jewish minority in Poland. Hitler's decision that 1942 should be the year in which at least half of Polish Jews are to be killed is being implemented with a total ruthlessness and barbarity unprecedented in the history of the civilised world. The figures speak for themselves: of the approximately 400,000 Jews in the Warsaw Ghetto, more than 260,000 have been murdered since 17 July, thus in just under three months. Mass murders are taking place across the entire country. Polish Jews are being exterminated together with Jews from other [German] Occupied countries who have been transported to Poland for this purpose.

Vigorous protests against these murders and pillage are being made by Poles from all parts of the country. These protests are motivated by feelings of common humanity and are also expressions of helplessness in the face of such atrocities. Poles throughout the country are well aware . . . that the accelerated pace of murder concerning the Jews today will tomorrow affect those who remain.

Source: From the London-based newspaper *Dziennik Polski*,
28 November 1942

Document 117

An official memorandum to the United Nations on the plight of the Jews in Poland from the Polish Ministry of Foreign Affairs in London, 10 December 1942:

The most recent reports that have been received here present an appalling picture of the position in which the Jews in Poland now find themselves. It is impossible to estimate the precise number of Jews who have been murdered . . . but all reports suggest that the total number killed runs into many hundreds of thousands. Of 3,100,000 Jews in Poland before the start of the war, over a third have died during the last three years.

New methods of mass extermination introduced in the last few months confirm that the German authorities aim to systematically wipe out the entire Jewish population of Poland, as well as thousands of Jews sent into Poland from West and Central Europe and also from the German Reich.

The Polish Government, as the legitimate representative of authority in the country in which the Germans are carrying out the systematic extermination of Polish citizens . . . considers that its duty is to inform the governments of all civilised countries of this extermination, and to appeal to the governments of the United Nations. The Polish Government trusts that they will share its own strong belief in the need not only to condemn the crimes being committed, but also to find effective and assured means of preventing the Germans from continuing this mass murder.

Source: Archive of the Centre for Research in Polish History, File A.3

Document 118

Emmanuel Ringelbaum (1900–44), a severe critic of Polish attitudes towards Jews during the Second World War, wrote in his diary, spring 1943:

In these conversations among the Poles about what was happening in the ghetto, the anti-Semitic tone was predominant in general, satisfaction that Warsaw had in the end become *judenrein* [free of Jews], that the wildest dreams of Polish anti-Semites about a Warsaw without Jews were coming true. Some loudly and others discreetly expressed their satisfaction at the fact that the Germans had done the dirty work of exterminating the Jews.

157

Sympathy was given expression in the sense that though it was Jews that were being murdered, still they were human beings. The blocks of flats that were burned down aroused more regret than the live human torches. Joy over Warsaw's being cleansed of Jews was spoiled only by fear of the morrow, the fear that after liquidating the Jews, the Germans would take the Poles in hand . . .

A direct outcome of the liquidation of the Warsaw Ghetto was that Jews living in flats on the Aryan side were given notice *en masse*. It was feared that after the liquidation of the ghetto by fire and sword, an analogous 'action' would take place on the Aryan side. Fear set in lest the rumoured German threats might be carried out that every block of flats where a Jew was found would be razed to the ground.

Source: E. Ringelbaum, *Polish–Jewish Relations During the*
Second World War, ed. J. Kermish and S. Krakowski
(Evanston, IL: Northwestern University Press, 1992), pp. 184–9

Document 119

From a letter written shortly before he committed suicide by Szmul
Zygielbojm (1895–1943), the representative of the Jewish Bund political
party on the National Council of the Polish Government-in-Exile, 11 May
1943:

The latest news that has reached us from Poland makes it clear beyond any doubt that the Germans are now murdering the last remnants of the Jews in Poland with unbridled cruelty. Behind the walls of the ghetto the last act of this tragedy is now being played out.

The responsibility for the crime of the murder of the whole Jewish nationality in Poland rests first of all on those who are carrying it out, but indirectly it falls also upon the whole of humanity, on the peoples of the Allied nations and on their governments, who up to this day have not taken any real steps to halt this crime. By looking on passively upon this murder of defenceless millions . . . they have become partners to the responsibility.

I am obliged to state that although the Polish Government contributed largely to the arousing of public opinion in the world, it still did not do enough. It did not do anything that was not routine, that might have been appropriate to the dimensions of the tragedy taking place in Poland . . . And the murder continues without end.

I cannot continue to live and to be silent while the remnants of Polish Jewry, whose representative I am, are being murdered . . . By my death I wish to give expression to my most profound protest against the inaction in which the world watches and permits the destruction of the Jewish people . . . perhaps I shall be able by my death to contribute to the arousing from lethargy of those who could and must act in order that even now, perhaps at the last moment, the handful of Polish Jews who are still alive can be saved from certain destruction.

I yearn that the remnant that has remained of the millions of Polish Jews may live to see liberation together with the Polish masses in a world of freedom and socialist justice . . .

Source: *Documents on the Holocaust*, ed. Y. Arad, I. Gutman and A. Margaliot (Lincoln, University of Nebraska Press and Yad Vashem, 10th edition, 1999), Document 154, pp. 324–7

Document 120

An appeal by the Council for Aid to the Jews (Żegota), September 1943:

Poles! The German murderer is trying to tell the world that it was we who set fire to the Warsaw Ghetto and we who murdered Jews . . . We and our children, who are suffering all the terror of bloody Occupation and are unable at present to defend ourselves, could not give the Jews effective aid in their struggle at this time of crisis.

No Pole who is faithful to Christian morality has taken part or will take part in this terrible crime. In the record of glowing deeds of heroism performed by underground Poland will be engraved, no less than other deeds, deeds of heroism in the saving of people from the Hitlerite beast. The late Prime Minister of the Polish Republic in London, General Sikorski . . . sent a message of gratitude to the [Polish] fatherland for its fine stand, and for the help it is giving to the Jews in their terrible situation.

Source: *Documents on the Holocaust*, ed. Y. Arad, I. Gutman and A. Margaliot (Lincoln, University of Nebraska Press and Yad Vashem, 10th edition, 1999), Document No. 155, pp. 327–8

Document 121

From an article written by the Polish academic, Jan Błoński, on Polish–Jewish relations, January 1987:

It was nowhere else but in Poland, and especially in the twentieth century, that anti-Semitism became particularly virulent. Did it lead us to participate in genocide? No. Yet, when one reads what was written about the Jews before the war, when one discovers how much hatred there was in Polish society, one can only be surprised that words were not followed by deeds. But they were not (or very rarely). God held back our hand. Yes, I do mean God, because if we did not take part in that crime, it was because we were still Christians, and at the last moment we came to realise what a devilish undertaking it was. This still does not excuse us from sharing responsibility. The desecration of Polish soil has occurred, and we have not yet carried out our duty of seeking expiation. In this graveyard, the only way to achieve this is to face up to our duty of considering our past honestly.

Source: From the Catholic periodical *Tygodnik Powszechny*, 11 January 1987

10

DEFEAT IN VICTORY

The fate of the Second Republic was always bound to be determined mainly by the course of the Second World War and the international diplomacy that accompanied it. That the Poles themselves would play no more than a secondary role was made clear by the increasingly weak position of the Polish Government, based initially in France and from June 1940, following the total collapse of her long-standing ally, in London.

In General Władysław Sikorski, who had been appointed Prime Minister and commander-in-chief of the Polish armed forces in autumn 1939, and thus underlining the legal continuity of the Second Republic, the Poles at least had a leader of outstanding ability and genuine international stature. He had played a prominent and influential part in the Polish victories over the Ukrainians in 1918–19 and then, more importantly, over the Soviet Bolsheviks in 1919–20, and had acquired high-level political experience as Prime Minister in 1922–3 and Minister of Defence in 1924–5. However, Sikorski's career had stalled thereafter because he fell foul of Marshal Piłsudski, not only by supporting demands for more parliamentary control over the army, but also, more importantly perhaps, for his non-committal stance *vis-à-vis* the *coup* of May 1926. The *Sanacja* regime did not regard Sikorski as one of its supporters, and he soon found himself on the army reserve list – in effect, marginalised.

During the remainder of the pre-war period, Sikorski used his time to establish a solid reputation as a progressive-thinking military analyst and writer, and became associated with the political opposition, including the centre-right 'Morges Front' in the mid-1930s. By then, however, Sikorski, who regarded himself as the quintessential non-party patriot, had undoubtedly become rather frustrated at the unpromising path his career had taken, to the point where he made a few attempts to effect some sort of reconciliation with the post-Piłsudski regime. The overtures came to nothing, and he was further humiliated when war broke out in 1939, for his request to be given a military command post had been rejected. None the less, Sikorski retained sufficient self-confidence to continue to believe in his own ability.

Poland's collapse in September 1939 had discredited the *Sanacja* as far as many Poles were concerned, and provided Sikorski at the same time, therefore, with an exit route from his career impasse. To many but by no means all, he was an excellent choice as the new national leader, not least because he represented, as he himself was at pains to emphasise repeatedly, a clean break with the failed past. He emphasised his government's commitment in a restored, independent Poland to parliamentary democracy, social justice and equal rights for all ethnic minorities, including the Jews. There were also those, such as the celebrated pianist and former Prime Minister, Ignacy Paderewski, who even saw Sikorski as a man of destiny, chosen by Divine Providence no less, to lead Poland out of her current misery into a brighter future. For other Poles, however, Sikorski's disparagement of the *Sanacja*, and by implication the Second Republic as a whole, went too far and only served to confirm the British Government's generally unflattering estimate of Poland which had evolved during the interwar years. In addition, it was felt that Sikorski's judgement of the pre-war regime was fuelled to an unfortunate degree by his personal rancour at the way it had treated him, and also by his considerable vanity and inflated ego.

Although Sikorski and his entourage were accorded a warm welcome by the British Government and people, and the 20,000 or so Polish soldiers who, having made their way across Europe to continue the fight against Nazi Germany and the Soviet Union, were fêted as 'gallant allies', their situation, in reality, was unpromising from the outset. In the first instance, prior to the signing of the Anglo-Polish Treaty in 1939 Britain had not been a natural ally or even a particularly close friend of Poland. Relations between the two countries in the early 1920s had been informed by Britain's reservations until late in the day about granting independence to Poland, by her general support for Germany in the bitter disputes over the future of Upper Silesia and East Prussia, and by her attitude towards the Polish–Soviet War which the Poles regarded as decidedly unhelpful. Thereafter, Poland's principal ally had been France, while Britain, although observing the rules of diplomatic cordiality, continued to see Poland as a rather over-ambitious state that was attempting unrealistically to present herself to the wider international community as a Great Power. An example of Britain's outlook was her condemnation of Poland's forcible recovery of Cieszyn in October 1938 in the wake of the Munich crisis. Only when Britain finally decided that appeasement was an ineffectual policy of dealing with Hitler's imperialist expansionism and that her own continental interests were under severe threat had she concluded the alliance with Poland, which, like Czechoslovakia, had been dismissed until then as a 'far-away' country of little or no real importance for Britain.

In 1940, therefore, Poland and Britain were somewhat unnatural allies, brought together only by unprecedented circumstances of adversity. In the following years, these facts were sometimes forgotten, glossed over or obscured by other developments, but they did not disappear. Indeed, in so far as they added up to a certain ambivalence at best about Poland and her national interests, they arguably exercised a telling influence on British policy when an insistent *Realpolitik* came to dominate the international agenda in the last years of the war. Moreover, it was significant, especially in the longer term, that while Britain declared war on Germany, she did not do so in respect of Poland's other invader and occupier, the Soviet Union.

In the meantime, the Polish Government suffered from a large number of weaknesses which curtailed its ability to exert influence. These clearly included its financial, physical and diplomatic dependence on the British and its restricted and insecure lines of communication with Poland. Moreover, Sikorski had to face considerable opposition from within the ranks of his exiled fellow-countrymen. The officer corps of the army was thoroughly Piłsudskiite in character, and because Sikorski had been a prominent enemy of its beloved marshal before the war, he was regarded as something of an unwelcome interloper. Such was the degree of inter-necine friction that the British were obliged to set up two internment camps in Scotland in 1940 for the most outspoken of the general's critics among the officers.

This state of affairs was replicated to a considerable extent in the political sphere, where the Polish Government, composed of the four main political opposition traditions of the pre-war era – socialist, nationalist, populist and labour – plus *Sanacja* moderates, was never wholly united behind Sikorski. This was partly due to the continuation of pre-war tensions and personal rivalries, and partly to some of the government's policies, particularly regarding the question of Poland's eastern border and relations with the Soviet Union. It did not help matters that a number of leading figures, such as President Władysław Raczkiewicz (1885–1947) and Foreign Minister August Zaleski (1883–1972), grew increasingly opposed to some of Sikorski's policies. It might also be said that the general's rather aloof and autocratic personality, and inclination not to keep his cabinet colleagues fully informed of his political ideas and initiatives, contributed to the overall problematic situation of the Poles.

Prime Minister Winston Churchill (1874–1965) developed a good working and personal relationship with the general, whom he seems to have admired for his ability and integrity, but he formed a much less positive view of many other Polish representatives in government. Churchill frequently complained from an early stage that they were petty-minded, capricious and generally difficult to deal with. However, these views should not obscure the reality that he, great wartime leader of Britain that he assuredly was, had little innate understanding or appreciation of Poland's history and culture, or indeed of Eastern Europe as a whole.

Churchill's personal and political horizons embraced the British Empire and transatlantic relations. For those of such an outlook, and it was pervasive in the British Establishment, any East European country was seen simply as an element in the wider question of the balance of power on the continent, and to be treated accordingly whenever that balance broke down or threatened to do so. For all his gushing rhetoric over the course of the war about Sikorski and the Polish forces, therefore, Churchill had from the beginning only an extremely limited private commitment to the Polish cause, whether concerning her borders or even, when it came down to it, her national independence. This private attitude was exposed more and more publicly in reaction to the military and political vicissitudes of the war. The fundamental turning-point for all who were involved, however, came in 1941 when Germany launched her invasion of the Soviet Union, and later that year, when the United States entered the conflict. It then was made patently obvious when the Grand Alliance emerged in 1942 that the Poles were very much a junior, subordinate partner, which was to have devastating consequences for them and the national cause they embodied.

Churchill immediately saw the potential for a much strengthened anti-German alliance with the inclusion of the Soviet Union, and it also emerged very soon that he would not be deterred in any way by the inevitable difficulties that such a course of action would create for the Polish Government, for whom until now the Russians were as much the enemy as the Germans. Thus, while Churchill became the driving-force behind what subsequently took shape as the Polish–Soviet Pact of July 1941, he actually had an ally in Sikorski, whose main task was to convince his own government of the merits of the new friendship with the Soviets. Although he was a national hero of the Polish–Soviet War of 1919–20 and a staunch anti-Communist, the general had opposed the endemic anti-Sovietism of the *Sanacja* in the 1930s and had advocated, if only for tactical reasons, a Polish alliance with the Soviet Union directed against what he considered to be Poland's principal enemy, Germany.

In 1941, some members of Sikorski's government rejected any softening of the anti-Soviet line and, outraged by the July 1941 pact, resigned in protest. They criticised him for not taking advantage of the Soviet Union's relative weakness and vulnerability as the *Wehrmacht* recorded one victory after another over the Red Army in the second half of that year, and regarded his meeting with Stalin in Moscow in December 1941 as a missed opportunity because he failed to press the Soviet leader on the border issue.

Other members of Sikorski's government reluctantly accepted the realities of the new situation and supported the pact, which in any case brought some tangible benefits to the Poles, such as Soviet diplomatic recognition of the Polish Government, the release from prison of thousands of captured Polish soldiers and the creation of a Polish Army in the Soviet Union, though they remained wary of longer-term Soviet intentions towards Poland. This related in particular to the eastern border with the Soviet Union as defined in the Treaty of Riga (1921). But on this vital matter the pact was for the Poles disconcertingly vague and non-committal. Already a highly sensitive and controversial issue for the Poles, it became even more so in view of the repeated refusal of Churchill and Foreign Secretary Anthony Eden (1897–1977) to offer Britain's guarantee of the border.

The British concern from 1941, fully supported by President Franklin D. Roosevelt (1882–1945) of the United States, was to keep the Soviet Union in the anti-German alliance and to maintain a basis for peaceful postwar co-operation, which meant in practice that they were prepared to compromise or to sacrifice entirely, as deemed expedient, the Polish national interest as represented by Sikorski's government. Stalin's demands over Poland were to be met, if occasionally with minor adjustments or modifications or the odd display of ephemeral opposition. But the underlying orientation and character of Allied policy as regards Poland was now firmly set.

The attitude adopted towards Stalin by the British and American leaders was informed by factors which extended well beyond their innate disregard for Poland and her interests. Roosevelt and Churchill both feared that since Germany and the Soviet Union had joined forces once already, in 1939–41, circumstances might conceivably arise in the future when they would decide to link up for a second time – against the Western Powers. That was a nightmare scenario which Churchill and Roosevelt were resolved to avoid at all costs, even if this required Soviet interests to be given precedence over Polish ones. In other words, the Poles were ultimately expendable, whereas Stalin was not. Furthermore, as the war dragged on, Roosevelt often stressed the importance of extending the alliance with the Soviets into the postwar era. He had become convinced, especially following the Red Army's successes, that the Soviet Union was now a Great Power whose co-operation was essential for the longer-term peace and security of Europe and the wider world. Besides, he wanted Stalin's assistance in the war against Japan.

It is not at all certain that Sikorski appreciated the new realities, for the evidence indicates that he continued to place his trust in his British and American allies right up to his death in July 1943. By then, the balance of military power on the Eastern Front had shifted irreversibly in favour of the Red Army, given the earlier catastrophic German defeats at Stalingrad and Kursk. Notwithstanding the crucial information supplied by Polish military intelligence in 1939 to France and Britain concerning the German 'Enigma' coding machine, the outstanding role of Polish pilots in the Battle of Britain in 1940, and the later, equally important, performance of units such as the Second Corps under General Anders in the Italian campaign and of General Stanisław Maczek's (1892–1994) First Armoured Division in Normandy and the Low Countries, the Poles could make nothing like the scale of the Soviet military contribution to the overall war effort. And those with the most military power also wielded the most diplomatic and political authority. By 1943, that meant Stalin and Roosevelt, with Churchill tagging along some way behind. Consequently, an increasingly confident and assertive Stalin was able to use the Polish Government's demands for the International Red Cross to investigate the discovery in April 1943 of the Katyń Massacre to break off diplomatic relations with it and to forge ahead virtually unimpeded with his plans for eventually transforming Poland into a satellite state of the Soviet Union. For example, he was already sponsoring, on Soviet territory, the misleadingly named Union of Polish Patriots (ZPP) under Wanda Wasilewska (1905–64), as well as a Polish Army led by Colonel Zygmunt Berling (1896–1980) under overall Red Army control.

In the interests of political expediency, Churchill eschewed objectivity and instead did his best to downplay the Katyń atrocity, despite being almost certainly aware of Soviet culpability. He exerted the strongest pressure he could muster on the Poles to follow suit. But the Poles were now in a quite impossible position. How could they continue to work with an ally who was responsible for murdering the elite of the Polish nation? What were they to do in the light of the unsympathetic and unsupportive British and American reaction to Katyń? In effect, even before Sikorski's death, the Polish cause which he personified had been cast into the diplomatic wilderness: the Poles were stranded and eventually were to be crushed between the evils of Stalinism and the apathy and disregard of the Western Powers. Sikorski could not have materially changed the direction that international affairs were now taking. Symbolically, his death was the *coup de grâce* of the Polish cause, particularly as his successors, however honest and well-meaning, lacked stature as well as his qualities of leadership, and hence carried little weight in the Allied corridors of power.

With Stalin set on his destructive course towards Poland and Churchill more and more a player of diminishing significance in the international arena, the only possible way that the Polish cause could have been saved was if President Roosevelt had intervened. Thus, while Poland's fate is usually discussed in relation to Stalin's attitudes and policies, the role of Roosevelt in this regard has not usually been fully appreciated, whereas it ought to be. After all, the issue of Poland's independence had been taken up with determination and enthusiasm by one of his predecessors, President Woodrow Wilson (1856–1924), resulting in a warm relationship between both countries, which continued despite the subsequent withdrawal of the United States into isolationism. Wilson demonstrated that he was a man of high moral and ethical principle, underpinned by an idealistic conviction that the underdog, a category into which Poland fell easily before 1914, should be helped where possible. Consequently, his famous Fourteen Points in January 1918 included a commitment to the restoration of an independent Polish state. Domestic political considerations, specifically the votes of the substantial Polish community in the United States, played only a very secondary role in Wilson's calculations.

President Roosevelt was similarly confronted a quarter of a century later with Poland's future as an independent state and he was well aware of the Polish electorate in the United States. The fundamental difference, however, was that he emphatically did not share Wilson's personal and political sympathy for Poland. On the contrary, underneath the diplomatic niceties he punctiliously observed when meeting General Sikorski, for instance, during the Polish leader's last visit to the United States, in December 1942, Roosevelt was rather dismissive of Poland as a factor in American global strategy. While he has many admirers, of course, there are others who have a rather different, less flattering view, stressing his considerable capacity for hypocrisy, deceit and inconsistency. He had apparently a conceit about his ability to persuade others by his patrician charm, which resulted in a tendency to put on a different face for different audiences, as circumstances demanded. Sikorski and the Poles unwittingly fell victim to this unprepossessing characteristic.

While Roosevelt (and Churchill), in formulating in August 1941 the Atlantic Charter, which enunciated the Four Freedoms of speech and worship, and from want and fear, stipulated that territorial changes could not be enforced against the wishes of those concerned, and affirmed the right of every nation to decide its own form of government, gave encouragement to countries like Poland, the President had no compunction two years later, at the Tehran Conference, in secretly agreeing to Stalin's demands to have a more or less free hand over Poland. Even Churchill was not informed of this assurance until a year later. It also caused Roosevelt no discomfort whatever that the Poles themselves should not have been invited to a conference that went a long way towards deciding Poland's fate.

Roosevelt's attitude is best understood in the context of his resolute conciliation of the Soviet Union since 1941, bolstered from 1943 by due recognition of the political implications of the Red Army's advances on the Eastern Front. This explains, for instance, his muted response to the discovery of the Katyń Massacre in April 1943. Particularly from 1943 onwards, his administration went to considerable lengths, with the eager support of the liberal Establishment on the East Coast, to inform American public opinion in a pro-Soviet manner. Stalin's personal popularity ascended to unprecedented heights, while the Polish Ambassador to Washington, Jan Ciechanowski (1887–1973), complained personally to Roosevelt that American radio broadcasts to Occupied Poland were tantamount to Soviet Communist propaganda.

The complementary objective of this campaign was to depict the Poles in the most unfavourable light possible: they were increasingly denigrated as reactionaries, fascists and anti-Semites who were undermining the cohesion of the anti-Hitler coalition. The President allowed this to continue, privately criticised Sikorski and his government, and gave assurances to, among others, Foreign Secretary Eden, that he would not intercede with Stalin on Poland's behalf. A similar anti-Polish propaganda campaign was launched at the same time in Britain, with the notable support of the Foreign Office, the BBC, *The Times*, and large sections of both the Labour Party and trade unions. The Poles had, of course, few resources to effectively counter this campaign, so that the once 'gallant allies' were now cast in quite antithetical terms.

Roosevelt continued none the less with his two-faced stance towards the London Poles and American Polonia, assuring them that he was on their side and that they would reap their due reward for their heroism and sacrifices at the end of the war. As a President seeking his third term of office in November 1944, he wanted as many of the six million or so Polish-American votes as possible, as he cynically confided to Stalin at Tehran, and when Prime Minister Stanisław Mikołajczyk (1900–66) visited Washington in June 1944, Roosevelt told him that he stood solidly behind him and the Polish cause. Anthony Eden, for one, knew better, and remarked that the President 'will do nothing for the Poles . . . the poor Poles are sadly deluding themselves if they place any faith in him'. Remarkably, Roosevelt himself was perfectly aware of his breathtaking duplicity, admitting in May 1942 to a 'willingness to mislead and tell untruths'.

It should have been no surprise, therefore, that the President did not give serious consideration to responding positively to the Polish Government's frantic appeals for American and other Allied aid to the Warsaw Rising in August–October 1944. He had long decided that Poland lay wholly in Stalin's sphere of interest, and he saw no reason to help a Polish government and its armed wing, the Home Army (AK), which he had discounted as a meaningful factor in international affairs. Not until the rising was well under way and heading for heroic failure did he authorise, in a merely token gesture, the dropping of a limited amount of munitions and food-stuffs to the insurgents. He, along with Churchill and Stalin, had betrayed their Polish ally, and not for the last time either. They all appreciated that the failure of the rising dealt a final, crushing blow to the Polish Government and its supporters, and at the same time cleared the path for Stalin to do as he wished in Poland.

Already in place, after all, since July of that year, was the Soviet-sponsored Polish Committee of National Liberation (PKWN), known in the West as the Lublin Committee, which had issued a manifesto for the future government of Poland. Despite this ominous development for the Poles, Roosevelt's cynicism and duplicity continued into the presidential election, when he shamelessly maintained the myth that he was a true friend of Poland. The ruse paid off, for he won overwhelming backing from the Polish-American electorate. Only after he had been safely returned to office did he at last allow the mask to fall. Above all, his conduct at the Yalta Conference in February 1945 revealed the stark and awful reality of his treachery and betrayal of the Poles.

The major theme for discussion by the 'Big Three' at Yalta was the future of Poland, though in many ways the substantive decisions had already been taken at the Tehran Conference. Yalta was designed essentially to confirm arrangements, and, as at Tehran, in the absence of Polish Government representatives. Roosevelt's main concern was not Poland, anyway, for he would entertain no deviation from the pro-Soviet approach that he had faithfully pursued since 1941. Rather, he was keen to secure agreement on the Far East, specifically for the war against Japan, and on the United Nations organisation. He lost little time, therefore, in agreeing to the so-called Curzon Line, with only minor changes, as Poland's new eastern border, which meant that the Soviet Union was able to annex nearly half of the territory of the pre-war Second Republic, including the historically Polish cities of Wilno and Lwów. By way of 'compensation', but also as punishment for the Third Reich, Poland was to receive former German areas in the West, as decreed by the Potsdam Conference later that year. Yalta also agreed on the creation in Warsaw of a 'Provisional Government of National Unity' (TRJN), which was supposed to include democratic representatives from the Polish Government in London: in practice, this body was dominated by Polish Communists, their fellow-travelling left-wing allies, and Soviet placemen. Free elections were also to be organised as part of the package, but, of course, never were.

Roosevelt warmly commended the Yalta Agreement to Congress on 1 March 1945, and most of the American media endorsed it, too. Churchill behaved in like manner in the Commons. Stalin was naturally elated, though had undoubtedly believed for a long time that the Western leaders were a 'soft touch'. The Polish Government, on the other hand, was shocked and outraged, and, with total justification, quickly denounced Yalta as a 'sell-out' of a loyal ally and as a Fifth Partition of Poland. It rightly warned that the Provisional Government of National Unity would simply provide Stalin with the means to effect complete Soviet control over Poland. Leading Polish military figures, notably General Anders, wholly endorsed this response and interpretation, and made sure that Polish troops knew about it.

The Poles elicited support and sympathy largely from some conservative sections of British and American opinion, especially when the Western Allies added insult to injury in July 1945 by withdrawing their recognition of the Polish Government in London while recognising the Provisional Government in Warsaw, and at the same time, under pressure from Stalin, by not allowing Polish troops to participate in the Victory Parade in London. The American Ambassador to Poland in 1944–7, Arthur Bliss Lane (1894–1956), attacked Roosevelt for capitulating to Stalin, but he had not properly understood that this had been the President's line all along. Similarly, the British Ambassador to Poland in 1941–5, Sir Owen O'Malley (1887–1974), revealed a certain naivety in denouncing his government's treatment of the Poles. In any case, such criticisms changed nothing on the ground, and having done his worst, Roosevelt died a few weeks later, leaving it to others to deal with the unholy mess to which he had so signally contributed.

There can be no question that the Polish national interest, as defined and upheld throughout the war by the Polish Government under General Sikorski and his successors, had been completely and shamelessly betrayed, first at Tehran and then, finally, at Yalta, by her Western allies, especially by the most powerful, the United States. Roosevelt had for years engaged in a exercise of prodigious duplicity towards the Poles, pretending to be their friend when, in fact, he was really as much their enemy as Stalin. The President's approach ensured that Poland, part of the victorious alliance against Nazi Germany from beginning to end, ended up, perversely, as one of the principal and most conspicuous losers of the war, no better in many ways than defeated and disgraced Germany. This outcome resulted, *inter alia*, in almost half a century of exploitative and comprehensively ignominious Soviet-controlled Communist rule in Poland, and the permanent establishment of a substantial Polish émigré community in Britain. The Second Republic, once so valiant, optimistic and indeed successful, thus came to its final, sad and undeserved end at the hands of Stalin, but also with the connivance of its Western allies.

Document 122

In his address to the inaugural meeting of the Polish National Council in Paris on 23 January 1940, General Sikorski stressed his government's break with the pre-war Sanacja:

Every government draws its vital energy from the people supporting its activity. In Poland it was otherwise . . . Poland bravely resisted the united destructive forces that sought to annihilate the world. She accepted a struggle too uneven to be won. But that she lost it so quickly was the fault of the system, which was out of touch with the nation and used its energy in a useless and detrimental manner.

The government over which I preside has broken radically with these methods. It avoids exercising uncontrolled authority . . . Rejecting totalitarian models so absolutely foreign to the Polish spirit, and following the admirable examples of our allies, Great Britain and France, we are preparing the basis for a truly democratic, and consequently just and orderly, Poland.

**Source: Archive of the Polish Institute and
Sikorski Museum, Rada Narodowa, A.5. 1/1**

Document 123

General Sikorski's reaction on 23 June 1941 to news of the German attack on the Soviet Union:

What we have been anticipating has occurred, though sooner than expected. The Nazi–Bolshevik combination which was at the source of the terrible disaster that brought about the fate of Poland has been shattered . . .

Such a sequel is very favourable to Poland. It changes and reverses the previous situation . . . I am convinced that in the field of international politics, the Russo–Polish problem will disappear entirely. At this moment, we are entitled to assume that in these circumstances Russia will cancel the pact of 1939. That should logically bring us back to the position governed by the Treaty of Riga . . . Will it not be natural, even for Soviet Russia, to return to the traditions of September 1918, when the Supreme Soviet Council solemnly declared null all previous dictates concerning the Partitions of Poland rather than participate actively in her Fourth Partition?

For the love of their country, their freedom and honour, thousands of Polish men and women, including 300,000 prisoners-of-war, are still suffering in Russian prisons. Should it not be deemed right and honest to restore to these people their liberty?

Source: *Documents on Polish–Soviet Relations, 1939–1945*
(London: Sikorski Historical Institute, 1961), Volume I, p. 108

Document 124

From a declaration by the Polish Government on the future Poland, July 1941:

An independent Poland, with a completely democratic political system, is the chief aim of the Polish Government . . .

The government is an instrument in the service of all Polish citizens and of the republic. There can be no return to any system of personal, clique, or oligarchic rule. There can be no return to irresponsible government which evades democratic, popular control as expressed through the elected representatives of the nation.

The main, immediate task of the government is to participate fully and actively in the war and in the subsequent peace conferences, in order to ensure for Poland a direct and adequate outlet to the sea, and frontiers which will guarantee the future security of the republic.

Without undermining the inalienable right of the nation to decide what political and economic system Poland shall have after the war, the government pledges that:

1 The Polish State will be based on Christian principles and culture.
2 Poland will be a democratic state. All her citizens will enjoy equal rights and equal treatment by the administration and courts, regardless of race, creed or nationality. Personal liberty, the democratic rights of individual citizens, and the national rights of the minorities . . . will be fully respected.

3   Poland's administrative apparatus will be responsible to and controlled by the representatives of the nation, elected by the secret, equal, universal, and direct vote of all her citizens.

4   Economically and socially, Poland will strive to implement the principles of social justice. The right to work of every citizen will be assured and safeguarded, every peasant will own the land he tills. An equitable redistribution of the land will be effected by the government. Manual and white-collar workers will have a voice in the control of industrial production, and a share in its rewards. The system of production will be re-organised according to just and rational principles, and the workforce will be protected from exploitation and provided with a decent standard of living and health.

> **Source: Archive of the Polish Institute and**
> **Sikorski Museum, PRM 63/28**

Document 125

The Polish–Soviet Agreement of 30 July 1941:

1   The Government of the Union of Soviet Socialist Republics recognises that the Soviet–German treaties of 1939 relative to territorial changes in Poland have lost their validity. The Government of the Republic of Poland declares that Poland is not bound by any agreement with any third state directed against the USSR.

2   Diplomatic relations will be restored between the two governments . . .

3   The two governments mutually undertake to render one another aid and support of all kinds in the present war against Hitlerite Germany.

4   The Government of the Union of Soviet Socialist Republics expresses its consent to the formation on [its] territory of a Polish Army under a commander appointed by the government of the Republic of Poland, in agreement with the government of the USSR. The Polish Army . . . will be subordinated in operational matters to the Supreme Command of the USSR, on which there will be a representative of the Polish Army. All details as to the command, organisation and employment of this force will be settled in a subsequent agreement.

5   This agreement will come into force immediately upon its signature and without ratification . . .

Protocol: As soon as diplomatic relations are re-established, the government of the USSR will grant an amnesty to all Polish citizens who are at present deprived of their freedom on the territory of the USSR, either as prisoners-of-war or on other adequate grounds.

Source: *Documents on Polish–Soviet Relations, 1939–1945*
(London: Sikorski Historical Institute, 1961), Volume I, pp. 141–2

Document 126

General Klemens Rudnicki (1897–1992), latterly General Officer Commanding, the First Polish Armoured Division (1945–7), commented in his memoirs on the 1941 Polish–Soviet Agreement:

Our attempts at a long-term solution with Soviet Russia . . . were sincere. Although we were all former prisoners or deportees, we believed in this bold experiment in Polish–Soviet co-operation, and we tried to forget the terrible personal and national suffering. But the Soviets only needed us as a tool. They constantly gave us to feel that collaboration would only happen on their terms, which implied a complete surrender of our Christian principles, our traditions and our national sovereignty, and we rejected such a compromise . . .

Source: K. S. Rudnicki, *The Last of the War Horses*
(London: Bachman & Turner, 1974), p. 186 (adapted)

Document 127

The Soviet Government break off diplomatic relations with the Polish Government over the Katyń affair, April 1943:

The Soviet Government consider the recent behaviour of the Polish Government with regard to the USSR as entirely abnormal and violating all regulations and standards of relations between two Allied States. The slanderous campaign hostile to the Soviet Union launched by the German Fascists in connection with the murder of the Polish officers, which they themselves committed in the Smolensk area on territory occupied by German troops, was at once taken up by the Polish Government and is being fanned in every way by the Polish official press.

Far from offering a rebuff to the vile Fascist slander of the USSR, the Polish Government did not even find it necessary to address to the Soviet Government any enquiry or request for an explanation on this subject.

Having committed a monstrous crime against Polish officers, the Hitlerite authorities are now staging a farcical investigation, and for this they have made use of certain Polish pro-Fascist elements whom they themselves selected in Occupied Poland, where everything is under Hitler's heel and where no honest Pole can openly have his say.

For the 'investigation', both the Polish Government and the Hitlerite Government invited the International Red Cross, which is compelled, in conditions of a terroristic regime . . . to take part in this investigation farce staged by Hitler. Clearly, such an 'investigation', conducted behind the back of the Soviet Government, cannot evoke the confidence of people possessing any degree of honesty.

The fact that the hostile campaign against the Soviet Union commenced simultaneously in the German and Polish press, and was conducted along the same lines, leaves no doubt as to the existence of contact and accord in carrying out this hostile campaign between the enemy of the Allies – Hitler – and the Polish Government.

While the peoples of the Soviet Union . . . are straining every effort for the defeat of the common enemy of the Russian and Polish peoples, and of all freedom-loving democratic countries, the Polish Government . . . has dealt a treacherous blow to the Soviet Union . . .

All these circumstances compel the Soviet Government to recognise that the present government of Poland, having slid on to the path of accord with Hitler's government, has actually discontinued allied relations with the USSR, and has adopted a hostile attitude towards the Soviet Union.

On the strength of the above, the Soviet Government has decided to sever relations with the Polish Government.

Source: *Documents on Polish–Soviet Relations, 1939–1945*
(London: Sikorski Historical Institute, 1961), Volume I, pp. 533–4

Document 128

From a confidential note from the Polish Government to the British Government, 16 January 1944:

. . . the most urgent requirements of the Polish Government in connection with the fact of the crossing of the Polish frontier by Soviet troops [are].

1   The successful progress of the Soviet offensive makes it probable that soon it may become possible and opportune for the Polish Government to issue orders . . . for the launching of military action on

the largest scale by the underground Polish forces behind the lines of the German Army retreating across occupied Poland. Such action may have an important bearing, not only on the liberation of Polish territory from the enemy, but also on the speeding up of his ultimate defeat. The Polish Government feels, therefore, compelled to stress once more most earnestly the necessity for, and the exceptional urgency of, supplying the Polish underground army with indispensable arms . . .

2   The Soviet forces have crossed the Polish frontier . . . but without agreement with the Polish Government . . . and the political designs of the Soviet Government disclosed designs on which a number of symptoms and indirect pronouncements have shed a highly disquieting light. The Polish Government are on that account compelled to issue a protest safeguarding the territorial status of the Polish Republic, based on valid international treaties, against the political and legal consequences of possible unilateral decisions on *faits accomplis*.

3   . . . As the liberation of the territory of the Polish Republic progresses . . . there will arise the absolute necessity for the speedy reestablishment of a Polish administration . . . The Polish underground movement . . . is prepared, according to instructions issued by the Polish Government, to make itself known and to take over the government of the country. The Polish Government and the commander-in-chief of the Polish armed forces are also prepared to return at any moment to the liberated areas of the country.

The Polish Government are looking forward to HM Government for support and the necessary facilities in this respect, and also for co-operation in opposing possible attempts at violating Poland's sovereignty through forcing upon her illegal authorities by means of external pressure.

4   The progress of Soviet troops inside Polish territory is raising the urgent problem of the security of the Polish underground movement and of the life and property of the people of Poland . . . such security can be assured only if, together with Soviet troops, Polish, British, and American troops should simultaneously enter Poland . . . The Polish Government confidently expect that the British Government will concur in their views and that they will see their way to dispatching British troops to Poland . . .

Source: S. Mikołajczyk, *The Rape of Poland. Pattern of Soviet Aggression* [Memoirs] (New York: McGraw-Hill, 1948), pp. 273–5

Document 129

From the so-called 'Lublin Manifesto' of 22 July 1944 issued by the Communist organisation, the Polish Committee of National Liberation (PKWN), which had been set up the previous day by the Soviet-sponsored National Council of the Homeland (KRN):

The KRN, created by the fighting Polish nation, is the sole legal source of authority in Poland. The émigré government in London and its agency in Poland are an illegal and self-styled authority, derived from the illegal Fascist constitution of April 1935. That government has impeded the fight against the Hitlerite invaders through its policy of political opportunism, and is pushing Poland towards another disaster.

The KRN and PKWN are acting on the basis of the constitution of March 1921, the only legal constitution . . . which shall remain in force until a meeting of parliament, elected by a general equal, indirect, secret and proportional vote, which, as a representative of the national will, will vote for a new constitution.

The PKWN calls upon the Polish people and all bodies subordinated to its authority to co-operate very closely with the Red Army. Stand up and fight for the liberation of Poland, for the return to the Motherland of the ancient Polish territories of Pomerania, Silesia and East Prussia, for a broad access to the sea, for Polish frontier signs on the Oder! History and the present war prove that Poland can be saved from the German menace only by the establishment of a great defensive alliance of Slav nations, based on agreement between Poland, the Soviet Union and Czechoslovakia.

The Polish borders should be agreed by mutual consent. Poland's eastern border should be a border of neighbourly friendship, not a barrier between ourselves and our friends.

In order to promote the reconstruction of our country and to satisfy the peasantry's long-standing devotion to the soil, the PKWN will immediately proceed with a broad agrarian reform in liberated Polish territory . . . The estates of Germans and traitors to the nation will be confiscated. Large holdings of the above type will be taken over without any compensation . . .

The aim of the PKWN is to organise the quickest possible return home of all émigrés. The gates of the republic will be barred only to Hitlerite agents and those who betrayed their country in September 1939. We exclude the thuggish agents of the reactionary movement who, by their attempts to put Pole against Pole, have played into the hands of Hitlerism.

Source: Archiwum Akt Nowych, Warsaw, PKWN-URM
[Office of the Ministerial Council]

Document 130

Sir Cuthbert M. Headlam (1876–1964), a Conservative MP, wrote in his memoirs of the Poles:

[Stalin's] attitude towards the Polish Govt. in London is becoming very unpleasant and I am afraid that our Government may play the dirty on the decent Poles here, which would be a terrible mistake, . . . To allow the Russians to set up a Bolshevik form of government in Poland and set up what frontier they like would be a pitiable thing to do, ruinous to our prestige in Europe. (*Entry for 12 August 1944, pp. 415–16*)

Winston [Churchill] and Anthony [Eden] are busy talking in Moscow with 'Uncle Joe' . . . the next business I suppose is to try and get the decent Poles to give way to the indecent Poles who are being run by Uncle Joe. It really should begin to open people's eyes a bit about the brave new world to watch the way in which Russia is treating Poland – never was there a more bare-faced or grosser policy of aggression and interference by one country against another – not only do the Russians propose to take a big slice of Polish territory but they tell the Polish Govt. what it is to do with regard to the internal government of Poland. (*Entry for 12 October 1944, pp. 425–6*)

The leader in today's *Times* about Poland sickens me – a vain attempt to show that our pledge to the Poles only referred to German aggression! I agree that we cannot prevent Russia from doing as she likes with Poland . . . but we should not try to excuse ourselves on any other score than our inability to prevent the Russians from their acts of aggression – we should not attempt to condone them – what we are doing now is to make ourselves a partner in a new partition of Poland. The consequence of this policy will be to reduce our prestige in Europe and to lay the foundation for future trouble. We are really fighting this war to preserve the balance of power in Europe which is essential for our preservation – all that we have succeeded in doing is to knock out German hegemony and set up a Russian hegemony – which in the longer run may be much more dangerous to us both in Europe and Asia. (*Entry for 16 December 1944, pp. 436–7*)

Source: *Parliament and Politics in the Age of Churchill and Attlee: The Headlam Diaries 1935–1951*, ed. S. Ball
(London: Cambridge University Press, 1999)

Document 131

Stalin's remarks on Poland at the Yalta Conference, February 1945:

It is not only a question of honour for Russia, but one of absolute necessity, to have Poland independent, strong and democratic. It is for this reason that the Soviet Government has made a great change from the policies of the tsars, who wished to suppress and assimilate Poland.

> Source: *The Yalta Agreements. Documents prior to, during and after the Crimea Conference 1945*, ed. Z. C. Szkopiak (London: the Polish Government-in-Exile, 1986), p. xv

Document 132

Winston Churchill recounts his view of Stalin at the Yalta Conference, 1945:

The impression I brought back . . . , and from all my other contacts, is that Marshal Stalin and the Soviet leaders wish to live in honourable friendship and equality with the Western democracies. I feel also that their word is their bond. I know of no government which stands to its obligations, even in its own despite, more solidly than the Russian Soviet government.

> Source: W. S. Churchill, *The Second World War*, Volume Six, *Triumph and Tragedy* (London: Cassell, 1954), p. 351

Document 133

From the official response of the Polish Government in London to the decisions regarding Poland of the Yalta Conference, 18 February 1945:

Before the Conference began, the Polish Government handed to the government of Great Britain and the United States a Memorandum in which the hope was expressed that these Governments would not be a party to any decisions regarding the allied Polish State without previous consultation and without the consent of the Polish Government. At the same time, the Polish Government declared themselves willing to seek the solution of the dispute initiated by Soviet Russia through normal international procedure and with due respect for the rights of the parties concerned.

In spite of this, the decisions of the Three Powers' Conference were prepared and taken not only without the participation and authorisation of the Polish Government but also without their knowledge. The method adopted in the case of Poland is a contradiction of the elementary principles binding the Allies, and constitutes a violation of the letter and spirit of the Atlantic Charter and the right of every nation to defend its own interest.

The Polish Government declare that the decision of the Three Powers' Conference concerning Poland cannot be recognised by the Polish Government and cannot bind the Polish Nation.

The Polish Government will consider the severance of the Eastern half of the territory of Poland through the imposition of a Polish–Soviet frontier, following along the so-called Curzon Line, as a fifth partition of Poland, now accomplished by her Allies.

The intention of the Three Powers to create a 'Provisional Polish Government of National Unity' by enlarging the foreign-appointed Lublin Committee with persons vaguely described as 'democratic leaders from Poland itself and Poles abroad' can only legalise Soviet interference in Polish internal affairs. As long as the territory of Poland will remain under the sole occupation of Soviet troops, a Government of that kind will not safeguard to the Polish Nation, even in the presence of British and American diplomats, the unfettered right of free expression.

The Polish Government, who are the sole legal and generally recognised Government of Poland, and who for five and a half years have directed the struggle of the Polish State and Nation against the Axis countries, both through the underground movement in the Homeland and through the Polish Armed Forces in all the theatres of war, have expressed their readiness . . . to co-operate in the creation of a Government in Poland truly representative of the will of the Polish Nation. The Polish Government maintain this offer.

> Source: *The Yalta Agreements. Documents prior to, during and after the Crimea Conference 1945*, ed. Z. C. Szkopiak (London: the Polish Government-in-Exile, 1986), pp. 30–1

Document 134

Sir Cuthbert M. Headlam (1876–1964), a Conservative MP, records his reaction to the Yalta Agreement of 1945:

Winston [Churchill] spoke for 2 hours today . . . it was a fine performance – but his line about Poland annoyed several people, self included. He tried to ride off criticism by assuring us that the agreement was in the best interests of the Polish nation and that they ought to welcome losing their eastern territory, etc., in view of what they were to get from Germany. His assurance that the new Polish Government would be fully representative of Polish political views was not very convincing and one is left with the feeling that he and Roosevelt have given way to Stalin. It is a bad business I think . . . Winston is so much obsessed by the beating of Germany that he seems to be oblivious of the new danger he is creating for us in eastern Europe by assisting the aggrandisement of Russia and the promotion of Communism as far west as Vienna.

Source: *Parliament and Politics in the Age of Churchill and Attlee: The Headlam Diaries 1935–1951*, ed. S. Ball (London, Cambridge University Press, 1999), entry for 27 February 1945, p. 448

Document 135

A message from King George VI (1895–1952) to Polish President Władysław Raczkiewicz on the day of Germany's unconditional surrender, 8 May 1945:

Mr President, it is with deep emotion that I send you this message of greeting on the day of final triumph over Germany.

It will always be to Poland's honour that she resisted, alone, the overwhelming forces of the German aggressor. For over five tragic years, the British and Polish nations have fought together against our brutal foe, years of terrible suffering for the people of Poland, borne with a courage and endurance which has won my sincere admiration and sympathy.

The courageous Polish soldiers, sailors and airmen have fought alongside my forces in many parts of the world, and everywhere have won their high regard. We in this country remember with gratitude, in particular, the part played by Polish airmen in the Battle of Britain, which all the world recognises as a decisive moment in the war.

It is my earnest hope that Poland may, in the tasks of peace and international co-operation now confronting the Allied nations, reap the reward of her bravery and sacrifice.

Source: Archive of the Polish Institute and Sikorski Museum, A.48. Z. II

CONCLUSION

The evidence presented in this study demonstrates without any doubt that the Second Republic, far from being a failure as so many historians have claimed since the end of the Second World War, was, when all relevant factors and perspectives are duly taken into account, a rather remarkable success during the years from 1918 until 1939. This verdict is based not simply on the already acknowledged cultural brilliance, intellectual vigour and educational advances of the interwar era. There were, in addition, a host of other conspicuous achievements in a variety of spheres.

In defiance of the most inauspicious circumstances, the republic managed to defend and then consolidate its independent status in the early 1920s, for which the Polish Army's stunning victory over the Soviet Bolsheviks in 1920 was the exhilarating inspiration. The victory not only kept at bay the menace of revolutionary Bolshevisn for a generation and thwarted incipient German imperialist aggression, but also instilled in the hearts and minds of ethnic Poles a new self-belief and confidence in the future of their country. A deep-seated sense of national consciousness, pride and patriotism was the enduring legacy of that triumph.

The economy, ravaged by the exploitative policies of the partitionist powers and the destructive impact of the First World War, lacked substantial material resources for investment, and then had to withstand the crises of hyperinflation and the Depression. None the less, comparatively significant progress was recorded. While agriculture continued to suffer from the serious problems of under-mechanisation, low productivity and over-population, the introduction by the government of the ambitious Central Industrial Region in 1936 showed the way ahead. In the brief time before the war, it had already begun to realise, thanks to astute management and a clear sense of purpose, some of Poland's industrial potential, with concomitant consequences for the standard of living of the general population. It goes without saying, of course, that what the economy needed most of all was a prolonged period of stability, which it was cruelly denied, unfortunately, by the outbreak of war. In any case, the condition of the Polish economy cannot be fairly measured if it is compared only with those of the advanced industrial countries of the West, which had a start of many decades, if not centuries, as with Britain.

The creation of a progressive public welfare system, which was closely modelled on the much-acclaimed version of Weimar Germany, was another striking development, even if its provisions could not be fully implemented because of the various economic crises. But the intent was securely in place and would have been acted upon more effectively in time. Alongside this innovation, the republic emphasised the importance of family values within a Christian framework, fostered respect for religious institutions and organisations, and encouraged the dissemination of a gentry-type civility in society as a whole. The relatively low incidence of serious crime, excluding acts of Ukrainian terrorism, the integrity of the family unit, and the relative absence of physical and sexual abuse, including pornography, were unequivocal indications of a fundamental contentment and wholesomeness in Polish society which the emergence of Warsaw as a vibrant European capital city may be said to have encapsulated. The country, in general, often exuded a vitality that was all the more striking for being wrapped up in an inimitable Polish sense of style. On the other hand, the alleged failures, in respect of the political situation, the position of the ethnic minorities, the conduct of foreign affairs, and the role of the army, do not stand up wholly to objective analysis, particularly as mitigating factors must be taken into consideration.

It is undeniable, of course, that the system of parliamentary democracy proved to be unsuited to a politically inexperienced nation caught up in extreme economic and political turbulence and struggling for its very existence in the early and mid-1920s. Through no fault of the Poles, the essential foundations for democracy were simply not in place. This failure, however, has unduly overshadowed historians' overall assessments of the republic.

The case for the defence extends also to what the 1926 *coup* meant for Poland. At least the increasingly authoritarian regime of the *Sanacja* which replaced parliamentary democracy in 1926 at last brought a large degree of stability, albeit at the cost of an emasculated parliamentary system. However, it should be stressed that the *Sanacja* was not a 'terror regime' in the mould of the Third Reich, Stalinist Russia or Fascist Italy. The Polish people did not feel cowed by an overbearing state which knocked on doors at midnight to haul away suspected miscreants. The regime acted toughly and justifiably in protecting the national interest against Poland's internal political enemies, especially Communists and Ukrainian subversives, though admittedly it did respond on occasion with disproportionate vigour.

But the overall impact of the *Sanacja* was beneficial to Poland, while in Marshal Piłsudski, for all his faults and despite fierce criticism from the *Endecja* and others, she had a statesman of international eminence.

In addition, it may also be unfashionable to point out, without prejudice, that the republic's admittedly imperfect political life also produced an outstanding and highly influential ideologue in Roman Dmowski. The *Endek* philosophy of which he was the leading exponent authentically articulated the views of an important segment of Polish opinion, and has to be understood, not as a kind of proto-fascism, as has frequently been claimed, but as a genuine product of its times. Above all, perhaps it would be more appropriate that Dmowski is understood and respected as a wholehearted patriot and that his conservative, Catholic ideology is not denigrated out of hand as one of racial hatred. It should not be overlooked either that even the postwar Communist regime in Warsaw paid him and his ideology a backhanded compliment by trying for a time to depict itself as their natural successor, in so far as it presided over an ethnically homogeneous Polish state, pursued an anti-German foreign policy, and was allied to Soviet Russia.

Faced with German revanchism, Ukrainian subversion and widespread Jewish hostility, the republic's treatment of its ethnic minorities, for which it has been invariably excoriated, was, in fact, generally even-handed, equitable and restrained. The provocations it had to put up with would have elicited a quite different response from most other regimes at that time in Europe. The real failure in this area was that far too many of the minorities were determined not to reciprocate the flexible Polish attitude, even when one concession after another was granted. But, a pattern of behaviour emerged where no concession, however generous, was ever going to satisfy them. Instead, they gave little or no thought to fulfilling their duties and responsibilities as citizens. They made demands without giving serious consideration to what they could contribute to Poland's development. Criticism, carping and confrontation was what they knew best. Consequently, while it is true that the minorities had not been reconciled to the state by 1939, the blame for the negative relationship lies mainly with them, not the republic.

In foreign affairs, it is impossible to see what course of action Poland could have pursued in place of the 'Doctrine of Two Enemies', for the incontrovertible reality was that she was irrevocably hemmed in between two much larger and stronger powers who were resolved to destroy her as soon as the opportunity arose as an essential part of their campaign against the whole postwar Versailles settlement. How could any state have avoided the machinations of the two most ruthless dictators of the twentieth century, Hitler and Stalin? Criticism of Foreign Minister Beck's policy as 'pro-German' is simplistic and unjustified, even if the *Sanacja* regarded the Soviet Union as Poland's principal adversary. And what was so wrong with that, anyway? Polish foreign policy was left with the invidious choice of either the Nazi devil or the Bolshevik devil. In other words, there was, in effect, no choice and no room for manoeuvre, a point underlined by the pusillanimous policy of appeasement embraced so stubbornly and for so long by Britain and France.

The further criticism, that Poland's endeavours to assert her 'Great Power' status somehow clouded her judgement, has very little hard evidence to commend it. Piłsudski hit the nail on the head, as he invariably did, when he affirmed perspicaciously during his final years that it was only a matter of time, regardless of what policies Poland adopted, before Germany and the Soviet Union pounced on her. Moreover, in such circumstances, no army, modernised and mechanised or not, could have withstood their combined assault and invasion. Thus, the Polish Army, which had been so outstanding in battle in the early 1920s and which had developed thereafter as the veritable 'school of the nation', embodying the best patriotic values of service and loyalty, cannot be reasonably saddled with responsibility for Poland's defeat in 1939. In any case, a coherent Polish battle strategy was in place to meet German aggression. Unfortunately, it was based on the not unreasonable expectation that Poland's allies, Britain and France, would quickly fight alongside her, as defined in their treaty obligations. This was not, of course, to be the only great betrayal that she was to endure as events unfolded during the Second World War.

By 1939, there is no good reason to believe that, while Poland was certainly suffering a serious political crisis, it would not have been resolved sooner or later, as all other similar crises had been resolved in the past, particularly as throughout that last year before the war, ethnic Poles and some of the minorities had been rallying together in response to the darkening international situation. They proved eminently capable of putting aside their political and other disputes in the common cause of defending the fatherland from the gathering menace of external aggression. The fundamental reason for such a reaction is that by then Poland had greatly matured as a nation, so that there was no question whatsoever of her viability as a state being endangered from any domestic source. The republic was defeated on the battlefield exclusively because of the unprecedented evil and power represented by totalitarian Nazism and Bolshevism; only at that point was its impressive development brought to a halt.

The military and diplomatic course of the Second World War, especially after the Soviet Union joined the Western Allies against Hitler and began to gain the upper hand on the Eastern Front, determined that in 1945 the

Second Republic did not resume in Poland. It is clear that the Polish national interest, as represented by the government led by General Sikorski and his successors, was, in time, cynically regarded as expendable by the 'Big Three' – the United States, the Soviet Union, and Britain – whose attitude was shaped by the exigencies of international power politics and by their own selfish concerns and agendas. The Poles were therefore marginalised from 1941 in the anti-Hitler coalition, subordinated to junior status after 1942/3, and finally betrayed at the Tehran and Yalta conferences. Stalin's plans to strip Poland of genuine independence and reduce her to a satellite state through a proxy Communist regime in Warsaw proceeded ultimately with virtually no opposition worthy of the name from President Roosevelt and Prime Minister Churchill. The Poles, already traumatised by the primeval brutality of the Nazi and Soviet Occupations of their country, were compelled to endure a catastrophic political defeat amidst military victory over Germany.

That such an outcome was unjust and undeserved is further underlined by the fact that neither the republic before the war nor the exiled government during it can be held responsible in any way for the tragedy of the Jewish Holocaust, which was rather the grotesque culmination of Nazi racial anti-Semitism. The anti-Semitism which did regrettably exist in Poland during the interwar era was of a quite different type altogether – economic and cultural – and was not nearly as extensive in society as has frequently been alleged. Accordingly, there is no question of the Jews of Poland having been somehow prepared in advance by the republic for their appalling fate under Hitler.

In sum, the achievements and strengths of the Second Republic had by 1939 considerably outweighed its failures and weaknesses by dint of the efforts of a single 'Great Generation'. It ensured that Poland, having had to surmount just about every conceivable obstacle at home and abroad, had none the less finally emerged as a justifiably proud, important and increasingly successful nation at the heart of European affairs. But if her interwar development can be characterised overall as the 'Heroic Age', so the period of the Second World War in its history may be termed the 'Age of Martyrdom and Betrayal'.

Poland was not lost, of course, as the first line of the stirring national anthem reminds us (*'Jeszcze Polska nie zginęła'*), for the republic did continue to exist in London, in the form of the Government-in-Exile, from July 1945 until December 1990, when it handed over the seals of office to the President of a Poland which had once again regained her freedom and independence, this time from Communist tyranny.

Perhaps the best and most telling endorsement which can be made of the Second Republic is that its example inspired patriotic Poles everywhere in the years after the Second World War to help finally bring about the present-day Third Republic, which enjoys the added bonus of now being securely anchored in the West, Poland's natural home, through its membership of NATO and the European Union.

BIBLIOGRAPHY

General texts

Ascherson, N., *The Struggles for Poland*. London: Granada 1987.

Davies, N., *Heart of Europe. A Short History of Poland*. Oxford: Oxford University Press 1984.

Halecki, O., *A History of Poland*. London: Routledge & Kegan Paul 1977.

Lerski, G. L., *Historical Dictionary of Poland*. New York: Hippocrene 1996.

Leslie, R. F. (ed.), *The History of Poland since 1863*. London: Cambridge University Press 1983.

Lukowski, J. and Zawadzki, H., *A Concise History of Poland*. London: Cambridge University Press 2001.

Roos, H., *A History of Modern Poland*. London: Eyre & Spottiswoode 1966.

Stachura, P. D. (ed.), *Themes of Modern Polish History*. Glasgow: The Polish Social and Educational Society 1992.

Stachura, P. D. (ed.), *Perspectives on Polish History*. Stirling: The Centre for Research in Polish History 2001.

Tymowski, M., *History of Poland*. Paris: Editions Spotkania 1986.

1 Independence regained

Blanke, R., *Prussian Poland in the German Empire, 1871–1900*. Boulder, CO: East European Monographs 1981.

Blejwas, S. B., *Realism in Polish Politics. Warsaw Positivism and National Survival in Nineteenth Century Poland*. New Haven, CT: Yale University Press 1984.

Blit, S., *The Origins of Polish Socialism. The History and Ideas of the First Polish Socialist Party, 1878–1886*. Cambridge: Cambridge University Press 1971.

Blobaum, R., *Feliks Dzierżyński and the SDKPiL. A Study of the Origins of Polish Communism*. Boulder, CO: East European Monographs 1984.

Blobaum, R., *Rewolucja: Russian Poland, 1904–1907*. Ithaca, NY: Cornell University Press, 1995.

Brock, P., *Nationalism and Populism in Partitioned Poland. Selected Essays.* London: Orbis Books 1968.

Brock, P., *Polish Revolutionary Populism. A Study in Agrarian Socialist Thought from the 1830s to the 1850s.* Buffalo: University of Toronto Press 1977.

Bromke, A., *Poland's Politics. Idealism versus Realism.* Cambridge, MA: Harvard University Press 1967.

Chmielewski, E., *The Polish Question in the Russian State Duma.* Knoxsville, TN: University of Tennessee Press 1970.

Clements, K. A., *The Presidency of Woodrow Wilson.* Kansas: University Press of Kansas 1992.

Corrsin, S. D., *Warsaw Before the First World War. Poles and Jews in the Third City of the Russian Empire, 1880–1914.* Boulder, CO: East European Monographs 1989.

Davies, N., *God's Playground: A History of Poland,* Volume I: *The Origins to 1795*; Volume II: *1795 to the Present.* Oxford: Clarendon Press 1981.

Eile, S., *Literature and Nationalism in Partitioned Poland, 1795–1918.* London: Macmillan 2000.

Fedorowicz J. K. (ed.), *A Republic of Nobles. Studies in Polish History to 1864.* Cambridge, MA: Harvard University Press 1982.

Fountain, A. M., *Roman Dmowski. Party, Tactics, Ideology 1895–1907.* Boulder, CO: East European Monographs 1980.

Friedrich, K., *The Other Prussia: Royal Prussia, Poland and Liberty, 1569–1772.* Cambridge: Cambridge University Press 2000.

Hagan, W. W., *Germans, Poles and Jews. The Nationality Conflict in the Prussian East, 1772–1914.* Chicago: Chicago University Press 1980.

Janowski, M., *Polish Liberal Thought up to 1918.* Budapest: Central European University Press 2001.

Jedlicki, J., *A Suburb of Europe. Nineteenth-Century Polish Approaches to Western Civilization.* Budapest: Central European University Press 1998.

Kaminski, A. S., *Republic vs Autocracy: Poland-Lithuania and Russia, 1686–1697.* Cambridge, MA: Harvard University Press 1993.

Kaplan, H. H., *The First Partition of Poland.* New York: Columbia University Press 1962.

Knock, T. J., *To End All Wars. Woodrow Wilson and the Quest for a New World Order.* New York: Oxford University Press 1992.

Komarnicki, T., *The Rebirth of the Polish Republic. A Study in the Diplomatic History of Europe, 1914–1920.* London: Heinemann 1957.

Kutołowski, J. F., *The West and Poland. Essays on Governmental and Public Responses to the Polish National Movement, 1861–1864.* Boulder, CO: East European Monographs 2001.

Link, A. S., *Woodrow Wilson, Revolution, War, and Peace.* Wheeling, IL: Harlan Davidson 1979.

Lukowski, J. T., *Liberty's Folly: The Polish-Lithuanian Commonwealth in the Eighteenth Century, 1697–1795.* London: Routledge 1991.

Lukowski, J., *The Partitions of Poland 1772, 1793, 1795.* London: Longman 1999.

Naimark, N. M., A *History of the 'Proletariat'. The Emergence of Marxism in the Kingdom of Poland, 1870–1887*. Boulder, CO: East European Monographs 1979.

Porter, B., *When Nationalism Began to Hate. Imagining Modern Politics in Nineteenth-Century Poland*. Oxford: Oxford University Press 2000.

Scott H. M. (ed.), *The European Nobilities in the Seventeenth and Eighteenth Centuries*, 2 volumes. London: Routledge 1995.

Snyder, T., *Nationalism, Marxism and Modern Central Europe. A Biography of Kazimierz Kelles-Krauz, 1872–1905*. Cambridge, MA: Harvard University Press 1997.

Trzeciakowski, L., *The Kulturkampf in Prussian Poland*. Boulder, CO: East European Monographs 1990.

Walicki, A., *Philosophy and Romantic Nationalism. The Case of Poland*. Oxford: Oxford University Press 1982.

Wandycz, P. S., *United States and Poland*. Cambridge, MA: Harvard University Press 1980.

Wandycz, P. S., *The Lands of Partitioned Poland, 1795–1918*. Seattle: University of Washington Press 1993 edn.

Zamoyski, A., *The Last King of Poland*. London: Jonathan Cape 1992.

Zawadzki, W. H., *A Man of Honour. Adam Czartoryski as a Statesman of Russia and Poland, 1795–1831*. Oxford: Oxford University Press 1993.

2 Consolidation

Boemeke, M. F., Feldman, G. D. and Glaser, E. (eds), *The Treaty of Versailles. A Reassessment After 75 Years*. Cambridge: Cambridge University Press 1998.

Carsten, F. L., *The Reichswehr and Politics, 1918–1933*. Oxford: Oxford University Press 1966.

D'Abernon, Lord Edgar V., *The Eighteenth Decisive Battle of the World*. London: Hodder & Stoughton 1931.

Davies, N., *White Eagle, Red Star: The Polish–Soviet War, 1919–20*. London: Macdonald 1972.

Dziewanowski, M. K., *Jósef Piłsudski. A European Federalist, 1918–1922*. Stanford, CA: Hoover Institution Press 1969.

Fiddick, T. C., *Russia's Retreat from Poland, 1920. From Permanent Revolution to Peaceful Coexistence*. London: Macmillan 1990.

Hunt Tooley, T., *National Identity and Weimar Germany. Upper Silesia and the Eastern Border, 1918–1922*. Lincoln, NB: University of Nebraska Press 1997.

Jędrzejewicz, W., *Piłsudski. A Life for Poland*. New York: Hippocrene Books 1982.

Lundgreen-Nielsen, K., *The Polish Problem at the Paris Peace Conference. A Study of the Policies of the Great Powers and the Poles, 1918–1919*. Odense: Odense University Press 1979.

Macmillan, M., *Peacemakers. The Paris Peace Conference of 1919 and Its Attempt to End War*. London: John Murray 2001.

Mayer, A., *The Politics and Diplomacy of Peacemaking. Containment and Counterrevolution at Versailles, 1918–1919*. New York: Knopf 1967.

Musialik, Z., *General Weygand and the Battle of the Vistula, 1920*. London: Józef Piłsudski Institute of Research 1987.

Piłsudski, J., *Year 1920*. London and New York: Piłsudski Institute 1972.

Riekhoff, H. von, *German–Polish Relations, 1918–1933*. Baltimore, MD: Johns Hopkins University Press 1971.

Schulz, G., *Revolutions and Peace Treaties, 1917–20*. London: Methuen 1974.

Schwabe, K., *Woodrow Wilson, Revolutionary Germany, and Peacemaking 1918–1919. Missionary Diplomacy and the Realities of Power*. Chapel Hill, NC: University of North Carolina Press 1985.

Sharp, A., *The Versailles Settlement: Peacemaking in Paris, 1919*. London: Macmillan 1991.

Stachura, P. D., (ed.), *Poland Between the Wars, 1918–1939*. London: Macmillan 1998.

Wandycz, P. S., *Soviet–Polish Relations, 1917–1921*. Cambridge, MA: Harvard University Press 1969.

Zamoyski, A., *The Battle for the Marshlands*. New York: Columbia University Press 1981.

3 Society and the economy

Jaworski, R. and Pietrow-Ennker, B. (eds), *Women in Polish Society*. Boulder, CO: East European Monographs 1992.

Kaser, M. C. and Radice, E. (eds), *The Economic History of Eastern Europe, 1919–1975*. Oxford: Clarendon Press 1986.

Kieniewicz, S., *The Emancipation of the Polish Peasantry*. Chicago: Chicago University Press 1969.

Landau, Z. and Tomaszewski, J., *The Polish Economy in the Twentieth Century*. London: Routledge 1985.

Latawski, P. (ed.), *The Reconstruction of Poland, 1914–23*. London: Macmillan 1992.

Narkiewicz, O. A., *The Green Flag. Polish Populist Politics, 1867–1970*. London: Croom Helm 1976.

Roszkowski, W., *Landowners in Poland, 1918–1939*. London: Cambridge University Press 1991.

Skrzypek, S., *The Problem of Eastern Galicia*. London: Polish Association for the South-Eastern Provinces 1948.

Słomka, J., *From Serfdom to Self-Government. Memoirs of a Polish Village Mayor, 1842–1927*. London: Minerva 1941.

Taylor, J. J., *The Economic Development of Poland, 1919–1950*. Ithaca, NY: Cornell University Press 1952.

Thomas, W. and Znaniecki, F., *The Polish Peasant in Europe and America*, 2 volumes. New York: Dover 1958.

Wellisz, L., *Foreign Capital in Poland*. London: George Allen & Unwin 1938.

Wynot, E. D., *Warsaw Between the Wars. Profile of the Capital City in a Developing Land, 1918–1939.* Boulder, CO: East European Monographs 1983.
Zweig, F., *Poland Between Two Wars. A Critical Study of Social and Economic Changes.* London: Secker & Warburg 1944.

4 Politics

Brzeziński, M., *The Struggle for Constitutionalism in Poland.* London: Macmillan 1998.
Dziewanowski, M. K., *Joseph Piłsudski: A European Federalist, 1918–1922.* Stanford, CA: Hoover Institution Press 1969.
Dziewanowski, M. K., *The Communist Party of Poland. An Outline of its History.* Cambridge, MA: Harvard University Press 1976.
Garlicki, A., *Józef Piłsudski, 1867–1935.* New York: Scolar Press 1995.
Jędrzejewicz, W., *Piłsudski. A Life for Poland.* New York: Hippocrene Books 1982.
Polonsky, A., *Politics in Independent Poland, 1921–1939: The Crisis of Constitutional Government.* Oxford: Clarendon Press 1972.
Rothschild, J., *Piłsudski's Coup d'Etat.* New York: Columbia University Press 1966.
Schatz, J., *The Generation. The Rise and Fall of the Jewish Communists of Poland.* Berkeley, CA: University of California Press 1991.
Shelton, A. K., *The Democratic Idea in Polish History and Historiography.* Boulder, CO: East European Monographs 1989.
Simoncini, G., *The Communist Party of Poland, 1918–1929: A Study in Political Ideology.* New York: Edwin Mellon Press 1993.
Stachura (ed.), P. D., *Poland Between the Wars, 1918–1939.* London: Macmillan 1998.
Stachura, P. D., *Poland in the Twentieth Century.* London: Macmillan 1999.
Watt, R. M., *Bitter Glory. Poland and Its Fate, 1918 to 1939.* New York: Simon & Schuster 1979.
Weydenthal, J.B. de, *The Communists of Poland. An Historical Outline.* Stanford, CA: Hoover Institution Press 1978.
Wiles, T. (ed.), *Poland Between the Wars, 1918–1939.* Bloomington: Indiana University Polish Studies Center 1989.
Wynot, E. D., *Polish Politics in Transition. The Camp of National Unity and the Struggle for Power, 1935–1939.* Athens: University of Georgia Press 1974.
Żółtowski, A., *Border of Europe. A Study of the Polish Eastern Provinces.* London: Hollis & Carter 1950.

5 The ethnic minorities

Abramsky, C. *et al.* (eds), *The Jews in Poland.* Oxford: Blackwell 1986.
Bartoszewski, W. and Polonsky, A. (eds), *The Jews in Warsaw. A History.* Oxford: Blackwell 1991.

Blanke, R., *Orphans of Versailles. The Germans in Western Poland, 1918–1939.* Lexington: University Press of Kentucky 1993.

Dawidowicz, L., *The War Against the Jews, 1933–45.* Harmondsworth: Penguin 1975.

Fishman, J. A. (eds), *Studies in Polish Jewry, 1919–1939.* New York: Yivo Institute for Jewish Research 1974.

Gutman, Y. *et al.* (eds), *The Jews of Poland Between Two World Wars.* Hanover, NH: University Press of New England 1989.

Heller, C. S., *On the Edge of Destruction. Jews of Poland Between the Two World Wars.* New York: Columbia University Press 1977.

Hoffman, E., *Shtetl. The Life and Death of a Small Town and the World of Polish Jews.* London: Vintage 1999.

Horak, S., *Poland and Her National Minorities, 1919–1939.* New York: Vantage Press 1961.

Hunczak, T. (ed.), *The Ukraine, 1917–1921: A Study in Revolution.* Cambridge, MA: Harvard Ukrainian Research Institute 1977.

Hunt Tooley, T., *National Identity and Weimar Germany. Upper Silesia and the Eastern Border, 1918–1922.* Lincoln: University of Nebraska Press 1997.

Johnpoll, B. K., *The Politics of Futility. The General Jewish Workers' Bund of Poland, 1917–1943.* Ithaca, NY: Cornell University Press 1967.

Levene, M., *War, Jews and the New Europe. The Diplomacy of Lucien Wolf, 1914–1919.* Oxford: Oxford University Press 1992.

Lewin, I. and Gelber, N. M., *A History of Polish Jewry during the Renewal of Poland.* New York: Shengold Publishers 1990.

Marcus, J., *Social and Political History of the Jews in Poland, 1919–1939.* New York: Mouton 1983.

Melzer, E., *No Way Out. The Politics of Polish Jewry, 1935–1939.* New York: Cincinnati Hebrew Union College Press 1997.

Mendelsohn, E., *Zionism in Poland. The Formative Years, 1915–1926.* New Haven, CT: Yale University Press 1981.

Mendelsohn, E., *On Modern Jewish Politics. The Interwar Years in Poland and America.* Oxford: Oxford University Press 1993.

Modras, R., *The Catholic Church and Antisemitism. Poland, 1933–1939.* New York: Harwood Academic 1994.

Opalski, M. M. and Bartel, I., *Poles and Jews. A Failed Brotherhood.* Hanover, NH: University Press of New England 1992.

Palij, M., *The Ukrainian–Polish Defensive Alliance, 1919–1921. An Aspect of the Ukrainian Revolution.* Toronto: Canadian Institute of Ukrainian Studies Press 1995.

Piotrowski, T., *Poland's Holocaust. Ethnic Strife, Collaboration with Occupying Forces and Genocide in the Second Republic, 1918–1947.* Jefferson, NC: McFarland 1997.

Polonsky, A. (ed.), *Jews in Independent Poland, 1918–1939*, Volume 8, *Polin.* New York: Littman Library 1994.

Redlich, S., *Together and Apart in Brzezany. Poles, Jews, and Ukrainians, 1919–1945.* Bloomington: University of Indiana Press 2002.

Reid, A., *Borderland. A Journey Through the History of Ukraine*. London: Weidenfeld & Nicolson 1997.

Richmond, T., *Konin. A Quest*. London: Jonathan Cape 1995.

Rosenthal, H. K., *German and Pole. National Conflict and Modern Myth*. Gainesville: University Presses of Florida 1976.

Skrzypek, S., *The Problem of Eastern Galicia*. London: Polish Association for the South-Eastern Provinces 1948.

Tigne, C., *Gdańsk. National Identity on the Polish–German Borderlands*. London: Pluto Press 1990.

Żółtowski, A., *Border of Europe. A Study of the Polish Eastern Provinces*. London: Hollis & Carter 1950.

6 Culture and education

Carpenter, B., *The Poetic Avant-Garde in Poland, 1918–1939*. Seattle: University of Washington Press 1983.

Dyboski, R., *Poland in World Civilization*. New York: J. M. Barrett 1950.

Eisenstein, M., *Jewish Schools in Poland*. New York: King's Crown Press 1950.

Ficowski, J. (ed.), *The Collected Works of Bruno Schulz*. London: Picador 1999.

Grossman, E. (ed.), *Studies in Language, Literature and Cultural Mythology*. London: E. Mellon Press 2002.

Hertz, A., *The Jews in Polish Culture*. Evanston, IL: Northwestern University Press 1988.

Klimaszewski, B. (ed.), *An Outline History of Polish Culture*. Warsaw: Interpress 1978.

Kłoczowski, J., *A History of Polish Christianity*. Cambridge: Cambridge University Press 2002.

Krzyżanowski, J., *A History of Polish Literature*. Warsaw: Interpress 1978.

McCall, S., *Polish Logic*. Oxford: Oxford University Press 1967.

Miłosz, C., *A History of Polish Literature*. London: Macmillan 1969.

Olszewski, A. K., *An Outline of Polish Art and Architecture, 1890–1980*. Warsaw: Interpress 1989.

Wynot, E. D., *Warsaw between the World Wars. Profile of the Capital City in a Developing Land, 1918–1939*. Boulder, CO: East European Monographs 1983.

7 Foreign policy

Cannistraro, P. V., Wynot, E. D. and Kovaleff, T. P. (eds), *Poland and the Coming of the Second World War. The Diplomatic Papers of A. J. Drexel Biddle Jr., United States Ambassador in Poland, 1937–1939*. Columbus, OH: Ohio University Press 1976.

Cienciała, A. M., *Poland and the Western Powers, 1938–1939*. Toronto: University of Toronto Press 1968.

Cienciała, A.M. and Komarnicki, T., *From Versailles to Locarno. Keys to Polish Foreign Policy, 1919–1925*. Lawrence: University Press of Kansas 1984.

Debicki, R., *The Foreign Policy of Poland, 1919–1939*. New York: Praeger 1962.

Gromada, T. V. (ed.), *Essays on Poland's Foreign Policy, 1918–1939*. New York: Józef Piłsudski Institute 1970.

Jędrzejewicz, W. (ed.), *J. Lipski, Diplomat in Berlin. Papers and Memoirs, 1933–1939*. New York: Columbia University Press 1968.

Jędrzejewicz, W. (ed.), *Papers and Memoirs of Juliusz Łukasiewicz, Ambassador of Poland. Diplomat in Paris, 1936–1939*. New York: Columbia University Press 1970.

Karski, J., *The Great Powers and Poland, 1919–1945: From Versailles to Yalta*. New York: University Press of America 1985.

Korbel, J., *Poland Between East and West. Soviet and German Diplomacy Towards Poland, 1919–1933*. Princeton, NJ: Princeton University Press 1963.

Korczyński, A. and Świętochowski, S. (eds), *Poland between Germany and Russia, 1926–1939*. New York: Józef Piłsudski Institute 1975.

Lerski, G.J., *Herbert Hoover and Poland. A Documentary History of Friendship*. Stanford, CA: Hoover Institution Press 1977.

Newman, S., *March 1939: The British Guarantee to Poland*. Oxford: Clarendon Press 1976.

Pease, N., *Poland, the United States, and the Stabilization of Europe, 1919–1933*. New York: Oxford University Press 1986.

Prażmowska, A., *Britain, Poland and the Eastern Front, 1939*. Cambridge: Cambridge University Press 1987.

Riekhoff, H. von, *German–Polish Relations, 1918–1933*. Baltimore, MD: Johns Hopkins University Press 1971.

Wandycz, P. S., *Czechoslovak–Polish Confederation and the Great Powers, 1940–1943*. Bloomington: Indiana University Press 1956.

Wandycz, P. S., *France and Her Eastern Allies, 1919–1925*. Minneapolis: University of Minnesota Press 1962.

Wandycz, P. S., *Soviet–Polish Relations, 1917–1921*. Cambridge, MA: Harvard University Press 1969.

Wandycz, P. S., *The United States and Poland*. Cambridge, MA: Harvard University Press 1980.

Wandycz, P. S., *Polish Diplomacy 1914–1945: Aims and Achievements*. London: Orbis Books 1988.

Wandycz, P. S., *The Twilight of French Eastern Alliances, 1926–1936*. Princeton, NJ: Princeton University Press 1988.

8 Occupation and resistance

Bartoszewski, W., *Warsaw Death Ring, 1939–44*. Warsaw: Interpress 1968.

Bethell, N., *The War That Hitler Won*. London: Allen Lane 1972.

Bór-Komorowski, T., *The Secret Army*. London: Victor Gollancz 1953.

Chodakiewicz, M. J., *Between Nazis and Soviets. A Case Study of Occupation Politics in Poland, 1939–1947*. Kentucky: Lexington Books 2004.

Ciechanowski, J. M., *The Warsaw Rising of 1944*. Cambridge: Cambridge University Press 1974.

Coutouvidis, J. and Reynolds, J. (eds), *Poland, 1939–1947*. Leicester: Leicester University Press 1986.

Davies, N., *Rising '44: 'The Battle for Warsaw'*. London: Macmillan 2003.

Davies, N. and Polonsky, A. (eds), *Jews in Eastern Poland and the USSR, 1939–46*. London: Macmillan 1991.

Dobroszycki, L., *Reptile Journalism. The Official Polish-Language Press under the Nazis, 1939–1945*. New Haven, CT: Yale University Press 1994.

Garliński, J., *Poland in the Second World War*. London: Macmillan 1985.

Garliński, J., *The Survival of Love. Memoirs of a Resistance Officer*. Oxford: Blackwell 1991.

Gross, J. T., *Polish Society under German Occupation. The Generalgouvernement, 1939–1944*. Princeton, NJ: Princeton University Press 1979.

Gross, J. T., *Revolution from Abroad. The Soviet Conquest of Poland's Western Ukraine and Western Byelorussia*. Princeton, NJ: Princeton University Press 1988.

Gutman, Y., *Resistance. The Warsaw Ghetto Uprising*. New York: Holocaust Library 1994.

Hanson, J. K. M., *The Civilian Population and the Warsaw Uprising of 1944*. Cambridge: Cambridge University Press 1982.

Jolluck, K.R., *Exile and Identity. Polish Women in the Soviet Union During World War II*. Pittsburgh, PN: University of Pittsburgh Press 2002.

Korboński, S., *The Polish Underground State. A Guide to the Underground, 1939–1945*. Boulder, CO: East European Monographs 1978.

Krakowski, S., *The War of the Doomed. Jewish Armed Resistance in Poland, 1942–1944*. New York: Holmes & Meier 1984.

Lotnik, W., *Nine Lives. Ethnic Conflict in the Polish–Ukrainian Borderlands*. London: Serif 1999.

Lukas, R. C., *The Forgotten Holocaust. The Poles under German Occupation, 1939–1944*. Lexington: University Press of Kentucky 1986.

Malcher, G. C., *Blank Pages. Soviet Genocide against the Polish People*. Woking: Privately published 1993.

Ney-Krwawicz, M., *The Polish Home Army, 1939–1945*. London: The Polish Institute and Sikorski Museum 2001.

Okoński, W., *Wartime Poland, 1939–1945. A Select Annotated Bibliography*. London: Greenwood Press 1997.

Olson, L. and Cloud, S., *For Your Freedom and Ours*. London: Heinemann 2003.

Paul, M., *Neighbors on the Eve of the Holocaust. Jewish–Polish Relations in Soviet-Occupied Eastern Poland, 1939–1941*. Toronto: PEFINA Press 2002.

Piesakowski, T., *The Fate of Poles in the USSR, 1939–1989*. London: Gryf Publications 1990.

Pinchuk, B. C., *Shtetl Jews under Soviet Rule. Eastern Poland on the Eve of the Holocaust*. Oxford: Blackwell 1990.

Piotrowski, T., *Polish–Ukrainian Relations during World War II*. Toronto: Adam Mickiewicz Foundation 1995.

Piotrowski, T., *Poland's Holocaust. Ethnic Strife, Collaboration with Occupying Forces and Genocide in the Second Republic, 1918–1947*. Jefferson, NC: McFarland 1997.

Piotrowski, T., *Genocide and Rescue in Wołyń. Recollections of the Ukrainian Nationalist Ethnic Cleansing Campaign against the Poles during World War II*. Jefferson, NC: McFarland 2000.

Pogonowski, I. C., *Jews in Poland: A Documentary History*. New York: Hippocrene 1998.

Salmonowicz, S., Ney-Krwawicz, M. and Górski, G., *Polish Undergrounnd State*. Warsaw: RYTM Publishers 1999.

Sword, K. (ed.), *The Soviet Takeover of the Polish Eastern Provinces, 1939–41*. London: Macmillan 1991.

Sword, K., *Deportation and Exile. Poles in the Soviet Union, 1939–48*. London: Macmillan 1994.

The Crime of Katyń. Facts and Documents. London: Polish Cultural Foundation 1965.

Zawodny, J. K., *Death in the Forest. The Story of the Katyń Massacre*. London: Macmillan 1971.

Zawodny, J. K., *Nothing but Honour. The Story of the Warsaw Uprising*. London: Macmillan 1978.

9 The Jewish Holocaust and the Poles

Abramsky, C., Jachimczyk, M. and Polonsky, A. (eds), *The Jews in Poland*. Oxford: Blackwell 1986.

Bartoszewski, W. and Lewinówna, Z. (eds), *Righteous Among Nations. How Poles Helped Jews, 1939–1945*. London: Earls Court Publications 1969.

Bartoszewski, W. T. and Polonsky, A. (eds), *The Jews in Warsaw*. Oxford: Blackwell 1991.

Burleigh, M. and Wippermann, W., *The Racial State. Germany, 1933–1945*. Cambridge: Cambridge University Press 1991.

Burrin, P., *Hitler and the Jews. The Genesis of the Holocaust*. London: Edward Arnold 1994.

Chodakiewicz, M. J., *After the Holocaust. Polish–Jewish Conflict in the Wake of World War II*. Boulder, CO: East European Monographs 2003.

Cooper, L., *In the Shadow of the Polish Eagle. The Poles, The Holocaust and Beyond*. London: Palgrave 2000.

Dawidowicz, L. S., *The Holocaust and the Historians*. Cambridge, MA: Harvard University Press 1981.

Deák, I., Gross, J.T. and Judt, T. (eds), *The Politics of Retribution in Europe: World War II and Its Aftermath*. Princeton, NJ: Princeton University Press 2000.

Engel, D., *In the Shadow of Auschwitz. The Polish Government-in-Exile and the Jews, 1939–1942*. Chapel Hill, NC: University of North Carolina Press 1987.

Engel, D., *Facing a Holocaust. The Polish Government-in-Exile and the Jews, 1943–1945*. Chapel Hill, NC: University of North Carolina Press 1993.

Gilbert, M., *The Holocaust. The Jewish Tragedy*. Glasgow: Collins 1986.

Gross, J. T., *Neighbors. The Destruction of the Jewish Community in Jedwabne, Poland*. Princeton, NJ: Princeton University Press 2001.

Gutman, I. and Krakowski, S., *Unequal Victims. Poles and Jews During World War II*. New York: Holocaust Library 1986.

Iranek-Osmecki, K., *He Who Saves One Life*. New York: Crown Publishers 1971.

Korboński, S., *The Jews and the Poles in World War II*. New York: Hippocrene 1989.

Kurek, E., *Your Life is Worth Mine. How Polish Nuns Saved Hundreds of Jewish Children in German-Occupied Poland, 1939–1944*. New York: Hippocrene 1997.

Lukas, R.C. (ed.), *Out of the Inferno. Poles Remember the Holocaust*. Lexington: University of Kentucky Press 1989.

Paulsson, G.S., *Secret City. The Hidden Jews of Warsaw, 1940–1945*. New Haven, CT: Yale University Press 2002.

Polin, Volume 13 2000: *The Holocaust and its Aftermath*.

Polonsky, A. (ed.), *'My Brother's Keeper?' Recent Polish Debates on the Holocaust*. London: Routledge 1990.

Steinlauf, M. C., *Bondage to the Dead. Poland and the Memory of the Holocaust*. Syracuse, NY: Syracuse University Press 1996.

Szonert-Binienda, M., *World War II Through Polish Eyes*. New York: Columbia University Press 2003.

Tec, N., *When Light Pierced the Darkness: Christian Rescue of Jews in Nazi-occupied Poland*. London: Oxford University Press 1985.

Tomaszewski, I. and Werbowski, T., *Żegota: The Rescue of Jews in Wartime Poland*. Montreal: Price-Patterson 1994.

Trunk, I., *Judenrat. The Jewish Councils in Eastern Europe under Nazi Occupation*. Lincoln: University of Nebraska Press 1996.

Zimmerman, J. D. (ed.), *Contested Memories. Poles and Jews during the Holocaust and Its Aftermath*. New Brunswick, NJ: Rutgers University Press 2003.

10 Defeat in victory

Bennett, E. M., *Franklin D. Roosevelt and the Search for Victory. American–Soviet Relations, 1939–1945*. Wilmington, DE: SR Books 1990.

Clements, K. A., *The Presidency of Woodrow Wilson*. Kansas: University of Kansas Press 1992.

Dallek, R., *Franklin D. Roosevelt and American Foreign Policy, 1932–1945*. Oxford: Oxford University Press 1979.

Edmonds, R., *The Big Three. Churchill, Roosevelt and Stalin in Peace and War*. London: Hamish Hamilton 1991.

Garliński, J., *Poland in the Second World War*. London: Macmillan 1985.

Jenkins, R., *Churchill. A Biography*. London: Pan 2001.

Kacewicz, G. V., *Great Britain, the Soviet Union and the Polish Government-in-Exile (1939–1945)*. The Hague: Martinus Nijhoff 1979.

Karski, J., *The Great Powers and Poland, 1919–1945: From Versailles to Yalta*. Lanham, MD: University Press of America 1985.

Kemp-Welch, A. (ed.), *Stalinism in Poland, 1944–56*. London: Macmillan 1999.

Kennedy-Pipe, C., *Stalin's Cold War. Soviet Strategies in Europe, 1943 to 1956*. Manchester: Manchester University Press 1985.

Kersten, K., *The Establishment of Communist Rule in Poland, 1943–1948*. Berkeley: University of California Press 1991.

Kimball, W. F., *The Juggler. Franklin Roosevelt as Wartime Statesman*. Princeton, NJ: Princeton University Press 1991.

Kimball, W. F., *Forged in War. Churchill, Roosevelt and the Second World War*. London: HarperCollins 1997.

Kitchen, M., *British Policy Towards the Soviet Union during the Second World War*. London: Macmillan 1986.

Knock, T. J., *To End All Wars. Woodrow Wilson and the Quest for a New World Order*. New York: Oxford University Press 1992.

Lane, A. and Temperley, H. (eds), *The Rise and Fall of the Grand Alliance, 1941–45*. London: Macmillan 1995.

Link, A. S., *Woodrow Wilson. Revolution, War, and Peace*. Wheeling, IL: Harlan Davidson 1979.

Lukas, R. C., *The Strange Allies. The United States and Poland, 1941–1945*. Knoxsville: University of Tennessee Press 1978.

Marks, F. W., *Wind over Sand. The Diplomacy of Franklin Roosevelt*. Athens: University of Georgia Press 1988.

Miner, S. M., *Between Churchill and Stalin. The Soviet Union, Great Britain and the Origins of the Grand Alliance*. London: Macmillan 1990.

Pease, N., *Poland, the United States and the Stabilization of Europe, 1919–1933*. New York: Oxford University Press 1986.

Polonsky, A. (ed.), *The Great Powers and the Polish Question, 1941–1945*. London: Orbis 1976.

Polonsky, A. and Drukier, B., *The Beginnings of Communist Rule in Poland, December 1943-June 1945*. London: Routledge & Kegan Paul 1980.

Prażmowska, A. J., *Britain and Poland, 1939–1943. The Betrayed Ally*. Cambridge: Cambridge University Press 1995.

Raack, R. C., *Stalin's Drive to the West, 1938–1945*. London: Macmillan 1995.

Sainsbury, K., *The Turning Point*. London: Oxford University Press 1985.

Sword, K. (ed.), *Sikorski. Soldier and Statesman*. London: Orbis 1990.

Terry, S. M., *Poland's Place in Europe. General Sikorski and the Origin of the Oder–Neisse Line, 1939–1943*. Princeton, NJ: Princeton University Press 1983.

Torańska, T., *'Them'. Stalin's Polish Puppets*. New York: Harper & Row 1987.

Wandycz, P. S., *United States and Poland*. Cambridge, MA: Harvard University Press 1980.

Wandycz, P. S., *Polish Diplomacy, 1914–1945: Aims and Achievements*. London: Orbis 1988.

Waszak, L. J., *Agreement in Principle. The Wartime Partnership of Władysław Sikorski and Winston Churchill*. New York: Peter Lang 1996.

Zochowski, S., *British Policy in Relation to Poland in the Second World War*. New York: Vantage Press 1988.

APPENDIX I

CHRONOLOGY: THE SECOND REPUBLIC, 1918–45

1918

1 November   Beginning of Polish–Ukrainian War over Lwów and Eastern Galicia.

7 November   'Provisional People's Republic of Poland' set up in Lublin under the Galician socialist, Ignacy Daszyński, but quickly superseded by events in Warsaw.

11 November   An independent Polish State proclaimed (later officially designated National Day of Independence); Jósef Piłsudski appointed commander-in-chief of Polish armed forces.

14 November   Piłsudski appointed provisional head of state.

18 November   First Polish Government established under moderate socialist Jędrzej Moraczewski.

22 November   Poland declared a republic.

23 November   Moraczewski government introduces a broad range of social reforms, including the eight-hour day.

27 December   Anti-German Polish Rising in Poznań and western Poland.

1919

5 January   Beginning of Polish–Soviet War in Wilno region.

23 January   Czechoslovakia reneges on diplomatic agreement with Poland and seizes the disputed area of Cieszyn.

26 January   Elections for a Constituent *Sejm*.

20 February   Provisional (small) constitution approved; Piłsudski confirmed as head of state.

28 June   Treaty of Versailles, signed on behalf of Poland by Ignacy Paderewski and Roman Dmowski.

20 July   Lwów and Eastern Galicia secured by victory of Polish forces.

16 August   First Polish Rising in Upper Silesia.

1920

19 March   Piłsudski awarded the title of 'First Marshal of Poland' (conferred in November).

21 April   Polish–Ukrainian anti-Bolshevik alliance.

10 July   The Spa Conference fails to assist Poland against the invading Bolsheviks.

11 July   Plebiscites in East Prussia (Allenstein and Marienwerder) in favour of union with Germany.

15 July   Agrarian Reform Act.

24 July   Government of National Unity under Wincenty Witos.

13–19 August   Battle of Warsaw – momentous Polish Army victory over the Bolsheviks.

15 August   Designated 'Polish Soldiers' Day' in annual commemoration of victory.

19 August   Second Polish Rising in Upper Silesia.

9 October   Polish forces retake Wilno, which is subsequently incorporated into the Second Republic.

1921

21 February   Franco–Polish alliance.

3 March   Polish–Romanian alliance.

17 March   New constitution passed by the *Sejm*.

18 March   Treaty of Riga ends Polish–Soviet War.

20 March   Plebiscite in Upper Silesia.

2 May   Third Polish Rising in Upper Silesia.

30 September   First national census reveals Polish population of 27.2 million.

1922

5–12 November   First parliamentary elections under the new electoral law.

9 December   Gabriel Narutowicz elected first President of Poland.

16 December   President Narutowicz assassinated in Warsaw by an ultra-nationalist, Eligiusz Niewiadomski.

16 December   General Władysław Sikorski appointed Prime Minister.

20 December   Stanisław Wojciechowski elected President of Poland.

1923

15 March   The Ambassadors' Conference recognises Poland's eastern borders.

30 May   Piłsudski resigns as the Chief of General Staff.

2 July   Piłsudski resigns as head of the Inner War Cabinet and retires (temporarily) from public life.

September–December   Hyper-inflation crisis causes social and political unrest.

1924

14 April   Bank of Poland set up and the *złoty* introduced as the new currency.

31 July   School reform legislation.

1925

10 February   Polish–Vatican Concordat.

15 June   Germany begins tariff war against Poland (until 1934).

7 July   Polish–Jewish Agreement (*Ugoda)* in the *Sejm*.

28 December   Second Agrarian Reform Act.

1926

12–14 May   Piłsudski *coup d'état*.

15 May   Kazimierz Bartel appointed Prime Minister.

1 June   Ignacy Mościcki elected new President of Poland.

27 August   Piłsudski appointed Inspector-General of the Polish armed forces.

4 December   The right-wing, anti-government Camp of Great Poland created and led by Roman Dmowski.

1927

14 October   'Stabilisation Loan' from the USA.

1928

20 January   Non-Party Bloc for Co-operation with the Government (BBWR) set up.

4–11 March   Parliamentary elections produce a partial victory for the

BBWR (130 of 444 seats in the *Sejm* and 46 of 111 seats in the Senate).

1929

16 May–30 September   National Exhibition in Poznań celebrating ten years of Polish achievements.

1930

January   The Depression begins in Poland.
29 June   Congress of opposition parties ('Centrolew') in Kraków.
10 September   Arrest and detention of prominent political opposition leaders.
16 September   Polish 'pacification' campaign against Ukrainian terrorists.
16–23 November   Parliamentary elections give the BBWR a majority of seats in both the *Sejm* and the Senate.

1931

13 March   Abolition of anti-Jewish legislation dating from the tsarist era.
9 December   Second national census reveals a Polish population of 31.9 million.

1932

25 July   Polish–Soviet Non-Aggression Pact.
2 November   August Zaleski replaced as Foreign Minister by Józef Beck.

1933

22 March   The Camp of Great Poland banned.
8 May   Ignacy Mościcki re-elected President of Poland.

1934

26 January   Polish–German Non-Aggression Pact.
2 July   Internment camp for political subversives opened at Bereza Kartuska.

13 September   Poland repudiates the 1919 Minorities' Treaty.

1935

23 April   A new constitution introduced.
12 May   Death of Marshal Piłsudski.
30 October   Dissolution of BBWR.

1936

21 February   Oppositional 'Morges Front' announced.
29 February   Pastoral letter on the 'Jewish Question' from Cardinal Hlond, Primate of Poland.
1 July   The Central Industrial Region established by the government.

1937

21 February   Camp of National Unity (OZON) sponsored by the government.
19 October   Introduction of 'ghetto benches' in some Polish universities.

1938

August   The Communist Party of Poland dissolved by Stalin.
2 October   Poland recovers Cieszyn.

1939

2 January   Death of Roman Dmowski.
31 March   British guarantee to Poland.
23 August   Nazi–Soviet Pact.
25 August   Anglo-Polish Treaty.
1 September   Germany invades Poland; Nazi terror begins.
3 September   Britain and France declare war on Germany.
17 September   The Soviet Union invades Poland; 'Red terror' begins.
29 September   Fall of Warsaw to the Germans.
30 September   General Sikorski, now in France, appointed Prime Minister.
7 November   General Sikorski also appointed commander-in-chief of the Polish armed forces; he establishes in Poland an underground military organisation, the Union for Armed Struggle (ZWZ); the Polish Government is moved from Paris to Angers.

1940

18–21 June   Arrival of the Polish Government in London.

25 June   Formal capitulation of France to Germany

August–September   Battle of Britain, to which Polish pilots under Royal Air Force command make a major contribution.

1941

22 June   German invasion of the Soviet Union.

30 July   Polish–Soviet Pact.

14 August   Atlantic Charter.

3 December   Stalin–Sikorski meeting in the Kremlin.

8 December   The USA declares war on Japan following Pearl Harbor.

11 December   Germany declares war on the USA.

1942

5 January   A new Communist group, the Soviet-backed Polish Workers' Party (PPR), is formed in Warsaw.

14 February   Sikorski orders the creation of the Home Army (AK).

September   The right-wing National Armed Forces (NSZ) military organisation is established in German-occupied Poland.

4 December   Council for Aid to the Jews (*Żegota*) set up.

1943

31 January   German Sixth Army surrenders at Stalingrad.

1 March   The Union of Polish Patriots set up in Moscow.

13 April   German radio announces discovery of the Katyń graves.

19 April   Jewish Ghetto Rising in Warsaw (ends on 16 May).

4 July   General Sikorski killed in an air crash off Gibraltar.

28 November–1 December   The Tehran Conference.

1944

1 January   The Communist Polish National Council (KRN) set up in Warsaw.

3–4 January   The Red Army crosses Poland's eastern border.

18 May   The Second Polish Corps victorious at Monte Cassino.

21 July   The Soviet-sponsored Polish Committee of National Liberation established.

22 July   The Lublin Manifesto issued by Polish Communists.

1 August   Beginning of the Warsaw Rising; the First Polish Armoured Division lands in Normandy, soon winning the crucial Battle of Falaise Gap.

2 October   The Warsaw Rising ends in defeat.

24 November   Resignation of Polish Prime Minister Stanisław Mikołajczyk.

1945

19 January   Dissolution of the Home Army.

4–11 February   The Yalta Conference.

7 May   Germany's unconditional surrender.

21 June   The Soviet-sponsored, Communist-dominated Provisional Government of National Unity established in Warsaw.

5 July   The Western Allies withdraw recognition from the Polish Government in London, in favour of the new Warsaw regime.

17 July–2 August   The Potsdam Conference.

APPENDIX II

SOME STATISTICAL DATA
ON POLAND, 1918–45

(i)   Size (1939): 389, 700 square kilometres, of which 21.9 per cent was forested.

(ii) Population (1931): 31.9 million, of whom 8.7 million were urban-based and 23.2 million rural.

(iii) Religious affiliation (1931): Roman Catholic   20.6 million
                                    Greek Catholic   3.2 million
                                    Greek Orthodox   3.7 million
                                    Protestant   0.7 million
                                    Other Christian   0.1 million
                                    Jewish   3.1 million
                                    Atheist   0.5 million

(iv) Birth rate (1938): 24.5 births per 1,000 inhabitants
      Death rate (1938): 13.8 deaths per 1,000 inhabitants
      Both rates were among the highest in Europe.

(v)   Age groups (1938):

	0–14	15–49	50–64	65+
Poland	33.4	51.8	9.9	4.9
Britain	24.2	53.2	15.2	7.4
Germany	21.7	55.5	15.0	7.8
France	23.0	51.6	16.1	9.3
Italy	30.6	49.6	12.3	7.5

(vi) Population of the largest towns (over 100,000 in 1939):

Warsaw	1,289, 000
Łódź	672,000
Lwów	318,000
Poznań	272,000
Kraków	259,000
Wilno	209,000
Bydgoszcz	141,000
Częstochowa	138,000
Katowice	134,000
Sosnowiec	130,000
Lublin	122,000
Gdynia	120,000
Chorzów	110,000

(vii) There were 17 administrative districts (voivodships) in 1939: Warsaw City, Warsaw District, Łódź, Kielce, Lublin, Białystok, Wilno, Nowogródek, Polesie, Wołyń, Poznań, Pomorze, Silesia, Kraków, Lwów, Stanisławów and Tarnopol.

(viii) The gainfully employed population on average 1930–3 in percentages:

	Agriculture	Mining & Industry	Commerce	Transport
Poland	64.9	16.3	5.2	2.2
Britain	5.2	46.5	19.0	7.9
Germany	24.5	43.0	14.4	5.1
France	34.5	34.6	12.8	6.0
Hungary	49.7	24.2	7.1	3.1
Italy	39.2	34.0	9.6	5.0

(ix) The total number of handicraft workers in 1937 was 373,529, of whom the most numerous were tailors (57,359), shoemakers (57,194), butchers (47,548), blacksmiths (932,360), joiners (29,423) and bakers (18,904).

(x) Poland's most important trading partners (1937) in percentages:

	Imports	*Exports*
Britain	11.9	18.3
Germany	14.5	14.5
USA	11.9	8.4
Belgium	4.5	5.8
Netherlands	4.6	5.1
Austria	4.6	4.9
Sweden	3.0	6.3

(xi) Frontiers: 34.5% with Germany, 25.5% with USSR, 17.8% with Czechoslovakia, 9.2% with Lithuania, 6.3% with Romania, 2.2% with Gdańsk, 2.0% with Latvia and 2.5% sea coast.

(xii) The most important rivers, according to length in Poland: Wisła (Vistula), Bug, Warta, Horyń, Dniestr, Niemen, Narew, San, Wilia.

Sources: Extrapolated from *Polska w Liczbach*, comp. J. Jankowski and A. Serafiński (London: 1941); and *Statistical Atlas of Poland*, ed. E. Szturm de Sztrem (London: Polish Ministry of Information, n.d. [1942]).

INDEX